TECHNO FUNDAMENTAL TRADING

A Revolutionary Approach To Combining Technical & Fundamental Analysis

PHILIP GOTTHELF

PROBUS PUBLISHING

Chicago, Illinois
Cambridge, England

ISBN 1-55738-541-6

Printed in the United States of America

BB

1 2 3 4 5 6 7 8 9 0

CB/BJS

This book is dedicated to my father
the late Edward B. Gotthelf

with special thanks to the people who helped:
my wife, Paula Gotthelf;
my dedicated employees, Judi Harnick, John Ball,
David Orr, and Kimo Solis;
my friends, Jerry Becker and Lou Mendelsohn;
and finally, my sources—Knight-Ridder,
Commodity Trend Service, and the
U.S. Department of Agriculture.

TABLE OF CONTENTS

A NEW LOOK AT A LOST ART

The computer age has brought about unprecedented change. Even now it is altering the way we transact business, interpret events, gather information, and keep ourselves entertained.

While computers can expand our intellectual horizons, they can also limit creative interpretation. There is a tendency today to let computers do the work of designing and discovering rather than relying upon intuition and imagination. In a business context, computers reduce problems to statistical probabilities without necessarily considering broad effects of events and relationships.

This is not to say that computers should not be used to prove or disprove theories. However, it is important to remember that the intuition of the human mind has not yet been duplicated by electronic circuitry. Moreover, our educated intuitions are the critical tools with which to learn how markets work and why price trends develop.

Successful trading means first forming sound opinions about markets. Once you understand how trends develop, you can program a computer to recognize patterns or solve complex supply/demand equations.

The fact is, prior to the late 1970s, fundamental analysis—done with pencil and paper—was the tried and true method for properly evaluating financial markets. Technical analysis was considered foolhardy, a "hocus-pocus" approach to the market not worthy of serious consideration.

In today's world, ironically, fundamental analysis is almost a lost art. New "neural networks" (linking multiple computers) and "quantum market models" are the cutting edge of price forecasting technology. Multi-colored real-time charts are on every trader's desk. Screens are able to draw instant trend-lines and compute any moving average.

Traders can resort to Fibonacci ratios, Gann squares, advance/decline indices, and a host of other technical indicators to glean potential price direction. These exercises in technical analysis would have horrified the traditional and "Before Personal Computer" analysts.

Some "New-Age" market gurus make cryptic forecasts based upon higher highs, lower lows, and the position of Venus relative to Jupiter. The same gurus, interestingly, are hard pressed to answer basic fundamental questions like, "How many pounds are in a bushel of soybeans?" Is such a question important?

If we do not know the number of pounds in a bushel of soybeans, how can we translate millions of tons into bushels per acre? How can we comprehend the meaning of exports in tons, acres planted, and yield per acre?

The technician will say these figures are not important. Yet, even if simply an intellectual exercise, it is helpful to know whether a "technical market reaction" can be sustained relative to fundamental supply and demand. After all, few individuals will challenge the fact that every major trend has its source in fundamental changes.

Even with a new bias toward technical trading, you'll notice that newspapers, magazines, television, and other media continue to explain price movements in terms of fundamental developments. We cannot divorce ourselves from the cause and effect aspect of fundamental economic events.

Obviously, there is merit in technical analysis. Measuring potential imbalances between buyers and sellers using "technical patterns" can be extremely valuable for short-term trading and timing. However, the value of technical analysis should not distract you from the importance of fundamentals.

A New Way to Play an Old Game

Thus, a new science has emerged which I call "TechnoFundamentals." By combining technical timing and evaluation with fundamentals, you can gain a broad market perspective while avoiding the pitfalls of poorly executed strategies. All too often, traders follow a rumor and are devastated by the news. In many instances, technical analysis can save us from jumping to conclusions.

Frequently, traders hear about pending fundamental developments which fail to materialize as a price trend. Again, using technical insights can help you avoid these kinds of unnecessary losses.

By the same token, a breakout from a technical trading range can be correlated to known fundamental events. If no fundamental cause seems to exist, there is reason for investigation.

Is the breakout a false signal? Could the price movement be the result of converging technical signals with no basis in fundamental fact?

If so, we can avoid a technical trap by using fundamentals to filter out trades doomed to failure.

My purpose in this book is to step back and reintroduce principles of fundamental and technical analysis *in combination* to create a more comprehensive market perspective. How should we arrange pieces of a complex supply and demand puzzle so as to create a rational market approach or trading plan? How do we create a hybrid approach combining fundamentals with technicals to achieve better performance?

I recall a conversation some years ago my father was having about the relationship between farm subsidies and general economic conditions. Long before I ever began watching the impact of Federal Reserve actions or the performance of government interest rates and debt, my father was deriving a fundamental relationship between farm subsidies and Treasury borrowing needs.

After the drought of 1988, a newly elected President George Bush boasted major reductions in government spending. Indeed, government interest rates began declining in response to smaller than expected Treasury auctions and government borrowing.

Suddenly, I recalled my father's analysis and suddenly the fundamentals became clear. There was, in fact, a subtle relationship between soybeans and bonds. It was not necessarily the new president's skills that brought down interest rates. High farm prices caused by the 1988 drought lowered borrowing requirements by reducing Federal farm payments.

Could this relationship be useful for formulating a trading plan? Would it be helpful to know that high grain prices could reduce government spending? The answer is obvious.

High grain prices also translate into a rising Commodity Research Bureau Index (CRB). This number reflects raw commodity prices and is a barometer of inflation that is carefully watched by the Federal Reserve. Thus, grain prices impact monetary policy and affect decisions on adjusting interest rates. The extent to which the CRB influences Federal Reserve policy can be measured over time by observing the index and interest rates. While some of the correlation may be circumstantial, the study can set a foundation for monitoring monetary policy and interest rate trends.

With this knowledge at hand, it was possible to watch price patterns for technical clues that the relationship was taking effect. At some stage, fundamental influences revealed themselves in the form of a breakout in interest rate contracts.

Grain prices can be linked or correlated with interest rates. Interest rates can determine currency parities. Currency values can impact gold prices. The list of possible linkages goes on and on.

When you seek out these relationships you are developing tools to create significant trading strategies. At the very least, potential correlations between markets, politics, Mother Nature, and economic conditions are a challenging intellectual exercise. (Sometimes they can add up even more profitably than that.)

In the following chapters I'll take you, beginning from the ground up, through the definition of fundamental analysis within a modern framework. What is modern fundamental analysis? Are there differences between modern and traditional fundamentals?

What are the inputs for fundamental analysis?

Where can you obtain reliable information?

How can you automate fundamental analysis to make it less subjective?

Should you try to make fundamental analysis less subjective?

How can you apply fundamentals or build fundamental models?

How do you adjust your own thinking to incorporate fundamentals?

I'll go on in other chapters to examine just how market forces are reflected by "technical" trading patterns. How do fundamental changes in supply and demand show up in price action? How do we interpret changes in volume and open interest? Is it important to measure the amount of cash entering or leaving a market?

With the plethora of new books, journals, and articles on technical analysis, it is important to go "back to basics" so that we can properly digest the new directions of this artful science.

Consider simple concepts like, What makes a price rise and how is it reflected in chart patterns? What are trendlines and why are they useful? Are chart patterns reliable?

After covering basics, we can examine modern approaches like neural nets, chaos theory, multiple probability models, Monte Carlo simulation, expert systems, and a host of other sophisticated methods.

An important aspect of TechnoFundamental analysis is its ability to expand our perspectives beyond the obvious and even beyond the probable.

Consider a forecast for the 30-year Treasury Bond yield to drop below 6.25%—made in 1981. Would we consider such a decline possible after seeing consumer and business rates peak above 21%?

It is likely our subjective reaction would foreclose any acceptance of a forecast for a 6.25% 1993 T-Bond yield. In fact, computer models based upon yields from 1977 through 1990 placed a floor on T-Bond rates above 7%. Predictive parameters held a 6.25% yield "beyond the realm of possibility." Historical data did not reflect such a decline in interest rates.

Several computer models have failed because the historical data they relied upon placed events outside probability parameters. Consequences have been serious. The 1993 Midwest floods were "beyond the realm of possibility." Computers were used to design water control systems for any contingency. Yet rains of improbable proportions proved there is no such thing as "beyond the realm of possibility."

From an investment standpoint, we were concerned with the impact of floods upon grain prices, lumber, interest rates, insurance premiums, and an entire host of investment vehicles. (See Figure Intro-1.)

Without fundamental knowledge of where, how, and when grains are grown, it would be difficult to extrapolate a pattern for grain prices subsequent to the 1993 floods. Without technical interpretation, it would have been difficult to time market entries, place appropriate stops, and withdraw profits from roller-coaster price fluctuations.

Before Midwest storms subsided in late July 1993, soybeans dramatically reversed a bull trend and thwarted many technical systems and investors.

Was the market reaction understandable? More importantly, could price gyrations be anticipated? How might we have interpreted government and private reports on crop damage, quality, and progress? Is it really necessary to know when corn is in its critical pollination and tasseling stage? Fundamentals hold vital clues.

Figure Intro-1

1993 summer floods drove corn prices to extreme levels.

An exploration of fundamentals will take us through basic supply and demand relationships. We will examine cycles, seasonal tendencies, and weather patterns. We will see how government policies and programs can impact supply and demand.

Our examination will include an evaluation of technology and its role in determining fundamentals. How can new production methods affect supply and demand? What about new mining techniques? Can a unified European economic system be anticipated? What precedents can we rely upon? When must we develop new and original theories about supply and demand?

We are interested in relationships between various commodities and economic sectors. That is why we must understand how energy prices can influence gold, currencies, and interest rates.

We will demonstrate why a bond trader would be more savvy following agricultural trends as well as unemployment.

No modern review of fundamental analysis would be complete without considering hybrid approaches like "TechnoFundamentals." We will define this new term and provide examples of how TechnoFundamentals are developed.

Finally, we will discuss strategies and implementation. How can we take advantage of old crop and new crop differences? What about spreads and arbitrage? New financial vehicles like options on futures and index contracts provide unique trading opportunities which can enhance the profitability of fundamental analysis.

This is an exciting time to expand investment horizons. Over the past two decades, investment markets have been redefined by a host of new and innovative markets. From financial futures to stock index contracts . . . from energy futures to currencies . . . the world of investing has changed and continues to expand.

I hope this book will provide you with new insights and new tools that will increase profit opportunities through better understanding of these markets.

Now, on to the fundamentals.

CHAPTER 1

WHAT FUNDAMENTAL ANALYSIS IS (AND IS NOT)

Fundamental analysis is an art, a science, and . . . a pleasure, according to some observers. You'll find that the pleasure is keenest when art and science combine to produce profitable trading results. Indeed, there is surely a kind of artistry involved in assembling different pieces of data into a winning market prediction.

However, you'll also find that solid fundamental analysis has its foundation in cold, hard empirical facts and statistically measurable outcomes.

To begin with, here's a good, basic definition of fundamental analysis:

"Fundamental analysis is the evaluation of probable price direction or level based upon *supply and demand correlations*."

That's a pretty broad definition: let's refine it a little to make it useful. After all, many things affect supply and demand. In addition, there are several levels of complexity in any study of supply and demand.

Prospective Fundamental Analysis

First, keep in mind that it is not enough simply to know the *current* supply of a commodity relative to demand. You'll need some historical perspective against which to compare current statistics—i.e, a frame of reference.

A traditional fundamental approach considers *progressive* (i.e., over time) supply and demand developments. In the case of agricultural commodities, for example, I might begin by examining planting intentions to derive a potential yield. Then I'll look at a typical best-case/likely-case/worst-case weather scenarios in order to predict a final crop. Next, I'll compare our anticipated crop with past years to see if yields are above normal, average, or below normal. This process is called "prospective fundamental analysis."

I might then compare current domestic inventories with global inventories. (See Figure 1-1.) Turning my attention to demand, I'll look at historical demand relative to current supplies. If I want to forecast feed grain prices, for example, signs of growth in cattle, hog, and poultry production are important. If I'm interested in bread grains, baking consumption will be a key factor.

Categories can be refined further to determine the specific type of commodity and its uses. For example, if you're trading wheat, are you tracking hard red winter wheat or the soft spring variety?

I might then turn my attention to export potential. I would apply to the foreign markets the same analysis I did for the domestic situation. That would mean a look at export programs and financing to round out my projections.

After covering primary supply and demand factors, I might also consider "secondary" factors including inflation, interest rates, and the cost of inputs. As a matter of terminology, primary factors are usually associated with "macro fundamentals." Secondary factors are referred to as "micro fundamentals."

Finding the Minimum Selling Price

Keep in mind there are different philosophical approaches to fundamental price analysis. Some experts claim that macro fundamentals are all we need for useful forecasting. Others claim that micro fundamentals are required to fully evaluate potential macro trends.

Is the price of fertilizer relevant to the eventual corn price? To some extent, the answer is yes. However, a drought is more likely to dictate price direction than subtle changes in "input" prices. Thus, a macro fundamentalist may contend that micro considerations are a waste of time.

When you attempt to derive average potential selling prices, you'll need to understand profit margins. Obviously, farmers are not going to grow crops at a loss. (The exception might be when government programs make up for deficient profit margins.) If you know input costs such as fertilizer, irrigation, labor, equipment, seed, insurance, storage, interest rates, land rental, main-

Figure 1-1
World Production of Corn or Maize (in Millions of Metric Tons)

Crop Year	Argen-tina	Brazil	Can-ada	China	France	Hun-gary	India	Indo-nesia	Italy	Mexico	Rom-ania	South Africa	Thai-land	United States	Former USSR	Yugo-slavia	World Total
1980-1	12.9	22.6	5.4	62.6	9.2	6.5	7.0	4.0	6.4	12.5	10.3	14.6	3.2	168.8	9.5	9.3	406.7
1981-2	9.6	22.9	6.7	59.2	9.0	7.0	7.0	4.5	8.2	12.5	11.9	8.4	4.5	208.3	8.0	9.8	441.2
1982-3	9.0	19.5	6.5	60.3	10.4	7.8	6.3	3.2	6.8	7.0	12.6	4.1	3.5	212.3	13.5	11.1	440.4
1983-4	9.4	20.5	5.9	66.3	10.1	6.4	6.8	5.0	6.6	9.3	11.1	4.1	4.0	106.8	16.2	10.7	344.1
1984-5	11.5	22.0	7.0	73.4	10.4	6.7	8.4	5.3	6.8	9.9	13.3	7.8	4.4	194.9	12.5	11.3	457.0
1985-6	13.0	19.0	7.4	64.0	12.3	6.5	7.8	4.6	6.4	10.0	14.0	8.5	5.2	225.2	13.5	9.9	480.0
1986-7	9.5	26.5	6.7	69.0	11.3	7.0	7.2	5.4	6.5	10.0	15.5	8.5	4.1	209.6	12.5	12.5	477.2
1987-8	9.0	23.0	7.0	76.0	12.3	7.0	5.5	4.8	5.6	9.9	10.5	7.5	2.7	179.4	14.8	8.8	439.3
1988-9	5.0	26.1	5.4	77.4	14.6	6.0	8.3	5.2	6.3	10.1	10.0	12.4	4.2	125.2	16.0	7.7	400.7
1989-90	5.2	21.8	6.4	78.9	13.4	6.7	9.4	5.0	6.4	9.8	9.0	8.9	4.1	191.2	15.3	9.4	462.5
1990-1	7.6	23.7	7.4	96.8	9.5	4.5	9.0	5.2	5.7	14.1	6.8	8.3	3.8	201.6	9.8	6.7	477.2
1991-2 (1)	10.6	28.5	7.4	98.8	12.9		8.0	5.3	6.2	14.5	10.5	3.3	3.6	190.2	9.3	11.6	484.6
1992-3 (2)	10.0	25.0	5.3	93.0	13.6		9.4	5.3	7.6	15.0	8.5	8.0	3.6	240.8	9.1	7.1	524.1

(1) Preliminary. (2) Estimate.

The table above provides a 13-year history for world corn production broken down by major producing countries. This perspective gives a fundamental framework for evaluating the impact supply has upon prices. In addition, the table allows us to evaluate the relative importance of production from each country. A drought or other adversity in a particular country can be measured against the contribution that country makes to total world production.

Source: Foreign Agricultural Service, U.S.D.A. Table provided through Knight-Ridder CRB InfoTech™ CD-ROM.

tenance, insecticides, energy, and transportation, you can extrapolate a *minimum selling price.*

An assumed minimum selling price can be a reference point from which to estimate other price levels. Thus, if you assume corn costs $.98 per bushel to grow, you might conclude farmers will seek a 20% profit margin for a final price of $1.17¼ per bushel.

The analysis becomes more complex when you consider that input costs can vary with location. Is it better then to use an average cost for all locations or a proportional formula weighting each location according to production?

Prospective fundamental analysis is extremely useful for long range planning and arriving at a "trading bias." If your analysis reveals tight global supplies relative to usual demand, your "bias" would be toward higher prices. If carryovers or existing inventories were plentiful, you would have a downward bias.

Reactionary Fundamental Analysis

Prospective fundamentals also establish a baseline against which you can measure current events. For example, assume you've got an upward bias based upon tight supplies. Suddenly, you discover that the South American crop is much larger than originally expected. This new information can change your trading outlook and bias.

A change in forecast based upon new information or immediate developments is called a "reaction." Thus, the evaluation of immediate news is called "reactionary fundamental analysis."

It is important to note the difference between reactionary and prospective analysis. Reactionary analysis does not necessarily change the prospective forecast. Market response to a reaction is frequently exaggerated. The particular news item may come at a time when liquidity is thin (few participants) or a market is enjoying popularity. A thin market is likely to be bid up or down more significantly because price transitions take place between a small number of investors. On the other hand, a very popular market may experience a "bandwagon" effect which pushes prices beyond reasonable levels relative to the specific news. Therefore, a reaction may only have an impact over a short time interval. The prospective forecast often remains valid.

Consider a 90-day weather forecast for dryer than normal conditions across central corn growing regions. (See Figure 1-2.) A likely reaction to such a forecast would be a rise in corn prices in anticipation of drought damage. If dry conditions fail to materialize, an opposite reaction is likely to bring prices back down.

For better or worse, the business media and traders have a strong tendency to emphasize reactionary fundamentals. Their focus is often upon an immediate event or announcement. This emphasis tends to increase near-term price volatility while adding credibility to less subjective technical systems.

Even a quick scan of the Wall Street Journal will indicate the market's virtual addiction to reactionary fundamentals in the sheer number of articles highlighting new data of all kinds. As the government releases monthly unemployment statistics and revisions for the previous month, for example, traders instantly convert that information into opinions which are reflected in market action.

You'll often see an initial reaction followed by a reconsideration or correction. In the long run, however, the statistics are eventually forgotten in favor of a general consensus that probably existed before statistics were released.

Figure 1-2
Reactions to Weather Forecasts—Spring 1994

Certainly, if you see a pattern of growing unemployment, you might conclude that the economy is in a recession. This, in turn, affects opinions on corporate performance, consumer confidence, spending, borrowing, business failures, inflation, and more. However, the data show historically that reactions to statistics do not frequently change an underlying fundamental trend.

Combining Types of Analysis

Unfortunately, a student of the market may have to decide the validity of fundamental analysis when faced with the choice between reactionary and prospective fundamentals. In that situation, one obvious solution is to use a combination of the two analytical approaches whereby they become complementary.

Consider a prospective forecast for sugar which assumes 103 million metric tons of production and 98 million metric tons in consumption. Suddenly, there's news of a hurricane that threatens Cuba's crop.

The first question that comes to mind is, "How much sugar does Cuba produce?" (See Figure 1-3.) With such information you can calculate supplies in the absence of Cuban production. Your new supply assumption would be used to form a new prospective forecast.

Subtle nuances emerge when applying this analysis. Figure 1-3 reveals Cuba's output to be 6% to 8% of the world total. Production has remained relatively consistent since 1982. Notice how China and Thailand production has been growing in relation to total output. We see that the role of Cuba is remaining static while other nations account for current growth. You will discover that seasonal carryovers amount to approximately one-third of annual production. This implies that a loss of 7% of the gross crop would have a serious impact upon free stocks at the end of the season. Most production is consumed in the country of origin: i.e., only a small percentage is exported. Armed with this knowledge, we can focus upon the size of Cuban exports as well as total Cuban production. In the event of disaster, what would be the global impact?

Effective fundamental analysis must also consider the ultimate objective. If the purpose is to develop a successful trading plan, we must incorporate money management into our approach.

Understand that an accurate prediction of an eventual longer-term price is of no use to you if interim price movements completely deplete your capital.

Figure 1-3
World Production of Sugar (Centrifugal Sugar–Raw Value) in Thousands of Metric Tons

Crop Year	Australia Cane	Brazil Cane	Mainland China	Cuba Cane	South Africa Cane	India Cane	Indonesia Cane	Philippines Cane	Poland Beet	Germany Beet	Thailand	United States	USSR Beet	Mexico	France	World All
1982-3	3,535	9,300	4,132	7,200	2,256	9,508	1,731	2,521	2,009	3,591	2,305	5,359	7,392	3,078	4,833	101,342
1983-4	3,414	9,400	3,825	8,330	1,462	7,042	1,762	2,381	2,141	2,726	2,305	5,275	8,700	3,242	4,153	96,542
1984-5	3,548	9,300	4,627	8,100	2,514	7,071	1,709	1,767	1,878	3,146	2,533	5,289	8,587	3,436	4,301	100,183
1985-6	3,404	8,100	5,535	7,200	2,287	7,983	1,728	1,561	1,811	3,430	2,586	5,473	8,260	3,928	4,297	98,938
1986-7	3,457	8,650	5,774	7,220	2,289	9,474	2,024	1,350	1,891	3,469	2,639	6,246	8,700	3,970	3,707	103,271
1987-8	3,528	8,457	4,706	7,400	2,165	10,000	2,127	1,400	1,823	2,968	2,704	6,483	9,560	3,806	3,966	103,270
1988-9	3,680	8,582	5,312	8,100	2,240	10,150	1,889	1,600	1,825	3,003	4,055	6,089	8,900	3,678	4,372	105,485
1989-90	3,797	7,793	5,618	8,000	2,289	12,575	2,080	1,750	1,865	4,087	3,502	6,008	9,425	3,100	4,204	108,734
1990-1	3,515	7,900	6,765	7,620	2,152	13,748	2,120	1,718	2,214	4,675	3,954	6,273	9,047	3,900	4,736	113,967
1991-2 (1)	3,690	8,936	8,500	7,000	2,429	15,470	2,250	2,010	1,642	4,245	5,062	6,577	6,795	3,500	4,423	116,337
1992-3 (2)		9,100	8,500	6,000	1,600	14,750	2,100	2,000	1,400	4,550	5,000	6,804	7,500	3,620	4,900	115,785

(1) Estimated. (2) Preliminary.

Source: Foreign Agricultural Service, U.S.D.A. Table provided through Knight-Ridder CRB InfoTech™ CD-ROM.

However, if your analysis is to be used for long range planning or marketing, interim movements might not matter greatly. A bank may want to forecast the major or "secular" interest rate trend to plan marketing strategies. If rates are rising, banks want to attract deposits while delaying making loans. Falling interest rates suggest the opposite strategy.

The Three Tiers of the Markets

Good fundamental analysis should also include examining the specific trading vehicle. For example, many markets today have three tiers known as cash, futures, and options. All are related, but each must be examined differently.

Futures are contractual commitments between buyers and sellers. The contract requires making or taking delivery of a specific quantity and quality of a commodity at a particular price on the delivery (expiration) date. These are the general contract terms. In addition, there is an associated "margin deposit" representing "consideration" that binds the parties. All futures contracts are standardized, allowing them to be easily transferred between parties without renegotiation. The only thing that changes is price. Each contract between buyer and seller represents one "open interest" or unsettled commitment. The total number of contracts between all buyers and sellers is called total open interest and is reported by the exchange clearing associations each day.

Options are also contracts, however, they provide the right rather than an obligation to buy or sell a futures contract or commodity at a specified price known as the "strike price." The "right" to buy or sell rests with the option buyer. A "premium" is paid for this right. Traders who sell options are known as "writers." They receive the premium in return for granting the right to buy or sell at the strike price. If the strike price is reached by the underlying futures contract, the option buyer can "exercise" his right to buy if he owns a call or sell if he has a put. The option writer must honor the request to exercise by providing the appropriate futures position; long if the exercise is on a call or short if the exercise is on a put.

Futures and options have "expiration months" when commitments must be honored. When the expiration is reached on a futures contract, the buyer must pay full price for the contract value and take delivery of the associated commodity or financial instrument. The seller must secure the commodity or financial vehicle and deliver it to the buyer. When the expiration date is reached on an option, the buyer must exercise his right or lose any opportunity to profit. Under almost all circumstances, an option will only be exercised if it has favorably moved beyond the strike price. If the strike has not been achieved, the option expires worthless and the buyer loses his premium to the seller.

Frequently, futures and options prices seem to be at odds with the actual or "cash" commodity. This is because demand for futures and related options is anticipatory while the cash market reflects immediate demand.

This is an important consideration. Many commodities have production cycles linked to the time required to grow and harvest crops, fatten an animal for slaughter, or the production season. Suppose a near-term shortage will not be relieved until new production comes to market. This might pressure current or "cash" prices higher.

However, if plentiful new supplies were projected, futures and options covering new deliveries (expiration months) could have much lower prices than the cash market.

Successful trading of futures and options means making many important timing considerations. Timing is itself a fundamental consideration. For example, contract expiration dates play a crucial role in futures and the critical role in options. The very *value* of an option is based upon the time before expiration, while the *liquidity* of futures contracts is determined by proximity to expiration.

Also keep in mind: *demand for futures contracts can at any moment be far different from demand for cash commodities.* A newspaper article might stimulate trading interest in coffee because it carries a bullish tone. Traders could decide to "take a shot" at buying futures, which might push futures prices higher.

In the cash market, however, weather, economic conditions, and policies among coffee producers could dampen near-term demand. Roasters might not be in the market for green coffee because of previously accumulated inventories. Cash prices could be depressed while futures prices move higher. Herein lies an argument for using technical analysis. Since fundamentals reflect forces in the cash market, it is possible for the supply and demand in futures to differ from supply and demand in cash. Technical analysis tracks futures independently from underlying cash commodities.

Of course, there is a rule that futures and cash prices *converge* upon contract expiration. In our coffee example, higher prices might encourage producers to sell. Selling, in turn, would counteract speculative buying. From a fundamental standpoint, analysis must determine which is correctly priced if it is to be useful for making a profit. Will futures move to cash or cash to futures? (A question we will address in later chapters.)

The Risks of Hedging Apples with Oranges

Nothing serves to illustrate the importance of understanding the specific trading vehicle better than early market histories of financial futures.

The first "interest rate" contract, introduced in the late 1970s, was the "Ginnie Mae" (i.e., government-backed mortgage certificates). It was designed to help hedge against adverse mortgage rate fluctuations. When the Ginnie Mae contract gave way to more popular Treasury instrument contracts (Treasury bonds, bills, and notes), fundamental interest rate relationships changed. Yet many traders attempted to hedge mortgage risk using Treasury instruments.

When interest rates began declining in the late 1980s, mortgage-backed securities lost value because they were vulnerable to refinancing redemptions. At the same time, principal values on Treasury instruments were rising. The results became extremely expensive for several brokerage firms.

The problem was that traders (generally, speculators who do not own a commodity) and hedgers (participants who usually hold inventories of a commodity) were working on the incorrect assumption that both types of interest rates would move in tandem.

Unfortunately, mortgage-backed securities did not follow in the wake of retreating Treasury rates. Strategies failed to consider the significant difference between securities that were created by stripping yields versus securities that were based upon principal. Spreads (i.e., price differentials) between the futures and the cash instruments (a relationship known as "basis") moved against these strategies and caused large losses.

Trading by Starlight and Grand Cycles

I've touched upon prospective and reactive fundamentals as well as macro and micro perspectives. I described the major differences between the futures, options, and cash markets and briefly covered the importance of understanding the specific contract details of the vehicle you are trading.

No description of fundamental analysis would be complete without considering "fringe" methodologies relying upon astronomical events and grand theories.

The most common astronomical considerations concentrate upon gravitational influences of the moon and planets along with studies of electromagnetic cycles caused by shifts in the earth's fields or sun spot activity.

While there is evidence that astronomical events influence weather and perhaps behavior, most traditional fundamental analysts consider causal correlations between events and effects too imprecise for trading purposes. Still, the potential effects of astronomical activity merit at least a look.

Among other unusual theories, many readers will be familiar with the "Kondratieff Wave," often called the "Grand Cycle." This approximately half-century long business cycle is linked to peaks and troughs in the U.S. stock market, inflation, and general economic activity.

The Grand Cycle is associated with a theoretical tendency for capitalist economic systems to encounter "natural economic constraints." According to the theory, the profit motive drives a capitalist economy to overproduce. When overcapacity is reached and supply begins to outpace demand, prices fall below feasible levels. In turn, capacity will contract until prices rise. Overreaction in both directions causes the cycle to go on repeating itself.

Since different economic systems still coexist in the world, it is almost impossible to draw a definitive conclusion about the Grand Cycle's sole relationship to capitalism. For this reason, the Grand Cycle has also been attributed to (or blamed upon) solar cycles, lunar cycles, magnetic field cycles, the Bible, and a host of other reasons.

The question arises, "Is the Kondratieff Wave useful for making market forecasts?" If so, how precise can such a forecast be when a cycle can last 50 to 60 years?

Certainly, one can examine current economic conditions in relation to a Grand Cycle. For example, if stocks seem overvalued and we are within the time frame when the Grand Cycle should peak, we might begin a defensive equity investment strategy.

There is little question that investors and traders pay close attention to the cyclical nature of economic systems. (See Figure 1-4.) Consider how frequently we see news reports analyzing "cyclical stocks." Why is a stock considered "cyclical?" What cycle does this refer to?

In Chapter 3, I'll review the criteria used to categorize investment vehicles as cyclical, seasonal, and interrelated. That discussion will illustrate how fundamentals can be specific or broad in nature.

Fundamentals Can Change, Too

Moving deeper into our examination of fundamental analysis, keep in mind that the historical perspective or baseline can change. Prior to the internal combustion engine, for example, oil was irrelevant. Today, fossil fuels appear indispensable. Tomorrow, a new discovery could render oil irrelevant once again.

Technology as well as changes in global politics and economic systems can completely alter fundamental relationships between supply and demand. In some cases, a commodity or investment can become obsolete. In other cases, entire economic sectors can spring anew and control global destiny.

Figure 1-4
Computer Cycle Analysis for Live Cattle

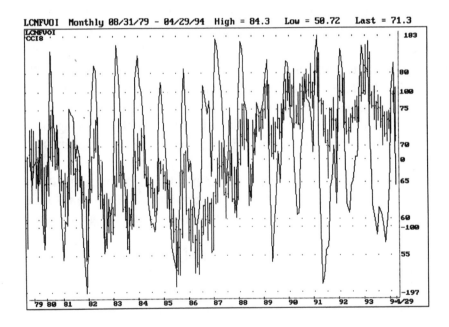

As mentioned in the Introduction, the personal computer has significantly changed our world. Consider that these machines were developed in the 1970s—not so long ago.

Yet the low cost/high speed microcomputer may be responsible for a complete shift in the relationship (or in economics jargon, correlation) between employment numbers and the health of the overall economy. Another example: the traditional positive correlation between employment and inflation may no longer hold true as computers replace more workers in more capacities.

When the compact disc was introduced as an alternative to records, initial reactions suggested that the new technology was "too exotic" for mainstream consumers. Many analysts believed the installed base of turntables for vinyl records was simply too large for CDs to have an impact.

Yet, within a few years, CDs have come to dominate the market. In addition, "multi-media" computer systems can transform video, music, and computing into highly integrated systems that continue to enrich and change our daily lives.

Technological advances, natural developments like disasters, diseases, or environmental changes as well as political shifts can alter "traditional" fundamental relationships within or between markets.

What would happen if diets in the industrialized West shifted away from red meat and toward vegetarian fare? Would we see changes in meat prices, grains, vegetables, and other foods? Suppose the Third World adopted the Western diet?

The point is that a fundamental study must provide tools for constructing new relationships. When there is a profound change, we want to evaluate the impact, why it occurred, and how much it should affect our analysis going forward.

In other words, it is not enough to simply review historic relationships between supply, demand, and price. We must recognize when old correlations are giving way to new. We must develop an intuitive sense for cause and effect, supply and demand.

How OPEC Changed the Fundamentals

This is particularly true in our new age of rapid technological advances. For example, gasoline prices spiraled upward after the Organization of Petroleum

Exporting Countries (OPEC) placed an embargo against the U.S. during the early 1970s. Shortly thereafter, global economies began making structural changes in energy production, distribution, and consumption. Conservation gave way to efficiency born out of technology.

The result was virtual stability in the fuel-based "price per mile." Vehicle fleet mileages increased from under 12 miles per gallon (mpg) in 1971 to more than 25 in 1993.

The math is obvious. Twelve miles at 55 cents per gallon equates to 4.58 cents per mile. Twenty-five miles at $1.35 per gallon translates into 5.4 cents per mile. However, after adjusting for more than 20 years of inflation, the change in fuel-based cost per mile is actually negative and continues to decline. Fleet mileage should surpass 30 mpg by 1997. In the meantime, the westernization of the former Soviet Union along with more rapid industrialization of other non-OPEC producers promises a substantial increase in world pumping capacity.

By early 1993, fundamentals suggested there could easily be a price war between OPEC and non-OPEC producers as demand for hard currency began to rise. At the same time, traditional relationships between production, pricing, and consumption were showing the effects of environmental concerns. Normally, a price war leads to an oil glut which, in turn, tempts consumers toward higher consumption.

However, new pollution restrictions are strong incentives to decrease consumption, regardless of how low oil prices may go. The supply/demand equation could permanently change for environmental reasons.

Quite honestly, the intellectual exercise associated with extrapolating old and new relationships is exciting and wonderfully satisfying. Moreover, the first one to arrive at the correct interpretation of these new relationships wins!

The Economic Impact of Structural Change

The twentieth century is likely to be called the era of "structural change." Unlike the mislabeled "Industrial Revolution," the past century really began the "Technological Evolution." This evolution has truly changed our economic, political, and social structures.

Thus structural change is now the most important long-term investment consideration. Biotech can structurally change medical treatments, lifespan, and product development. Exotic new processes can leach gold from soil and even extract this yellow metal from seawater. These kinds of developments change market structures.

Structural change also relates to new sources of supply and demand. As Brazil clears the rain forest to make way for cattle ranches or farms, a new supply of beef or grain comes to the world market. As Greenland discovers and develops gold fields, new supplies change the market structure. If taxol retards the growth of certain cancers, the structure of U.S. forest economics changes. The North American yew can easily become more valuable for medicinal applications than for wood. In general, structural changes have lasting effects upon pricing mechanisms.

Fundamental studies of production inputs often reveal subtle structural changes within the supply equation. Assume new farming techniques permanently reduce fertilizer requirements for soybeans, wheat, and corn. This alteration in the "input structure" for these grains will change their cost equations. Insect resistance will limit pesticides and boost yields.

Detailed studies of production inputs and outputs are common approaches to fundamentals. In later chapters I will touch upon "linear programs" that solve simultaneous equations for inputs and outputs. Input/output analysis attempts to define the role of each input or output in determining the eventual outcome. In our case, the outcome is a selling price. For other applications, the analysis might seek to balance an oil refinery's production between gasoline, heating oil, jet fuel, waxes, solvents, and other components. Depending upon the relative value of each component, there is an optimum mix the refinery would like to have between the output of each component. These relationships are usually linear. This means the solutions are defined using linear or "straight line" formulas.

You may recall "systems of simultaneous equations" from your high school or college math courses. Such systems are useful in determining price outcomes using different supply and demand inputs. As you will learn, computer technology allows us to approach these systems and problems with greater diversity and more powerful analytical tools. Relationships that are curvilinear and nonlinear can be approached using neural networks and artificial intelligence systems.

Even with new theories about structural correlations, fundamentals will nonetheless always focus upon factors influencing supply and demand.

Next, as I take you deeper into the subject of TechnoFundamentals, I'll open up my trading "toolbox" to show you how I evaluate various kinds of impacts upon supply and demand.

CHAPTER 2

LESSONS THE MARKET TAUGHT ME

Before we delve deeper into fundamental techniques, a short walk through market history will be helpful. Indeed, just reviewing several spectacular trends of past years serves to stimulate and inspire.

Can you spot the next great profit opportunity? To do so, you'll need to develop a framework for your own TechnoFundamental approach to the coming opportunities.

It is important to grasp the incredible profit potentials available when fundamental analysis is properly applied. Many younger traders will be surprised to learn how massive some moves have been . . . and in some surprising markets.

To get a sense of perspective—and some inspiration—let's compare some famous moments in the markets.

Sexy T-Bonds versus Dull Old Sugar

In 1972, the Chicago Mercantile exchange ventured outside traditional commodity boundaries and introduced currency futures through a newly formed International Monetary Market (IMM). The idea was to provide a new and more flexible way to hedge currency risk.

This group of "financial futures" were created in response to floating exchange rates. President Nixon had closed the gold window and currencies no longer enjoyed fixed parities with the U.S. Dollar. It was only a matter of time before the concept of nonagricultural futures contracts took hold, which they certainly did.

Shortly after the introduction of currency futures, exchanges introduced interest rate contracts like the Ginnie Mae, Treasury Bills, Bonds, Notes, and Eurodollars. (Today, we have stock indices, inflation contracts, and proposals for futures on insurance, freight rates, electricity, and other interesting concepts.)

In 10 short years, financial futures eclipsed the once dominant contracts like soybeans, corn, silver, and pork bellies. In fact, most trading interest today centers on financial contracts.

Yet here's the interesting point: history shows that financial contracts do not have the same enormous trend potential as agricultural commodities.

Consider sugar in 1974. Traded on the New York Coffee, Cocoa & Sugar Exchange, one contract represents 112,000 pounds of sugar and is quoted in cents per pound. Each penny movement translates into a profit or loss of $1,120. We arrive at this figure by multiplying the contract size of 112,000 pounds by $0.01. Further, the margin for sugar in 1974 was about $400 per contract.

From 1972 through 1973, sugar staged a stunning long-term rally from four cents to 13 cents. (See Figure 2-1.) While many traders were satisfied with a $9,960 move, the real trend was only beginning. A severe sugar shortage developed as back-to-back deficit production caused hoarding by middlemen. Just into the third quarter of 1974, prices had skyrocketed to $0.66 (66 cents).

This middleman squeeze in sugar produced a move worth over $60,000 per contract! In comparison, Treasury bond futures would have to move 60 full points to make an equivalent move. In other words, the 1974 sugar market offered a profit range equal to the gross distance Treasury bond futures prices traveled over their entire history through 1994.

Not surprisingly, sugar prices plunged the same distance in 1975. It is fair to say that if Treasury bonds exhibited similar volatility at any time, it would be a signal that the U. S. economy was in dire shape.

In 1975, a freeze in Brazil destroyed a major portion of that country's coffee crop. Coffee prices responded by moving from $0.45 to over $3.35 per pound! (See Figure 2-2.) The gross move was worth more than $108,000. (A longer discussion of this move appears later in this chapter.)

Figure 2-1

SBNFVOI Daily   08/02/72 - 12/31/73 High = 13.53   Low = 5.13   Last = 12.33

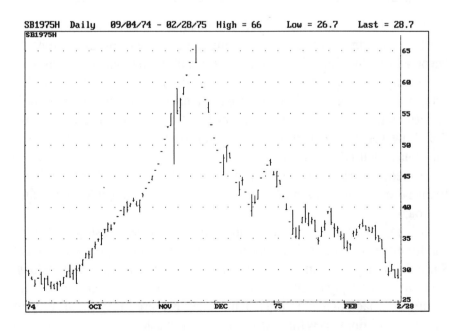

SB1975H Daily   09/04/74 - 02/28/75 High = 66   Low = 26.7   Last = 28.7

Figure 2-2

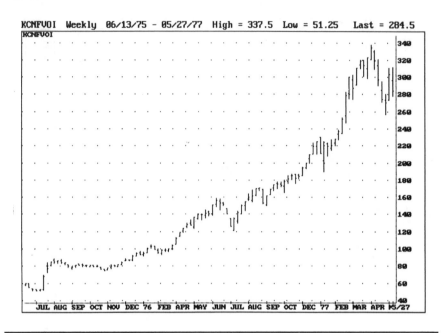

KCNFVOI Weekly 06/13/75 - 05/27/77 High = 337.5 Low = 51.25 Last = 284.5

Given the futures contract specifications for U.S. debt instruments currently, a Treasury bond trend producing the equivalent profit is probably beyond the realm of possibility. (Of course, I make this statement cautiously.)

Perhaps the popular S & P 500 stock index contract could match such a gain in so short a period. The disastrous October 1987 stock market crash yielded an impressive $75,000 gain for those who were short. (See Figure 2-3.) However, common sense tells us it is unlikely we will see a bull move of the same magnitude again any time soon.

Moreover, for better or (probably) worse, stock market crashes are the only financial trends that can match the potential of more tangible commodity contracts.

It's important to note that every major price trend has a basic prerequisite condition: the trading vehicle must be subject to extreme supply disruptions. Since the supply of financial instruments is controlled by human decisions, extraordinary supply disruptions are less likely than with traditional commodities. In fact, demand rather than supply is more likely to fall prey to extreme conditions, as is the case when markets crash.

Figure 2-3

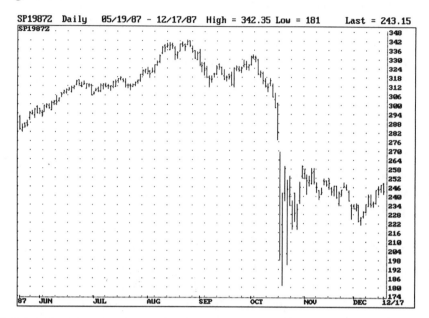

SP19872 Daily 05/19/87 - 12/17/87 High = 342.35 Low = 181   Last = 243.15

Only the 1987 stock market crash duplicated profit potential of traditional commodities.

With these principles in mind, let's explore more great trends and then analyze the fundamentals behind the moves.

1973: The "Year of the Grains"

For high financial drama at its best, few major price trends made as lasting an impression as the bull markets in grain of 1972/73. Billions of dollars were at stake as farmers, speculators, grain merchants, and even entire governments played against each other.

Mother Nature produced and directed the drama. The plot featured everything from supply disruptions and unexpected demand to adverse weather and misplaced government programs . . . all against an international backdrop of structural economic shifts.

To fully appreciate the story, imagine you are back in 1970. The U. S. remains involved in the Vietnam conflict. U.S. oil price controls are in place.

U.S. relations with Israel are about to precipitate the OPEC Oil Embargo which, in turn, will drive energy prices to unprecedented levels. U.S. citizens are no longer permitted to own gold. Richard Nixon is in the White House.

Global economic expansion has stretched the world monetary system to its limit. The U. S. can no longer afford to regulate currency flows through gold exchange. This situation is creating an underlying confidence problem as free world central banks are forced to wean themselves from gold-based exchange.

These conditions have set the stage for exaggerated price movements. In reality, shortages did not justify the tremendous price run-ups in corn, wheat, soybeans, and other grains that followed. In all probability, however, few analysts are likely to have taken these longer-term structural economic changes into consideration.

After all, the last such major economic change took place in the 1940s when President Franklin Roosevelt realigned the gold/dollar parity and declared gold illegal for domestic transactions or holdings.

Unless a structural change is dramatic or in response to crisis, there is a tendency to overlook or ignore its potential impact. Most people do not like change. Therefore, we take a long time to acknowledge change and adapt. When structural changes suddenly become apparent, we frequently experience panic because we are in uncharted territory. Usually the new rules, guidelines, relationships, and patterns have not yet been established.

With this latter point in mind, let's go back to the extraordinary events leading up to the unprecedented trends of 1972 and 1973.

Often the events leading to major moves take place over an extended period of time. For example, the bull market from 1972 through 1973 had its origins in 1970. (See Figure 2-4.) Despite enthusiastic planting, a severe corn leaf blight significantly reduced yields. Tight corn supplies pressured other feed grains like soybeans and barley.

From a low of approximately $1.20 per bushel, corn reached $1.60, a level not seen since 1954. At the time, the United States was the world's largest grain producer and exporter.

The corn leaf blight that season was a single, independent event that adversely affected feed supplies. Taken alone, the disruption was enough to touch off a 33% rise in corn prices. In addition, however, lower corn stocks forced users to find alternatives. This factor in turn raised prices for other feed stocks.

Figure 2-4

C-NFVOI   Weekly   01/23/70 - 12/28/73   High = 390   Low = 109.5   Last = 271.25

The 1971 corn leaf blight set the stage for a two-year bull market. A record 1972 crop was not enough to satisfy global needs into 1973.

Since there are alternative feeds, the overall impact of the corn leaf blight was held in check by other grains. Prices were "elastic" to the extent that an intolerable hike in corn would simply force users to other grains or protein products.

Still, corn prices spiked impressively higher. For traders recognizing the blight's impact, profit potentials ranged from $1,000 to $2,000 on a single futures position. This represented returns of as much as 1,000 to 2,000% considering minimum exchange margins were just over $100 per contract.

Once the 1970 harvest was complete and the damage assessed, traders turned attention to supplies on hand relative to historical demand. Among the factors considered were the number of cattle, hogs, chickens, and turkeys on feed. After evaluating domestic needs, export potential was the next focus.

As a seasonal commodity, there would be no new corn until a modest southern hemisphere harvest toward the end of the first quarter of 1971. Indeed, this seasonal consideration rallied corn prices from approximately $1.45 to just under $1.60 through 1970's last quarter.

In the meantime, soybean prices began declining from about $3.15 to about $2.80. Livestock producers determined that soybeans represented a cheaper alternative to corn. The forces of supply, demand, and price elasticity were in play.

Corn responded by declining sharply just after the beginning of 1971 until prices reached the interim 1970/71 support above $1.40. This raises two questions. First, what made $1.40 support? And second, isn't "support" a technical term?

To the latter, the answer is, yes, support is usually a technical concept. However, in the fundamental sense, traders were anxious to secure supplies at historically favorable prices. Having seen corn rally from levels near $1.40 several times since the 1970 summer breakout, they were concerned that they might not have another opportunity to buy at these relatively low levels, and that made $1.40 support level at that time.

Further, supplies dwindled as winter progressed. A modest amount of hoarding took place, followed by enthusiastic planting intentions for the 1971/72 season. There was little doubt that farmers would attempt to take advantage of attractive prices before the spring of 1971. Government programs encouraged additional planting and the stage was set for a retracement move downward.

Timing was tricky because prices rallied after a questionable planting period. Tight supplies, coupled with the fact that no new feed grains would be available until the fall, encouraged bulls right up until the summer.

By June of 1971, it was apparent the new corn crop was not going to suffer from blight. Farmers planted to capacity in corn, soybeans, and other grains to take advantage of the higher prices. The market reacted accordingly with a rapid sell-off as corn dropped to $1.10.

Indeed, 1971 yielded a record U.S. corn crop along with impressive soybeans, wheat, and other grains. The crisis seemed over . . . Or was it?

Although U.S. crops had recovered extremely well, other countries faced unusual weather problems. El Niño, a warming of the equatorial tides along South America's west coast, caused a shift in precipitation patterns that adversely affected the Soviet Union and southern hemisphere producers. (See Figure 2-5.) While South American grain crops only accounted for marginal production, gains in U.S. yields were still offset by declines in other countries.

Figure 2-5

S-NFVOI Daily   12/02/71 - 06/15/73 High = 1290   Low = 301.25   Last = 1050

El Niño combined with corn shortage to create a protein shortage as fish meal from Peru all but disappeared. Soybeans reached the "teens" for the first time in history.

More importantly, Peruvian fish meal was a major source of high protein animal feed. Anchovies were forced away from the coast by El Niño. This exacerbated a developing shortage of animal feeds for global consumption.

Large grain merchants were more aware of supply problems since they were filling export orders. In a counterseasonal move, grains began rallying during the 1971 harvest in response to large movements in government programs. At the same time, more than three million tons of feed grains were purchased by the Soviet Union.

As we will see when we look at conversion factors, three million metric tons translates into 118 million bushels—a significant purchase. (See Figure 2-6.)

We know the events leading to 1973's explosive grain markets were subtle. With the benefit of hindsight, we see that 1970 began a cumulative decrease in available supplies known as "free stocks." The 1971 recovery

Figure 2-6
World Production of Corn or Maize in Millions of Metric Tons (3)

Crop Year	United States	Argentina	Brazil	Mexico	South Africa	France	China	India	Italy	Bulgaria	Hungary	Yugoslavia	Romania	Indonesia	USSR	World Total
1961	3,598	210	373	219	220	1963—	1960—	168	155	45	107	179	215	91	500	7,465
1962	3,606	180	400	215	240	Avg.	64	180	128	61	128	208	194	126	385	7,470
1963	4,019	211	370	253	168	(3.6	Avg.	179	136	68	140	212	237	105	335	8,060
1964	3,484	202	465	295	177	M.T.)	(425)	179	156	81	138	274	263	161	360	7,835
1965-6 (3)	104.2	7.0	11.4	8.0	5.1	3.4	21.4	4.8	3.3	1.2	3.6	5.9	5.9	2.4	6.4	218.9
1966-7	105.9	8.0	12.8	8.2	9.6	4.3	21.7	4.9	3.5	2.2	3.9	8.0	8.0	3.7	6.8	239.4
1967-8	123.5	6.6	12.8	8.0	5.2	4.2	25.5	6.3	3.9	2.0	3.5	7.2	6.9	2.4	8.0	253.5
1968-9	113.0	6.9	12.7	8.5	5.0	5.4	23.5	5.7	4.0	1.8	3.8	6.8	7.1	3.1	7.4	243.3
1969-70	119.1	9.4	14.2	6.5	6.2	5.7	24.3	5.7	4.5	2.4	4.8	7.8	7.7	2.3	10.1	260.0
1970-1	105.5	9.9	13.5	8.7	8.6	7.6	26.4	7.5	4.8	2.4	4.0	6.9	6.5	2.9	7.8	255.1
1971-2	143.3	5.9	12.9	9.0	9.6	8.8	25.3	5.0	4.5	2.8	4.7	7.4	7.9	2.6	7.1	291.0
1972-3 (1)	141.1	9.2	14.3	8.1	4.2	8.2	22.0	6.2	4.8	2.9	5.5	7.9	9.5	2.0	9.8	286.8
1973-4 (2)	144.2	9.2	14.6	9.5	8.0	10.1	25.0	6.8	5.1	2.9	5.9	8.1	9.6	2.6	13.0	308.5

(1) Preliminary. (2) Estimate. (3) Data prior to 1965-66 are in MILLIONS OF BUSHELS.

Source: Foreign Agricultural Service, U.S.D.A. Table provided through Knight-Ridder CRB InfoTech™ CD-ROM.

created a deceptive interlude during which markets were lulled into a false sense of security.

As 1971 prices fell in response to record production, U.S. government support prices were triggered, funneling large free stocks into government storage. To avoid holding large inventories, the U.S. began unloading substantial amounts of wheat, corn, and soybeans in an export program known as the "Russian Wheat Deal."

Here is an interesting point. Despite seemingly record U.S. production, Russian purchases severely depleted global free stocks. Further, prices offered by the Russians and accepted by the U.S. were nominally above support. This was, in effect, a huge subsidy for the Soviet Union.

Political scientists have raised the question about whether the "subsidy" was intentionally orchestrated. Revelations of the early 1990s point to a hidden agenda whereby the United States had an interest in preventing the Soviet Union from suffering any severe food shortages. The power struggle was particularly sensitive. A famine could have precipitated internal conflict which could have easily been turned outward. An outright subsidy or "giveaway" would have been politically unwise because the U.S. was encountering its own inflationary problems. Therefore, a consequential increase in U.S. food prices on the heels of huge sales to the Soviets was more acceptable. Regardless of the method, the results are the same. U.S. consumers pay an inflated price for grain because the Soviet Union bought for less than true market value.

During summer 1972, the Soviets were buying everything in sight at below market prices. At the time, these deals seemed good for the U.S. The object was to recover a portion of the money spent on support payments. There were few indications that Mother Nature was about to turn the tide.

Russian purchases began the first stage of a massive bull market by mid-year, 1972. Wheat rallied from a low near $1.40 to a 20-year high just below $2.40. The large planting intentions caused a 1973 first quarter correction. Even with increases in potential production, free stocks remained critically tight.

At the time, it was difficult to imagine wheat prices rallying above $2.40. After all, most traders had never seen such high wheat prices. Soybeans were steadily moving higher as alternative high protein sources like fish meal disappeared.

The Russians were in a major program to upgrade their diet with expanded animal production; the herds were already in development. Large feed supplies were critical to their program—at any price.

When extremely wet weather hampered the 1973 spring planting, panic psychology overcame the grains. Traders suddenly realized just how low free stocks had become. Without a bumper crop, the world faced a possible disaster.

This psychology was fueled by the OPEC oil embargo and a seemingly out-of-control inflation brought about by currency devaluations and raw material shortages.

Was there good reason to believe that soybeans would top $13 per bushel, wheat more than $6.40, and corn above $4.00? In reality, shortages justified only half the rally. Just plain fear accounted for the rest.

What Happens if the Rules Change?

Many observers believe the 1972/73 bull markets in grains marked a new era of "SuperTrends." In addition to 1972/73 supply problems, the U.S. world moved away from a gold standard. The U.S. dollar could no longer be converted into gold. With that structural change, the greenback was also devalued between 10% and 15%.

Fixed currency parities were no longer the rule. An oil monopoly held the industrialized west hostage. There was a genuine fear that our way of life would be changed forever.

These factors contributed to the overreaction in wheat, corn, and soybeans. The daily question was, "When is a top likely?" while markets seemed out of control.

It is important to note that *extraordinary trends are more easily predicted than followed by fundamentals.* If a trader had been watching free stocks stagnate from 1970 through 1972, a bullish bias would have prevailed. It is difficult to believe that such a bias would have concluded with $13.00 high for soybeans—a price never before seen. (In later chapters, we will address the problem of "When is enough enough?")

As you can see from this review of market history from 1970 through 1973, the market action was nothing short of spectacular. Those fortunate enough to ride the trends amassed incredible fortunes. The process, however, was far from easy.

There are several broad lessons we gain from our retrospective. First, we see how a number of diversified developments contributed to the continuation of the same trend. We gain insight into recognizing and interpreting structural change. We also realize there is no such thing as "too high." Under certain circumstances, the unrealistic becomes reality.

The Sweetest Squeeze of '74

How many investment opportunities can you think of which can afford a $67,000 return on an investment of $400 in less than eighteen months? Such returns are usually storybook fantasies. At best, we can assume such circumstances rarely occur.

The sugar market afforded just such an opportunity during its greatest bull move of the twentieth century. Like the grain markets of 1970 through 1973, sugar experienced structural changes as well as cumulative events which precipitated its massive upward price surge.

Third World nations had been engaged in nationalization movements. Resources formerly under the control of industrialized nations were seized and converted to sovereign control.

These factors brought about two structural changes. First, income potential shifted from industrialized countries to resource owners. Second, it established a debtor relationship between new sovereign owners and former controlling interests.

With this new-found wealth and power, sugar-producing countries developed a sweet tooth, i.e., more sugar began to be consumed within the countries of origin. This pattern, coupled with back-to-back deficit production seasons, depleted global free stocks.

The world was accustomed to relatively low raw sugar prices from cane and beets. From a historical price perspective, there were few incentives to seek alternative sweeteners prior to 1974. Processing high fructose corn syrups was not a consideration. Corn prices and processing costs made such sweeteners uncompetitive.

U.S. import quota restrictions maintained an artificially high domestic raw sugar price while depressing world prices, creating the potential for price dislocation. The two-tiered system held crop expansion in check.

The main U.S. export crops (wheat, corn, soybeans) were fetching high prices from the previous season. This encouraged more grain acreage and less sugar beet production. In addition, the U.S. Sugar Act was expiring on December 31, 1974 and there was substantial uncertainty over import quotas and future supplies.

With hindsight, most analysts agree that the tremendous price surge was overdone. Rising prices precipitated a hoarding stampede that extended from industrial users all the way down to individual consumers.

At one point, supermarkets could not keep sugar stocked on shelves. Restaurants removed table sugar to prevent pilfering and soft drink companies scrambled to reformulate.

In the aftermath of the multi-billion dollar price rally that came (see Figure 2-7), some market philosophers speculate that there was a "hidden agenda." There is no question but that political actions of the European Community (EC) and the U.S. substantially contributed to the price surge.

Figure 2-7

Sugar experienced a major bull market ultimately leading to prices exceeding 60¢/lb.

With the pending expiration of the Sugar Act, the U.S. administration could have taken steps to relieve some of the concern over our policy.

However, no indications were given until mid-November when the President announced a global quota of seven million tons. Why was there no effort to alleviate pressure on domestic consumers? In addition, the International Sugar Agreement also expired at the end of 1973. With a potential shortage developing, why did participants fail to agree upon quotas and the release of buffer stocks prior to the crisis?

Third World economic reorganization was being funded by industrialized nations. Debt was rapidly building while income-generating infrastructure was not yet in place. Perhaps it was economically and politically more expedient to allow particular Third World commodities to "selectively inflate."

Whatever the case, U.S. sugar imports increased in value over 100% from 1973 to 1974. A substantial portion of the more than $2.25 billion went to developing nations. This extraordinary boost in income allowed these nations to meet their debt service. In effect, it was a transfer from industrialized consumers to Third World treasuries.

Obviously, this is a theory that is only circumstantially supported by the fact that higher sugar prices in fact helped Third World producers. The importance of this theory is that it may serve to explain seemingly inexplicable political behavior during times of extreme economic dislocation in any commodity market.

It is interesting to note that many erroneous fundamental conclusions were formed during the 1973/74 panic. At one point, for example, analysts suggested that sugar production was being curtailed by a lack of cheap labor to harvest cane. Had this been the case, we would have seen a major structural change in the sugar market. However, the subsequent decline in sugar and boost in post-1974 production proved this was not the case.

Difficulties with the 1974 European sugar beet crop was also thought to contribute to higher prices. It is true that the decline in beet sugar output placed further pressures on supplies. But the eventual "deficit" turned out to be far less than the later prices would justify.

Global carrying stocks of sugar are generally one-quarter to one-third of annual production. This has always been a sufficient buffer to prevent exceptional price gyrations. The two crop years preceding this one fell short of consumption. Even with optimistic forecasts for Soviet, Brazilian, and Philippine output, buffer stocks were reduced to less than one-fifth of anticipated usage.

An encouraging report released by the sugar-tracking firm of F. O. Licht predicted 1974 would return the market to near normal conditions. When this optimism faded, speculation overreacted.

As sugar topped $0.60 on the New York Coffee and Sugar Exchange, industrial users were convinced cane and beet sugar would not return to pre-1973 levels. As a result, they rapidly developed alternatives like high fructose corn sweeteners (HFCS). Even with the relatively high corn price, HFCS was competitive with raw sugar that exceeded $0.25 per pound.

What was the effect of the move toward HFCS? The development of this alternative provided a new fundamental consideration. The relationship between corn and sugar prices became significant in regulating raw sugar prices. Availability of HFCS structurally changed the sweetener market. Soft drink manufacturers, bakers, and food processors all developed formulas that could use either sugar or HFCS.

Thus, the upper limit on raw sugar was capped by HFCS substitution. All future sugar moves would be regulated by this alternative. In fact, when the 1979/80 crop year fell short of usage, sugar was unable to return to 1974 highs. Many believe prices were contained by the substitution of HFCS.

Could sugar move beyond 1974 highs? Anything is possible. However, such a move would require shortages and high prices for both white sugar and corn. Since industrial users are more flexible in their formulations, a return to 1974 would be more difficult.

The Time Coffee Was Really Perking

Immediately following sugar's spectacular 1974 run-up, coffee eclipsed the performance by soaring from approximately $0.65 a pound to more than $3.20. (See Figure 2-8.) This "Mega-Move" astounded market participants, with a single contract position yielding more than $100,000 over the course of the entire move!

An interesting aspect of this move was the deception prior to the announcement that Brazil's major coffee-producing region had suffered a severe freeze. While it is generally believed that Brazil's officials knew of earlier damage, the crop condition may have been withheld to permit Brazil's exporters time to cover commitments.

Figure 2-8

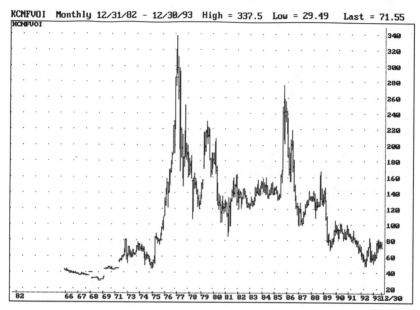

In 1975, coffee prices eventually reached $3.26/lb. This bull move structurally changed coffee for 15 years.

Knowing there would be a shortfall, Brazil bought futures to offset its delivery requirements. Once positions were in place, the really bad news hit the market.

This is an important consideration because it highlights the most glaring deficiency in fundamental analysis. Assuming you are collecting information from public sources, that means there's the chance of erroneous or misleading data.

If you can afford to place your own reliable scouts in Brazil, you might feel more confident about such information. Absent such resources, we'll all have to rely upon more public information channels.

The freeze was announced on July 17–18, 1975. However, coffee prices had been steadily climbing from the beginning of May through mid-June. Market historians believe problems materialized during the May/June rally. In fact, cold weather was reported during the second week in June.

Brazilian Coffee Institute reports contradicted indications that weather had become a problem. This campaign of reassurance in the media quelled fears and coffee settled back through the first two weeks of July.

Technically, there were long side accumulations through June as well as early July. In other words, buyers were accumulating positions from short sellers while prices were rising. As we will see in the chapter covering technical analysis, long side accumulation is a process whereby buyers bid prices higher while devoting increasing amounts of cash to their positions. This was the only indication that a major bull market was brewing. Conflicting reports held coffee in a trading range between 50 and 56 cents until the news broke. Thereafter, coffee made limit-up moves until the September contract resumed liquidity around 80 cents.

Obviously, fundamentals were the driving force behind the trend. In addition, a knowledge of seasonal coffee patterns provided insight into the bull market's potential. However, precise timing would have required tracking the actual mid-July breakout from the trading range.

There were two main factors to consider. First, what would be the impact of the freeze on the market? Second, was there a technical confirmation and follow-through?

Understand that there was no historical precedent for the move that was to take place. From a purely fundamental standpoint, traders would have abandoned long positions between 75 and 80 cents. Indeed, many did.

What was the reason for picking this exit point? A long-term chart shows 85 cents as the highest previous top back in 1955. (See Figure 2-9.) Since this was the only historical reference point, it made sense to assume prices would meet resistance at that same approximate area.

As with grains in 1973, it was almost impossible to predict how excessively far coffee prices would carry before stabilizing or reversing. Of course, I use the phrase "almost impossible" because there were some subtle clues. Strong long-side accumulation was measurable after coffee broke through 85 cent resistance. As we will learn in the chapter on "The Fundamentals of Technical Analysis," accumulation can indicate the strength and momentum of a bull or bear trend.

To this day, there are many market historians who believe the extremely high prices were more a result of manipulation than reality. Frankly, a trader does not care if a trend is fabricated or real—as long as he or she participates in the correct side.

Figure 2-9

KC1975U Daily   03/04/75 - 09/23/75 High = 88.75 Low = 48.3   Last = 82.5

Long-Side Accumulation Beginning in May was the First Indication of a Potential Bull Move

Run-Away Bull Market Develops After Freeze is Announced

Brazil's Officials Talk Down Freeze Scare

Consider that while Brazil's coffee crop was reduced from 23 million to 9.3 million 60-kilo bags, the price moved from 50 cents to $3.20 before retreating. The crop was reduced by 60% while prices increased 640%.

Here's the economics of the crop years. Each bag represents 132.276 pounds. At 50 cents per pound, then, each bag is worth $66.14. At $3.20, the value is $423.28 per bag. Thus the 23 million bag crop had an average value of $1,521,220,000. The smaller 9.3 million bag crop had a maximum value of $3,936,504,000.

Contract records reveal that much of the Brazilian crop fetched between $2.50 and $2.75 per pound over the following two seasons. While all predictions called for a minimum five-year recovery period, Brazil's production hit 17.5 million and then 20 million bags the following two seasons. (See Figure 2-10.)

Brazil's increased coffee revenues were not trivial. In combination with the boost in sugar income, Brazil was able to pay much of her debt service.

The 1975 freeze established a floor on coffee prices at approximately $1.25. It lasted almost through 1989. Many believed coffee would never drop

Figure 2-10
World Green Coffee (Total) Production in Thousands of 60-Kilo Bags (132.276 Lbs. per Bag)

Crop Year	Angola	Brazil	Camer-oon	Colom-bia	Costa Rica	Ethi-opia	Guate-mala	India	Indon-esia	Ivory Coast	Mexico	Salva-dor	Uganda	Zaire (Congo, K)	World Total
1973-4	3,200	14,500	1,260	7,800	1,570	1,700	2,200	1,535	2,750	3,255	3,300	2,378	3,100	1,317	62,459
1974-5	3,000	27,500	1,816	9,000	1,390	2,050	2,540	1,630	2,675	4,500	3,900	3,300	3,000	1,150	81,082
1975-6	1,180	23,000	1,482	8,500	1,276	2,677	2,043	1,498	3,049	5,266	3,856	2,530	2,214	1,072	73,008
1976-7	1,131	9,300	1,307	9,300	1,331	2,782	2,213	1,753	3,219	4,867	3,330	2,973	2,664	1,437	61,439
1977-8	1,047	17,500	1,371	11,050	1,449	3,143	2,550	2,147	3,911	3,393	3,401	2,700	1,868	1,129	71,374
1978-9	613	20,000	1,634	12,600	1,749	3,142	2,827	1,842	4,788	4,742	4,022	3,423	1,944	1,293	79,074
1979-80	260	22,000	1,658	12,712	1,522	3,188	2,647	2,495	4,803	3,973	3,600	3,322	2,042	1,316	81,908
1980-1	586	21,500	1,959	13,500	2,140	3,264	2,702	1,977	5,265	6,090	3,862	2,940	2,133	1,526	86,249
1981-2	392	33,000	1,953	14,342	1,782	3,212	2,653	2,540	5,785	4,084	3,900	2,886	2,885	1,425	98,195
1982-3 (1)	430	17,750	1,817	13,300	2,450	3,350	2,593	2,200	4,786	4,260	4,100	2,671	3,200	1,390	82,345
1983-4 (1)	350	30,000	1,900	13,000	2,070	3,350	2,340	2,000	4,895	3,667	4,200	2,453	3,100	1,400	91,657

(1) Preliminary. (2) Estimate.

Brazil's coffee production dropped from 23,000,000 in 1975/76 to 9,300,000 in 1976/77. However, production quickly recovered despite dire forecasts.

Source: Foreign Agricultural Service, U.S.D.A. Table provided through Knight-Ridder CRB InfoTech™ CD-ROM.

below $1.00 a pound again. Yet, more than one-and-a-half inflationary decades later, coffee returned to its pre-1975 levels. Will (market) wonders never cease?

When Some Metals Got Very Precious

Perhaps the most memorable super trends of this century occurred in the precious metals markets at the end of the roaring '70s. No discussion of TechnoFundamentals would be complete without reviewing the ultimate conclusion of several massive structural changes and the ensuing economic realignment.

The combination of going off the gold standard, floating currencies, the Energy Crisis, back-to-back bull markets in virtually all commodities, political uncertainty, and failing confidence all culminated in a wild flight to silver and gold. This panic, while unfamiliar to many of today's professional traders, stands as a lesson and a warning that physical, tangible, hard assets are inevitably the investment of last resort. That is, when faith in "the system" is challenged, we return to some primal instinct that holds gold and other precious metals above all other stores of value.

Traditional economic theory and market logic simply had to bow to the new rules. Suddenly, there could be inflation in the face of zero or negative economic growth; it was dubbed "stagflation."

The world had a new system for establishing currency values. But, industrialized nations did not know how to control floating exchange rates with enough assurance to protect international trade from adverse parity fluctuations.

I am not suggesting conditions during the 1970s and 1980s never existed in history. Certainly, there have been inflations and hyper-inflations. We have had depressions and financial panics. In all cases, we can identify a breakdown in old structures and the replacement with new ones.

However, I believe it is generally agreed that times had changed. The world had become far more complex. Economic systems had become more vast and interrelated. As the events of the 1970s led to the new markets of the 1980s, the scope of change was probably unprecedented in modern history.

To take an obvious kind of change, consider the automobile, perhaps the most significant and distinguishing foundation of our modern lifestyle. I say "was" because we do not know if that same lifestyle will remain intact in the

"Information Age." However, our society owes most of its mobility to the car, and that car has always relied upon oil.

From the turn of the nineteenth century until the Arab Oil Embargo of the early 1970s, oil prices remained stable and low. With the exception of war-time fuel rationing, most consumers in the industrial nations have enjoyed their automobiles with scarcely a thought of fuel costs or availability. When Arab oil producers placed an embargo on oil to the U.S. after the Arab-Israeli War, this relative abundance of fuel was threatened.

The fantastic surge in oil price during the 1970s affected all economic sectors in ways never anticipated. While it is true that some scientists warned the same situation would occur naturally when the Earth ran out of fossil fuels, this was viewed as a fantasy.

In an instant, the Energy Crisis was real. Our huge dependence upon energy was demonstrated in practically every economic sector of the Western world. Transportation, manufacturing, heating, cooling, chemicals, plastics, building materials, electricity, and a host of other basic building blocks of the economy were held hostage to oil. The fantasy predicted by some scientists seemed closer and the world was trying to adjust.

This was no easy task. However deserving of criticism the Nixon and Carter administrations and their European counterparts may have been, the industrialized nations did an enviable job of holding things together. Through uncharted waters, we managed to avoid shipwreck.

Almost immediately, however, oil-related inflation began to impact markets. Gold became the physical commodity traded against oil. There had been a standing correlation between the value of one ounce of gold and certain commodities. For example, an ounce of gold maintained the same value as a custom tailored man's suit. In the 1930s, the official price was $30 and a suit cost about $30. Today, it takes about two ounces to buy a good quality man's suit and just over three ounces to cover a custom tailored outfit. Thus, the valuation or parity has changed since 1982. An ounce of gold was associated with approximately 10 barrels of oil. When oil was about $3 per barrel, gold had 10-to-1 parity at $30 per ounce. When oil prices broke rank with gold, substantially more gold would have been needed to maintain historical parity. Unfortunately, the capacity to produce more gold was limited by technology and resources. With constraints on production, an alternative to fixing oil prices in gold was required.

Yet the world was not quite ready to be weaned away from a gold standard. You don't alter centuries of perceived value overnight. As a first step, President Nixon removed gold as a trading vehicle by closing the gold "window." Next was allowing individuals to own gold by lifting the gold ban in 1975.

Finally, our government flooded the market with gold reserves to convince the public that gold is not really worth the glitter. (In the process, it helped to take silver along for the ride.)

Much of the strategy worked because people trusted governments. More importantly, the Organization of Oil Producing Countries (OPEC) believed in assurances from the West that the "paper" they were receiving for their oil was "as good as gold."

When the paper began to devalue faster that the purchasing power could be replaced with new oil sales, OPEC decided the promises were no longer good. All the ingredients for panic were somehow quietly put in place. All that remained was a cook to stir them into the pot.

The cook turned out to be Texas oilman Bunker Hunt and his brother. Together, they devised a plan to buy silver as eventual backing for silver bonds or certificates. These certificates would potentially replace the dollar as the standard for oil trade and would more accurately reflect value in a world of unstable currencies.

Silver was chosen over gold because it remained relatively cheap and plentiful. Byproduct production was on the rise while silver recovery technologies were becoming more efficient.

This raises an important fundamental point. Supply and demand for precious metals appeared to be in equilibrium as long as investment demand remained stable. The prospect for silver-backed certificates implied a tremendous surge in demand for monetary use which would distort prices for industrial applications.

Recall how food processors changed formulations when sugar became too expensive. Just as HFCS was substituted for white sugar, so were alternatives considered for silver, gold, platinum, and palladium between 1979 and 1981.

Significant metal processing technology was developed as a result of the 1979/80 bull market. This technology has steadily increased the amount of silver, gold, platinum, and palladium mined from primary sources and recovered from scrap. At the same time, alternatives to these metals have been developed as a hedge against any repeat of the 1979/80 conditions. As we'll see, structural changes born out of the 1980 peak in prices are still inherent in today's markets.

The Hunts and their OPEC allies began accumulating silver during 1979. An all-out buying binge developed within the first quarter of that year and seemed to fundamentally peak in early August at approximately $10.50 per ounce. (See Figure 2-11.)

The expression, "You had to be there . . ." is appropriate when describing the utter amazement shared by the financial community when silver pushed to double digits. Entire computer systems came to a halt when preset formats could not accommodate prices over $9.99 per ounce. It was simply not thought possible.

Interestingly, the shock of $10.00 silver managed to stall prices as disbelief became skepticism. Forecasters called for a "top" in silver as resistance became apparent around the $10.50 mark.

Figure 2-11

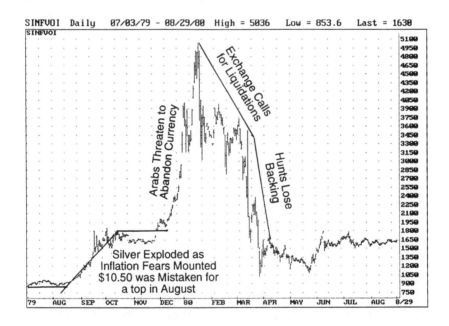

Analysts pointed out that many of the inflationary trends in raw commodities were ending. Conservation and exploration provided new energy resources, alleviating the prior crisis. Prices for coffee, sugar, grains, and other commodities had receded. The Commodity Research Bureau Index actually declined from more than 23000 to below 21000 by mid-1979. Things were looking better.

But the plan was already in play. The Hunt brothers and their followers were determined to make silver the new monetary standard. Their trading resources were bigger than anyone else's. For the remainder of 1979 and into 1980, the Hunts controlled silver's destiny and carried the other precious metals along for the ride.

By the second week of August 1980, silver bulls began another wave of long side accumulation. While other speculators were happy to take profits at the $10.50 mark, insiders knew the ultimate price would be much higher.

Essentially, the Hunts were attempting to corner the silver market. By the time the public became aware of the magnitude of the plan, silver was already on its way past $20 an ounce.

OPEC helped fuel the trend by threatening to require precious metals in return for oil. The OPEC/Hunt team worked together to keep precious metals on a fast track. In the process, they jeopardized the delicate arrangements established by Western nations to float and regulate exchange rates. Suddenly, all of the work associated with removing the world from a fixed standard was exposed to collapse—not a politically acceptable event.

Toward the end of 1979, governments began to exert pressure upon OPEC to end the attempt at changing monetary standards. Negotiations centered on resolving the problem of currency instability. Eventually, a compromise was reached which would allow OPEC to specify a "basket of currencies" for payment rather than a dollar standard.

In the meantime, the Hunts continued with their strategy. Ultimately, the bull trend was brought under control when the New York Commodity Exchange (or COMEX) changed its trading rules to force contract liquidation. The exchange called the Hunts' hand by preventing new accumulation of positions and requiring full margins in anticipation of taking delivery.

It is possible the Hunts could have emerged victorious, had they been permitted to complete their plan. However, OPEC backing was not forthcoming when the exchange applied pressure.

From the beginning of the 1979 trend through the 1980 top, silver amassed *almost $180,000 on a single contract position!* This assumes a trader bought at $5.50 and sold at $41.25. Such clairvoyance would have been remarkable, but not beyond all possibility.

Gold, platinum, and palladium also yielded phenomenal profits. (See Figure 2-12.) However, as quickly as profits mounted on the long side, almost equivalent short side opportunities were available after markets reversed.

The decline in prices came in three stages. First, as a correction of the enormous overextension of the uptrend. Then, as a result of unprecedented interest rates that made precious metals investments unattractive relative to yields on paper instruments.

Finally, new financial vehicles provided alternatives to the traditional roles of precious metals. That is, adverse fluctuations in interest rates and currency parities could be offset using futures and options rather than hedging with hard assets. Once "derivative" products—i.e., instruments like futures

Figure 2-12

Gold reached beyond $800/oz. as investors lost confidence in paper assets. Rising interest rates during the '80s tempted investors away from gold.

and options that have an underlying "cash" instrument—could emulate the function of gold and silver, metals were no longer a required safety mechanism. This was a structural change.

Events that generated the precious metal bull markets were ancillary rather than primary. This is to say that the basic supply and demand formula did not consistently apply. From a consumption standpoint, the threat of monetary usage drove silver and gold. There was no corresponding reason for platinum and palladium to follow.

If anything, the surge in silver and gold prices implied that platinum group metals would become byproducts. Certainly, there had been enough platinum and palladium to satisfy industrial needs before and during the run-up. The speculative frenzy served to curb industrial appetites and could have easily caused abandonment.

While this logic did not apply to the unique situation during 1979/80, it does reflect fundamentals from the 1980s through the mid-1990s.

Technically, both the upswing and downturn represented a trader's dream for those with the nerves and stomach to withstand this kind of market action. Anything from a liberally drawn trendline to moving averages could have followed precious metals to near their tops and bottoms.

Looking for the Right Signal

Oscillators and newly developed technical indicators did not fare as well, however. In 1978, J. Welles Wilder, Jr. introduced his concept for a "relative strength index," or the "RSI."

This index operates as an oscillator that normalizes price action on a theoretical scale from 0 to 100. For practical purposes, values rarely exceed 80 or fall below 20. Moves toward these extremes are presumed to indicate "overbought" or "oversold" conditions. (A more detailed discussion of oscillator techniques will be covered in Chapter 7.)

However, a preliminary review within the context of the 1979/80 metals markets reveals the most serious flaw of a price-based oscillator. When markets experience powerful trends with accelerating price movements, the RSI will indicate overbought or oversold far in advance of an actual top or bottom. Following loose rules associated with the RSI can cause premature entries against the trend. Since the RSI is only a technical "indicator," it does not give a comprehensive set of rules that include damage control when a false signal is followed.

In raging bull or bear markets, common sense and fundamental evaluation can override an apparent RSI signal. The key is to establish a standard whereby "common sense" is objective and unemotional.

As the chart illustrates (see Figure 2-13), the RSI would have sold in advance of the silver top with potentially devastating consequences. This is not to say the RSI is not a helpful tool. Price oscillators have considerable usefulness. It is also important to understand their inherent weakness, however.

The Russian Wheat Deal, 1974 sugar market, the coffee freeze of 1975, and the precious metals move of 1979/80 are examples of extraordinary trends. In each case, a series of fundamental events gripped the market and moved prices beyond all expectations. Thus, the examples serve to show *how fundamentals must be combined with technicals to strike a balance between the historical frame of reference and a totally new experience.*

Figure 2-13

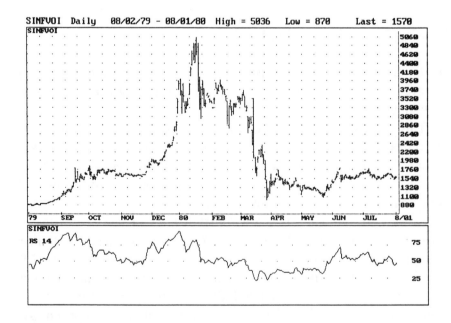

Our overview is not intended to demonstrate specific TechnoFundamental exercises. We have not examined techniques for building a fundamental model or applying technical analysis.

The purpose in this chapter was simply to acquaint you with some previous markets and illustrate the complexities associated with very large trends. In addition, the size of these unusual moves supports the adage, "Anything can happen . . ."

Now we're ready to examine some specific methodologies.

CHAPTER 3

TRENDS, CYCLES, SEASONS, AND THE RANDOM WALK

Each trend reviewed thus far has had several common elements. There were structural changes, crop seasons, and a tendency for cyclical behavior. There were random exaggerated movements and unexplained intermittent price changes.

These elements are the components of a "time series." In simple terms, a time series is a study of behavior or phenomena over time. A graphic representation of a time series is usually two-dimensional, with the X-axis (horizontal) representing time as a constant. The Y-axis (vertical) tracks observations at specific points in time. The most popular time series plots price against time. (See Figure 3-1.)

While there are many formats for a price time series, objectives remain the same. You will want to identify useful patterns for making predictions.

The Many Ways of Looking at Time and Trends

A time series can be evaluated technically or fundamentally. The technical approach attempts to identify patterns without regard for underlying fundamental events. The fundamental approach tries to link the time series to fundamental changes.

Figure 3-1
Price Time Series

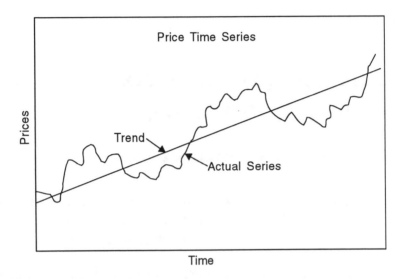

Recently the line between technical and fundamental interpretation has become confused. Often we hear a professed technician talk about "seasonal tendencies." The technician will acknowledge that seasonal tendencies exist, but he or she is not concerned with why such patterns occur. Nevertheless, seasonality is a fundamental concept.

It is obvious that crops respond to seasons. Certainly few would deny the existence of a "business cycle." We are all aware of the holiday season which is identified with the shopping spree that occurs between Thanksgiving and Christmas. And most of us would like to deny "tax season." Thus it is evident that seasons affect more than crops that are planted in the spring and harvested in the fall.

The fundamental analyst and technician also debate long-term structural or "secular" trends. In many cases the technician dismisses this trend as "too long" to be useful for trading. Yet when establishing long-term marketing programs or plans to build factories, the secular trend can be extremely important.

If you know why business cycles occur, you can attempt to recognize the precursors to recession, inflation, deflation, and other recurring economic conditions.

Random Walks and Noise Filters

Random events and associated reactions are also an important consideration. Anything from a political announcement to a natural disaster can occur randomly and result in substantial price changes.

Obviously, there is an enormous amount of data reflected in a simple time series. Despite its two-dimensional design, virtually all aspects of secular trend, business cycle, seasonality, and randomness can be gleaned from a study of price and time. (See Figure 3-2.)

The most popular tool for dissecting a time series is the simple moving average. However, the statistical application of moving averages has been obscured by the debate over fundamentals versus technicals.

Figure 3-2
Components of Time Series

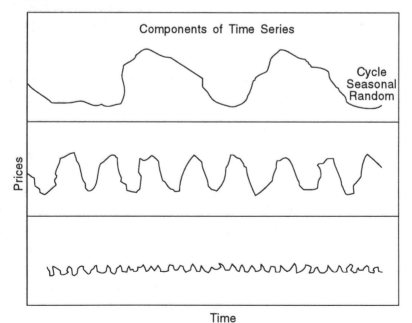

A moving average is a price average taken over a moving time window. For example, a 10-day moving average sums the past ten prices and divides by 10. The moving average itself is plotted over time and represents its own time series:

$$\Sigma \text{ (Last 10 Closes)} / 10 = 10\text{-Day Moving Average}$$

By its structure, a moving average lags behind a price trend while remaining flat under trendless circumstances. The statistical purpose of a moving average is to smooth out random price movements to identify underlying trends and cycles. Simply stated, the moving average removes "noise."

Early in the development of technical models, analysts discovered that moving averages could be used to filter out trends. An old physics law was assumed to apply to markets as follows: "A trend in motion will tend to remain in motion until acted upon by some countering force."

On this assumption, a moving average will follow a trend up or down and could conceivably identify a countering force by a change in price direction relative to the average.

Recall the example of a 20-day moving average (or 20MA) plotted against silver prices in the previous chapter (Figure 3-3). Notice how the 20MA tracks the price trend.

A simple set of rules has been established for interpreting moving averages: First, expect the market to continue rising when prices *exceed* a specific moving average.

Second, expect declining prices if a market falls *below* a moving average.

To my knowledge, there is no statistical basis for using moving averages as decision rules for trading. Yet the success of the approach popularized moving averages—along with price chart interpretation—as the most widely applied technical method.

Statistically speaking, the moving average can identify regular seasonal and cyclical patterns. Most of us are familiar with the term "seasonally adjusted." In many cases, the adjustment is based upon a moving average. There are variations on the standard moving average which include weighting "aged" data, exponential moving averages, logarithmic moving averages, and more. The goal is usually the same: to accurately identify time series components.

The application of moving averages to forecast or evaluate market behavior can be technical or fundamental, *depending on its use*. If the average is used

Figure 3-3
Silver with 20-Day Moving Average

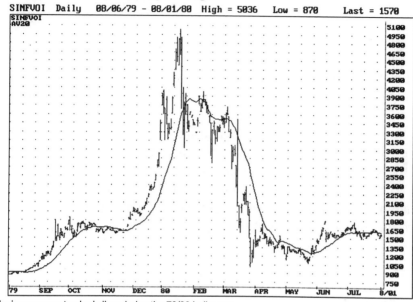

Moving average tracked silver during the 79/80 bull move.

alone as a trading decision rule, it is a technical approach. A moving average used to identify seasonal or cyclical tendencies is fundamental in nature.

It should be easy to see how technical and fundamental philosophies and tools share common ground. Hence, the need for TechnoFundamental analysis.

When you take a fundamental approach to analyzing a time series, you want to extract the trend, cycle, seasonal, and random components. A primary objective is to find reliable correlations to fundamental events or factors which can be used to make predictions.

Using known statistical techniques, you can identify recurring patterns within a time series. Even without the knowledge that grains are planted in the spring and harvested in the fall, a study of price action over time will clearly show a pattern of rising prices before planting and declining prices in the midst of harvest.

Logically, you can conclude there is a seasonal pattern to crop production. Extending the analysis further, you might want to see how the general infla-

tion rate affects crop prices. Should an inflation factor be built into a fundamental pricing model?

Interestingly, a study of prices from the early 1950s to the present reveals
that prices paid to farmers lag inflation and, in many cases, are unresponsive
to a general increase in retail consumer price levels.

You will find that increasing efficiency, technology, and productivity
have all worked to hold *average* grain prices in check. (See Figure 3-4.) Large
price swings are invariably linked to natural causes like droughts, floods,
insects, or disease.

How do we determine this? When we plot secular trendlines in soybeans,
corn, wheat, oats, cotton, and other crops, we will see that the slope is
relatively flat compared with the consumer price index.

What does this tell us about trading agricultural commodities? Any inflationary adjustment should be tempered. In short, you should never conclude
prices are "too low on an inflation-adjusted basis." A picture-perfect crop year

Figure 3-4
Corn Seasonality

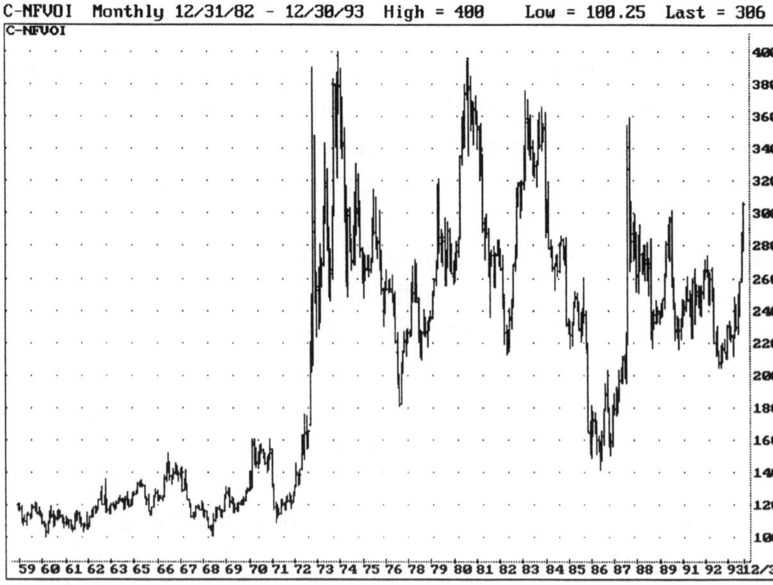

C-NFVOI   Monthly 12/31/82 - 12/30/93   High = 400   Low = 100.25   Last = 306

Source: Commodity Trend Service

may plummet grain prices to 10-year and even 20-year lows. This is particularly true if we experience structural change in global production or markets.

For example, when President Jimmy Carter imposed a grain embargo against the former Soviet Union as punishment for the invasion of Afghanistan, he forced the Soviets to seek grain from other markets. This, in turn, provided money and incentive for Third World countries to increase production. Within a few seasons, Brazil, Argentina, Western Europe, and Australia were filling the gap left by the United States. Once new production was in place, the United States lost its stronghold as the world's greatest food exporter.

The substantial increase in global capacity changed the pricing equation for grain. Fundamental analysis clearly shows the trend toward increasing global production and decreasing prices.

Other commodities are not as independent of inflation. Certainly, monetary metals like gold have kept pace with a rising price index. This is because gold is primarily used as a monetary standard. As a percentage of annual production, nonmonetary gold consumption is relatively small. The majority of this metal is used for investment or as a hedge against paper assets.

Thus, gold prices have been predicted on the basis of an inflation rate. In turn, the inflation rate can be determined using gold as a monetary standard.

Industrial metals like copper, aluminum, zinc, lead, and even silver reflect both inflation and changes in supply relative to consumption. You can adjust prices for inflation to forecast a most likely bottom. However, caution is always in order.

Prices and Trends

These commodities are also subject to structural changes that can counteract a secular inflationary trend. Advances in mining or declining applications can play an important role in determining how low prices can fall.

Modern copper production employs a process called "solvent extraction-electro-winning." This refining technique has lowered the cost of copper production to between 25 cents and 40 cents in 1993 dollars. Capital costs also have declined in recent years.

These trends should have suggested that the 1988 high of over $1.60 per pound was exaggerated and prices would eventually retreat to multi-decade lows. Indeed, copper retraced below $1.00 and further.

The fundamental influence could be used to predict a change in the price time series. It would have been fair to assume that technological break-throughs would reverse the secular price trend regardless of inflation.

Of course, this brings up an interesting question. If structural changes in core markets like grains, metals, and others cause a counterinflationary trend, shouldn't inflation abate or reverse?

Some might accuse this author of using 20/20 hindsight when pointing out that the early 1990s experienced negative inflation. In addition, the deflation or "disinflation" was largely due to a global recession brought about by high interest rates and changes in tax structure.

History will show that the recession in the wake of the 1987 crash in the U.S. stock market was only part of the deflationary drama. Worldwide expansion of production coupled with advancing technology combined to bring down basic commodity prices. In turn, profit margins diminished and world economies stalled.

At the same time, U.S. labor was forced to postpone its demands for wage and benefit increases as automated manufacturing joined forces with cheaper Third World competition to discourage hiring new workers.

Through turmoil and transition, fundamental equations for supply and demand held up reasonably well during this period. By carefully monitoring production and demand, accurate price forecasts could be constructed. We could see fundamental forces that were influencing prices of raw materials. Declining raw material prices in turn translated into low inflation.

Economists were perplexed when unthinkably low interest rates failed to stimulate the economy from 1989 through 1992. The recession persisted because structural changes were squeezing profit margins. Low interest rates did not benefit the public until the second half of 1992. Prior to that time, the rates served to shore up the banking system which was reeling from the worst real estate implosion since 1974/75.

Those who invested in fixed income vehicles watched their passive incomes dry up. Banks absorbed the spread between consumer rates and government paper to the detriment of liquidity.

Why all the history? It is important to see how a changing world can be followed in the trendlines. Monetary policy, alone, does not dictate price levels or economic health.

How to Cycle with Your Eyes Open

Of course, most traders will argue that long-term evaluations are fine, but near-term trading brings in the profits. The secular trend cannot be effectively traded unless we count upon a constantly rising stock market to reward a "buy and hold" strategy.

Cyclical and seasonal patterns have shorter durations and allow us to trade bull and bear movements.

While a trendline is usually expressed in terms of a straight line with a given slope or steepness, cycles and seasonal patterns are defined as waves. Those familiar with physics may recall that a cycle or wave has three basic attributes: frequency, amplitude, and phase.

Frequency, as the name implies, is the number of times a cycle or wave repeats within a given time. The *amplitude* defines the vertical height of the movement while *phase* defines the time interval for the frequency measurement. (See Figure 3-5.) Phase will determine the horizontal distance from peak to peak.

Using statistical tools, we can attempt to extract a regular cycle from a price time series. The cycle may be related to seasonal influences, production patterns, or monetary trends.

Cycle analysis has gained new respectability and a growing following. There are many advisory services and money managers who have researched seasonal patterns to derive predetermined cyclical trades. Studies appear to show that these trades could have yielded profits more than 80% of the time.

Unfortunately, when put to the test without regard to potential fundamental and technical aberrations, blind cyclical trading can have disastrous results.

The most common cause of failure is "phase shift." When the expected beginning of a cycle is delayed or advances, an investor could be trading at the wrong point along the cycle. Unless amplitude is extremely well defined and consistent, even a small phase shift can lead to undesirable results. (See Figure 3-6.)

It is important to note that cyclical studies in the absence of fundamental reasoning are technical in nature. Price history, alone, is used to determine cyclical patterns. If fundamentals are taken into consideration, it is possible to avoid the pitfalls of blind cyclical trading.

Figure 3-5
Components of a Cycle

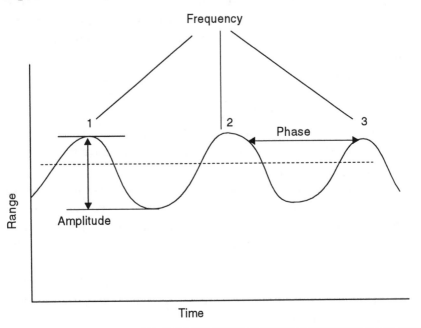

Consider the extreme winter of 1993/94. Normal seasonal energy patterns experience rising heating oil usage as winter approaches. Severe cold usually boosts the entire energy complex.

Yet in 1993/94, overproduction outweighed cold weather demand to cause a counterseasonal price movement. The North Sea opened production on eight new wells while dumping of Iraqi inventories was threatened. Even with heavy U.S. consumption through the first quarter of 1994, American Petroleum Institute statistics provided evidence that ample supplies existed.

In yet another challenge to seasonality, energy prices began to rise in 1994's second quarter. Some North Sea production was shut down for maintenance. A civil war in Yemen threatened Middle East production. As quickly as prices had declined, they returned to interim highs.

Combining short-term technical analysis might have supplemented a fundamental evaluation by clearly showing the energy complex in counterseasonal interim trends. Then what is an interim trend?

Figure 3-6

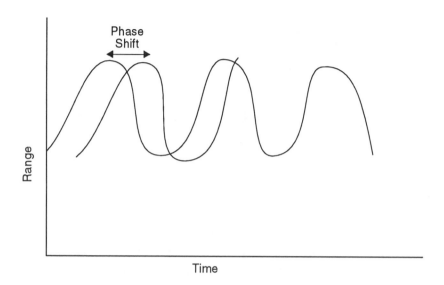

When a cycle advances its phase, tops and bottoms will occur at different times. This makes accurate prediction based upon phase very difficult.

Semantics play an important role in determining what trading philosophy is in place. Frequently, two analysts will track the same market phenomenon under different assumptions. Perspectives change depending upon the particular semantics.

The rising portion of a cycle can easily be viewed as an interim bull trend. Most analysts leave out the term "interim." We may hear descriptors like "short-term" or "long-term." A distinction between the upward or downward portion of a cyclical phase is not often considered.

Obviously, the time period under consideration defines the extent to which we might call price movement a cyclical event, random, or a trend. The argument has been carried down to the narrowest intervals. Personal computers around the world are concentrating on five-minute bar charts with the hope of identifying profit-making patterns. Under most circumstances, technical analysis is applied to spot "intraday" trends and cycles which can be based upon time intervals as short as five minutes.

Today, one man's intraday trend is another man's random noise. The line has been blurred by the use of sophisticated computer programs which fit curves to the slightest price gyration.

Increasingly complex studies suggest that it may not matter whether a price change is a trend or noise. Even random movements can be predicted based upon historical distributions of previous price changes called "histograms."

I want to examine approaches to predicting random movements more closely in later chapters. However, an overview is helpful to understand modern approaches to time series analysis.

The Fundamental "Spark"

TechnoFundamentals become increasingly important as the scope of our predictions expand. This is because the modern information explosion imposes a need for instant evaluation and action. When the U.S. Department of Labor releases monthly employment statistics, many thousands of investors stand ready to react.

The extent of any reaction will define that price movement as random, trending, cyclical, or even seasonal. The category is invariably determined well after the fact. However, the spark that ignites the reaction is fundamental.

Assume gold is trading at $350 per ounce with technical resistance at $365. An announcement by the Federal Reserve Chairman hints that inflation is heating up. Gold reacts by jumping higher. The reaction is based upon a fundamental development. The follow-through might depend upon whether the reaction pushes beyond $365 resistance.

A breakout above resistance is a technical event. Failure to penetrate resistance would indicate the fundamental reaction lacked sufficient strength to begin a trend. While technicians might argue that the fundamental development is irrelevant, we will see that *the degree of any breakout can be measured by fundamental forces*.

If inflation is heating up, a gold reaction is likely to be sustained. A false alarm would see gold retreat back to former levels. Therefore, we must be able to make a fundamental assessment of the Fed's action. Are commodity prices rising? What fundamentals are behind rising prices? Has employment been increasing? What is the extent of the increase? Has the money supply been expanding? What is the rate of growth in M1, M2, and M3?

Where are we relative to seasonal and cyclical patterns? Are we seeing a rally within the downward phase of an identified cycle? If so, how far might the rally carry? All of these questions relate to an analysis of one or more time series.

As mentioned in the Introduction, floods of improbable proportions plagued the U.S. Midwest throughout the summer of 1993. At the height of the floodwaters, grain prices pushed higher. When the flood level subsided, so did prices. Significant damage was obvious. So, too, was the strategy: buy grains.

However, the harvest exerted its customary pressures. Holding long positions through the fall would have required deep pockets and considerable patience. (See Figure 3-7.) Grain prices only began firming when news of poor quality and low yields was officially released by the Department of Agriculture.

Hence the question, "Where are we relative to seasonal and cyclical patterns?" Our fundamental bias may have been bullish. But a technical confirmation coupled with a keen awareness of seasonal tendencies might have avoided a premature market entry.

What about random price fluctuations? As recently as the mid-1970s, there was a prevailing belief that past price action could not be used with any degree of reliability to predict future prices. Markets were considered a "Random Walk." This assumption was supported by numerous studies which proved a lack of statistically significant correlations between a time series when compared against itself. The technique of "autocorrelation" lagged price data by various intervals to determine whether past price patterns provided any predictability. Most studies were conducted using stock data which, by nature, are less subject to seasonal and cyclical forces unless viewed in groups.

The formula uses price compared with previous price as follows:

$$P_t \text{ compared with } P_{t-1}$$

High speed computers have changed the Random Walk consensus. Even if accepted as random, price movements have associated probabilities. New models which employ multiple probability parameters seek to solve a basic

Figure 3-7
Soybeans—Summer 1993

S-NFVOI Daily 01/05/93 - 12/30/93 High = 755   Low = 561.75 Last = 704.25

As floods subsided, prices declined. It would have taken deep pockets to hold on.

Summer floods drove soybean prices to new highs.

Soybeans began recovering during the harvest when quality became an issue.

question, "If there have been six consecutive up-ticks, what is the probability of a down-tick?"

In theory, random price movements can still fall within known probability distributions. There is a historical precedent for consecutive unidirectional price changes. When consecutive price changes step outside the realm of probability, the chance for change rises.

Random market behavior has been modeled. In many cases, models predict random movements well. The key to profitable trading, however, requires sound money management conforming to probability parameters.

Just taken by itself, time series analysis is a subject for whole volumes. This brief introduction is designed to provide a perspective for further study while establishing guidelines for basic practical application.

With this in mind, let's look at the principles of technical analysis.

CHAPTER 4

THE BUILDING BLOCKS
OF TECHNICAL ANALYSIS

Let's begin with the simplest question. What makes a market move higher or lower? Here's an answer in the simplest terms: Prices move up when sellers become reluctant to sell at current price levels and buyers are willing to pay higher prices.

Prices move down when buyers are no longer willing to pay prevailing prices and sellers are willing to accept lower bids.

Too frequently, traders forget these simple explanations in their haste to interpret complex patterns and formations. The result is that they may formulate opinions out of their proper context.

For example, many market students are familiar with terms like "head and shoulders" or "ascending triangle." While many can describe the appearance of these formations, few are able to explain what they represent or why they might be significant.

To gain a better understanding of technical analysis, it's necessary to examine fundamental events that create technical changes. To do that, let's define market activity in the most basic terms and build an understanding from the ground up.

Market Tests and the Million-Dollar Painting

All interaction between buyers and sellers consists of a series of tests. Every "bid" and "offer" tests the willingness of a counterparty to consummate a transaction. Thus, if a trader offers silver at $5.4350 an ounce, he is testing to see if there are buyers willing to accept that price.

If the offer is accepted, the test has succeeded. A successful test appears as a trade on the ticker tape and an increase in volume. If the trade is in futures or options, you could observe an increase or decrease in open interest—the number of open, i.e., unsettled contracts between buyers and sellers.

If the test fails, the trader might make a new offer of $5.40. By lowering the price he hopes to attract buyers. Eventually, a transaction takes place.

When you observe testing and trading patterns you are comparative shopping. You can see the prices being offered and accepted by thousands of participants or "shoppers." At any moment, you know the best price being offered or the highest price someone is willing to pay.

Consider this information's importance. When you buy a car, house, or appliance you probably seek out reference prices. For example, you might look at a retail sticker price. Then, you would go to other dealers or stores to see if comparable prices are offered. Obviously you're looking for "the best price."

In the case of a home, you might make an offer less than the listing price. Of course, if the seller immediately accepts the offer, you will likely feel you paid too much. Nonetheless, it was the price you were willing to pay at that time with the knowledge available. If the seller rejects the offer, there is always the option of making a new and higher offer.

An astute buyer would not simply make an offer without checking home values. What were the most recent sales prices for comparable homes in the same location? You could visit the county tax offices to look up recent sales or ask several realtors. There are even computerized data services that provide transaction records.

When evaluating a trade, you are interested in the price relative to fundamental factors and in comparison to the latest transactions. You need Techno-Fundamental bearings to plot an appropriate course to trade.

When examining past data, you see prices that were successfully tested. When buyers are willing to pay increasing prices, a series of up-ticks appears as a rising price line. This is used to define a trend or pattern of buying and selling. If buyers and sellers agree upon a static price, the trendline will be flat. The market is in equilibrium. As first mentioned, if buyers are willing to pay more you'll see an uptrend. If sellers are willing to accept less, you'll see a downtrend. (See Figures 4-1 to 4-5.)

Figure 4-1
Price Action and Technical Patterns

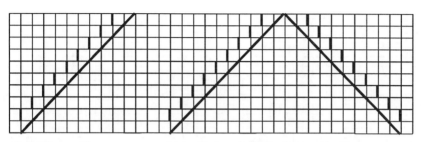

Each Time a Test
Succeeds it Appears
as a Trade

In an Uptrend, Each Succesive Test
Results in a Higher Price. Buyers
Continue to Buy.
A Downtrend Results When Sellers
are not Discouraged by Declining Prices.

Figure 4-2
Double Top

In the Bid for the Painting a Double Top was Seen at $20,000

$20,000 $20,000

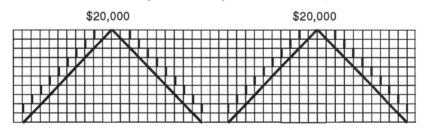

A Pattern Occurs when Two Formations are Seen That Identify
the Same Behavior

Figure 4-3
Technical Patterns

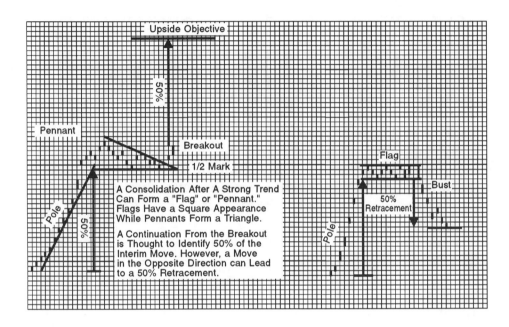

By combining observed patterns of rising, falling, and flat trends, you can look for formations that may indicate market sentiment or "bias." You can identify equilibrium areas that represent price support or resistance. You can predict levels where prices are likely to return.

Market strength or momentum can be assessed by measuring the slope or angle of a price line. If the angle is steep, opinion is rapidly changing. A gradual angle suggest a more stable environment. (See Figures 4-1 to 4-5.)

Suppose there is major disagreement between buyers and sellers. Under such circumstances, you could see wider "gaps" between price tests. These gaps can represent significant turning points because they reveal increasing divergence between buyers and sellers.

Figure 4-4

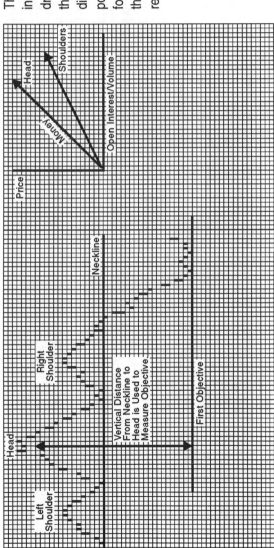

The amount of money entering the market is assumed to drive prices to tops forming the head and shoulders. If the distance prices travel is proportionate to money, then the force driving prices through the neckline should achieve a reaction of equal distance.

Figure 4-5

Rising open interest in futures and options during a trading range consolidation makes a market susceptible to strong breakouts or busts. When prices move above or below the range to cause margin calls, a large number of traders react at the same time. This is sometimes referred to as "congestion." However, this term also applies to similar conditions when tops and bottoms form.

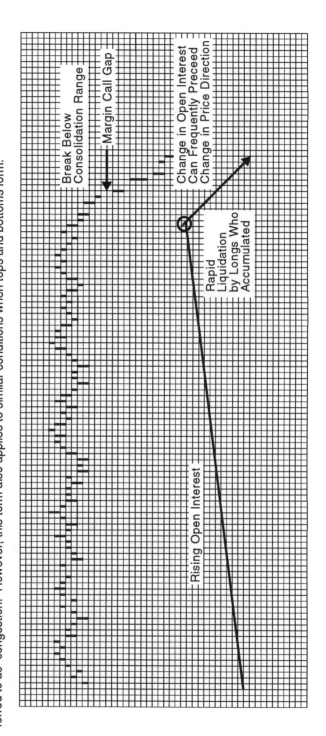

An auction provides an excellent analogy to technical analysis. In a room with 200 people, the auctioneer starts bidding at $100,000 for a painting. Suddenly, all hands go up. What is happening? What information is provided?

First, the auctioneer is testing a price of $100,000. When all hands go up, you know the price is too low and will move higher. The auctioneer has the advantage of testing another price. Since he observed universal interest, he knows he can substantially raise prices. The increment he chooses will be larger than if the audience showed less enthusiasm.

The auctioneer offers $150,000. Again, all hands go up. We know prices are on the rise. The next offer might be $250,000—a larger increase.

At $750,000, only five hands are raised. What information do you have? You know that the remaining five bidders can push the price higher. However, you are approaching the point where the last offer—say, one million dollars even—will be made and accepted. You are near a top.

When the final offer is accepted, you know there was only a single individual out of 200 who was willing to pay such a price. If this lone bidder were to try to sell the painting immediately after taking delivery, how many buyers would he find?

In all likelihood, the last bidder would, at best, be able to sell at the second to the last price bid by two participants. If the second to the last bidder bought the painting and, in turn, wanted to sell, he would probably be forced to accept the next best price prior to his bid.

You have just identified the process that leads to a "top" and subsequent turn in trend. While the absolute top may be based upon the final bidder's irrational desire to own the painting, you could identify where prices were meeting resistance—i.e., decreasing interest—by observing the decreasing number of raised hands.

Applying this to investments, you can draw a parallel between the number of hands at the auction and trading volume or changing open interest. The greater the volume, the more the interest. Under most circumstances, falling volume is a sign of fewer bids in a rising market and fewer offers in a falling market.

What else might we glean from our auction analogy? Price increments provide clues about potential volatility. Wide increments produce large gaps. If a large gap is followed by no decrease in interest, we can assume prices will continue higher. However, if you observe a significant drop in interest, you know the gap eliminated a large number of potential buyers.

Everything we've reviewed to this point about an auction has its corollary in technical analysis. You may already be familiar with terms like "breakaway gap," "measuring gap," and "exhaustion gap." Can you determine circumstances that differentiate these gaps?

Using the auction example, consider the first offer presented by the auctioneer. All hands went up. Knowing the interest level, the auctioneer substantially raised the bid. What would this look like on a price chart? Obviously, a gap would appear. (See Figure 4-6.)

Since this gap was generated by significant buying interest, you know prices will continue higher. If you were applying technical analysis to the situation, you might call the gap a "breakaway." Sometimes the distance between bids indicates the potential extent of a price move. Then this gap is used to measure the market move.

Assume the auctioneer observes no decrease in interest after the first substantial increase. He may decide to double the increment to arrive at a final

Figure 4-6

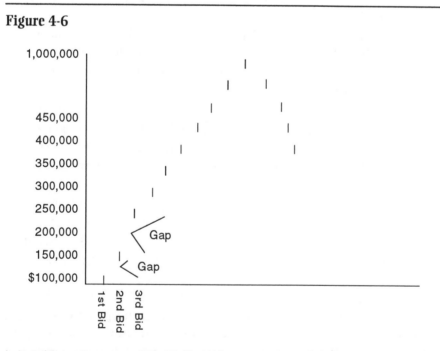

A chart of the auction process shows how the bidding appears as a technical pattern of gaps with an eventual top.

bid more quickly. The first increase or gap would be used to measure subsequent increases. Hence the term, "measuring gap."

When the last bidders battle for the prize, prices may still gap higher. However, you can see interest is exhausted because the number of bidders has diminished. Fewer and fewer buyers are willing to bid as prices move up. This condition leads to an "exhaustion gap."

Just as the hands at an auction help define gaps, market volume confirms possible price movement. Increasing volume in a gapping market implies further advances or declines.

Unlike an art auction, financial markets can gap down as well as up. Relationships are the same for declining prices as for advances. The only difference is price direction.

The auction illustration is an oversimplification compared with the many conditions that exist in financial markets. Obviously, daily and weekly interest as reflected by changing volume can wax and wane. The auction model assumes a steady decrease in the number of hands bidding as prices rise.

On the other hand, there are situations where the interest of bidders at an auction declines and reemerges. It is possible for bidders to regain courage if they observe other participants pushing up prices. Perhaps they say, "If they think the painting is worth more, maybe they are right. . . ."

Here we enter the realm of "herd psychology." There is a belief that traders or investors will act like herds following a leader. In the case of the Judas goat, however, the result is usually slaughter.

Herd psychology can also lead to logical patterns of price action. As the herd gathers momentum, we see rapidly rising or falling prices accompanied by surging volume. When volume peaks, we can assume a top or bottom is near.

The roller-coaster formations resulting from herd psychology have been identified as double tops, double bottoms, head and shoulders, rounded tops, rounded bottoms, and a host of other technical buzzwords. For the most part, these phrases apply to visual interpretations of charts. However, increasingly sophisticated computer models currently identify potential patterns and formations without graphic representations.

When we draw the analogy between an art auction and technical price patterns, it's clear that there is more than subjective interpretation to technical analysis. Technical relationships have fundamental foundations. Why is this important?

Unless the market student knows the basics behind chart formations, interpretation is likely to be a function of visual perceptions rather than market logic. A chart can appear as an ink blot test. Each individual sees a different shape in the ink blots.

Knowing the likely behavior behind a particular price formation or pattern provides substance for interpretation.

Tops, Bottoms, and Flags

In this chapter we have touched upon price formations and patterns. The question arises, "What is the difference between a formation and a pattern?"

The answer is simple, but extremely important. All too often, these terms are interchanged. The distinction is vital if we are to correctly interpret historical price, volume, and open interest events.

Assume the auction we're attending was dealing with early nineteenth-century American art. The auctioneer is offering five paintings of approximately the same composition and size from the same artist.

The first painting is bid to a selling price of $20,000. The rise from the initial offer to the final bid could be considered a formation with a top at $20,000. (See Figures 4-1 to 4-5.)

The second painting also reaches a final price of $20,000. Once the second sale is observed, we have a pattern consisting of two top formations reaching $20,000 each.

What might you assume from this observation? It seems clear that this particular artist's work is perceived to be worth $20,000. Thus, you might predict that the third painting would reach a price of approximately $20,000. Upon the sale of the fifth painting, you have an excellent basis for evaluating the value of the artist's overall works. This pattern of consecutive formations yields a perspective which we can rely upon for predicting future values.

There will always be circumstances that change the fundamentals affecting formations. For example, the artist may have different phases or periods which have different associated values. Works of living artists generally attract less than the deceased. If a painting tops out at $20,000 while an artist is alive, it is fair to assume it will fetch a higher price when the artist is dead. Death is a fundamental event that changes potential formations and eventual patterns.

Technical analysis of financial markets involves terms like pennant, flag, key reversal, island reversal, top, bottom, bear market rally, bull market correction, head and shoulders, double bottom, triple top, rounded top or bottom, and so on.

We could compare each of these terms to events we see in an auction. For expediency, we will dispense with the corollary and describe terms as they pertain to financial markets.

As I suggested earlier, price action consists of a series of tests. Each bid and asking price is presented to the market, is tested, and succeeds or fails. As you build a technical understanding, the concept of tests expands from this micro view to a macro context.

When successive testing of higher prices slows or stops, we identify a "top." What is a top?

Logic tells us that buyers are no longer willing to pay higher prices. A top is also called "resistance" because buyers are resisting price increases. A top formation is a macro test of a price area or range. By definition, it is a failed test because prices were not able to move higher.

A bottom is the same failed test for falling prices. Prices reach "support" because sellers refuse to offer lower prices and buyers are forced to support existing or better prices.

When buyers and sellers vacillate between the same tops and bottoms, prices are in a "trading range." This identifies a price band that accommodates the opinions of both sides of the market.

A trading range can be wide or narrow. A wide trading range is frequently called a "price envelope" or "trading window." A narrow range is often identified as "congestion."

If opinions of buyers and sellers converge, you are likely to see triangle, pennant, and flag formations. While there are many different subjective interpretations of such formations, their origin is fundamental and explained by behavior.

Tops and bottoms converge when opinions consolidate. The resulting formation is usually referred to as a "consolidation." Taken out of context, a consolidation simply means buyers and sellers agree upon almost the same prices during the consolidation period. These formations become significant when patterns emerge or when interpreted within the context of other market action.

Suppose you observe a consolidation in silver around $5.2550. Suddenly, silver retreats to $3.5000 in a major bear move. Over the next several months, prices rebound to $5.2550 for a second consolidation. Thereafter, silver breaks out to test $6.0000 and retreats back to $5.2550.

The conclusion you might draw is that regardless of breakouts and busts, silver has a tendency to consolidate around $5.2550. Any move above or below this consolidation represents an aberration which will eventually correct and prices will return to this agreed-upon level.

While this may sound simplistic and untradable, it is an accurate interpretation of the events. Obviously, a major move above or below the consolidation must be tracked with appropriate technical and fundamental tools. However, the consolidation area is an important reference. As prices close in on known equilibrium points, positions should be adjusted in anticipation of a potential consolidation.

These reference points serve as guides to the end of retracements. Thus, tops and bottoms give us a perspective as to how far trends may carry while consolidations can indicate where prices are likely to return.

During any given period, there are likely to be several "interim" consolidations. Herein lies a basic problem: When are consolidations significant?

If a consolidation is accompanied by uniform volume, we can assume continuing equilibrium and further consolidation. In the case of futures and options, static or level open interest confirms that an equal number of buyers and sellers are entering and leaving the market.

If, on the other hand, volume begins to rise or fall during a consolidation, you have an indication that a breakout is probable. Equally important is open interest which tells you about market cash flows and sensitivity. When these factors are taken together, you get a much better picture of market activity.

There has been a consensus among chartists that flag and pennant consolidations represent halfway points within the prevailing trend. Using the base of the flagpole as a measuring point, the distance between the base and the average within the flag or pennant is used to project the objective. Only recently has market participation been analyzed to reveal that the objective depends upon the amount of participation that takes place within the consolidation flag or triangle. A certain amount of force or fuel must be stored within the consolidation to propel prices halfway higher or lower.

Why You Should Care about Margins

This necessarily brings us to the topic of margin. There are three types of margin for futures and options:

1. **Initial Margin:** The amount required to initially open a position. For futures it is usually less than 10% of the total contract value based upon the contract size multiplied by the price.

2 **Variation Margin:** The amount associated with a change in price relative to the total contract size. For example, a contract of gold traded on the New York Mercantile Exchange represents 100 troy ounces. A move of $1.00 in the gold price represents a change of $100.00 in contract value reflected by variation margin. This amount is actually deposited into or taken out of an account.

3 **Maintenance Margin:** When the difference between initial margin and variation margin falls below a certain amount called maintenance margin, a margin call is issued which requires the account holder to deposit enough money to bring the balance back to initial margin levels.

Assume your initial gold margin is $2,000 with maintenance margin of $1,000. If you were long gold at $400 an ounce and prices fell to $390, you would have a $1,000 loss reflected in a negative move in your variation margin account. In other words, you would receive a margin call requiring the deposit of $1,000 to bring your margin balance back to the $2,000 initial level.

Margin plays a critical role in investment psychology. Investment decisions are governed by available margin and cash reserves dedicated to meeting margin calls. It is easy to understand that a commitment to a position requires sufficient cash to cover initial margin.

Similarly, the ability to hold a position during adverse market action depends upon funds available to meet calls.

This logic translates into potential behavior patterns that can supplement technical interpretations. If prices are rising and open interest is increasing, you know new cash is entering the market in the form of initial margins. Why is this important?

An accepted macro-economic principle is expressed by this equation:

$$\text{Price} = \text{Money} \times \text{Velocity}.$$

Price refers to the general price level while money represents the money supply and velocity is the turnover of the money supply. Although this formula expresses a theory about forces behind inflation, it applies to individual markets as well.

That is, the price of a commodity, stock, or bond is determined by the amount of money available to bid on the particular investment coupled with the number of bids made for the same investment.

When open interest rises in conjunction with volume and price, you can assume prices will continue higher based upon the formula's relationships.

However, there is more to this picture. Assume you are observing a consolidation formation in conjunction with rising open interest and volume. An understanding of variation and maintenance margins will tell you that participants are likely to become sensitive when prices move beyond the consolidation range by an amount equal to or greater than the maintenance margin differential.

In other words, you can approximate the point where buyers or sellers would receive margin calls. When a margin call is received, a decision is forced. The trader can either deposit more money or liquidate the position. (See Figure 4-7.)

When traders decide something in mass, a particularly strong force can develop. Obviously, the greater the number of traders making a decision together, the more money you see entering or leaving a market.

A breakout from a consolidation that is accompanied by large changes in open interest implies a continuation in the direction of the breakout. The greater the position accumulation during the consolidation, the stronger the breakout is likely to be.

Notice the long trading range consolidation exhibited on the September 1994 Feeder Cattle Chart. (See Figures 4-8 and 4-9.) At the time, initial margin was $675. Maintenance margin was approximately $100. Since each penny is worth $500, an adverse move of one cent will result in a margin call.

From mid-February through mid-April, prices consolidated around 8100 (81.00 cents per pound). When prices broke down below 7150 the week of April 11, traders who were long were forced to deposit more margin or exit positions.

Figure 4-7
Using Margin Call Clues

By observing position accumulation during a consolidation pattern (see below), you can measure intermediate trending potential and levels of "significant penetration" based upon margin call areas. The greater the accumulation during consolidation, the more likely a strong reaction when maintenance margins are violated. Each individual reacts differently to risk and exposure. However, within a group, there is likely to be a statistically consistent measurable number of individuals who will act in the same manner when faced with the same circumstances. Find a consolidation pattern (trading range, flag, triangle, etc.) on a chart. Place a compass point at the approximate middle of the consolidation (average price), measure the distance in points equal to maintenance margin using the chart scale and draw a circle. Extend parallel lines from the top and bottom of the circle. As long as prices remain within the lines, a trading range exists. If either line is penetrated, margin calls must be answered. A liquidation by large numbers of traders will accelerate the break-out and lead to a technical follow-through.

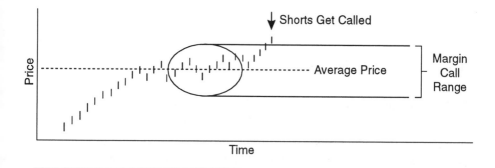

In fact, the chart shows a slight decrease in open interest as prices consolidated the week of April 18. Longs were liquidating instead of holding. This action precipitated a high volume confirmation of the break in prices on April 26. Thereafter, high volume and rising open interest accompanied rapidly falling prices. As sellers began losing confidence in the downtrend, volume decreased along with open interest.

However, we must be careful in our interpretation. The drop in open interest is partially the result of the expiration of the May contract. Even with this in mind, it is clear from the price action that uncertainty set in during the last week in May.

Figure 4-8

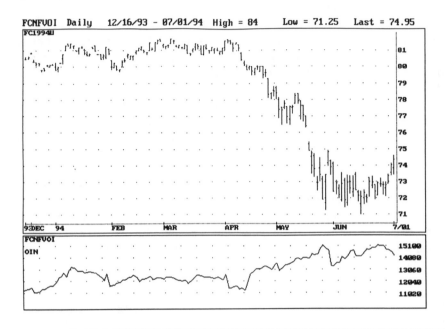

FCNFVOI Daily   12/16/93 - 07/01/94 High = 84   Low = 71.25 Last = 74.95

Flags, Pennants, Triangles

Feeder cattle offers a perfect example of the relationship between price, volume, and open interest as it relates to our description of market behavior. You can see how the logic translates into specific events. Understanding market logic is essential for a complete grasp of TechnoFundamental analysis.

TechnoFundamentals blend both disciplines in both directions. When you look at a chart formation or pattern, you want to be able to logically dissect "fundamental meaning." In the case of chart interpretation, fundamental behavior is reflected in technical patterns.

In addition, you want to identify fundamental changes in supply and demand that may be the cause of particular price action and understand behavior that leads to such action.

As early as the last quarter of 1993, feeder cattle inventories were growing while prices remained firmly within the trading range on the chart. In December '93 and February '94, prices dipped below 8000 to form an interim double bottom support.

Figure 4-9

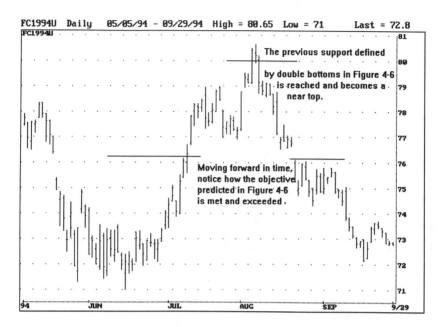

```
FC1994U  Daily   05/05/94 - 09/29/94  High = 80.65  Low = 71     Last = 72.8
```

The previous support defined by double bottoms in Figure 4-6 is reached and becomes a near top.

Moving forward in time, notice how the objective predicted in Figure 4-6 is met and exceeded.

In both cases, there was insufficient velocity to force a bearish reaction. At any time from January forward, prices could have broken through support based upon fundamental information. Yet, only after the downward thrust in mid-April did the market generate enough momentum to carry below the 8000 support. Thereafter, market participants agreed that feeder cattle was overpriced relative to supplies—a fact known for the previous six months.

The general equation of Price = Money × Velocity allows us to extrapolate conceptual variations that apply to futures and options, such as:

$$\text{Money} = \text{Initial Margin} + \text{Variation Margin}$$
$$\text{and Velocity} = \text{Volume.}$$

The formulas can be broken down further:
If Price = P, Open Interest = OI, Initial Margin = IM, and Variation Margin = VM, then:

$$\text{Total IM} = \text{OI} \times \text{IM}$$
$$\text{VM} = \Delta P \times (\text{OI} + \Delta \text{OI}).$$

The equations above provide us with a method for measuring how much money is entering or leaving a market. (See Figure 4-10.)

The same logic applies to equities; however, the price changes are correlated with transaction volume to measure cash flow. If we multiply money by volume, the product does not translate into a price. The equation only expresses relationships.

It is possible to solve the equation and correlate results against actual prices, however. This can establish a basis for a more exact relationship between the formula and an ability to predict prices. Solutions to the equation could be used to "train" a neural network—a topic for discussion later in this book. In the abstract, the equations help us fundamentally evaluate popular chart interpretations.

While dozens of formations and patterns are the topic of extensive studies, we will confine our review to the most common. We have already touched upon tops, bottom, gaps, and consolidation channels. There are also flags, pennants, triangles, and head and shoulders.

From a TechnoFundamental point of view, it is not sufficient to recognize these patterns. You'll want to know *why* they are significant. What behavior can you associate with these types of price activity?

Flags, pennants, and triangles are all consolidations. Taken out of context, these formations identify points where buyers and sellers agree upon a narrowing price range. For example, a triangle is also part of a pennant formation. The distinction is that a pennant appears after a steep rise or fall in prices which forms a "pole." A triangle can appear without a pole.

When prices narrow to a point, buyers and sellers are in their closest agreement. As with the consolidation illustrated by feeder cattle, accumulation during a consolidation conditions a market for a breakout or bust. (See Figures 4-8 and 4-9.) If the move out of the consolidation pattern (pennant, flag, or triangle) is in the direction of the trend, it confirms the trend. Hence, these consolidations are frequently referred to as "continuation patterns."

However, consolidations can also signal exhaustion reversals. One of the most sought after patterns is the head and shoulders. It is identified by three consecutive consolidation tops. The theory behind a head and shoulders is that three "waves" of buying (or selling) create an "overbought" or "oversold" condition where the highest (or lowest) trades are abandoned.

This action forms the "head." Abandoned traders are forced to exit positions and create a "downdraft" (or "updraft"). Thereafter, money associated

Figure 4-10

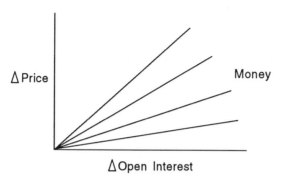

Any change in price coupled with a change in open interest results in money entering or leaving a market. The greater the open interest and price, the more money in the market. The amount available (accumulated) is important for forecasting potential squeezes, tops, bottoms, and momentum shifts.

Accumulation

1. ΔOI × initial margin = new margin
2. ΔOI × ΔP = new variation margin
3. OI × ΔP = variation margin from existing positions

Example:

OI = 1,000 gold contracts bought @ $400 per oz. average
1. 1,000 × ($400 × 100 oz.) × 10% = $4,000,000 margin existing
ΔOI = +100 contracts
100 × ($400 × 100 oz.) × 10% = $400,000 new margin
ΔP = $10
2. 100 × ($10 × 100 oz.) = $100,000 new variation margin
3. 1,000 × ($10 × 100 oz.) = $1,000,000 variation on existing margin
(Money enters market in cash and position accumulation.)

Distribution

If Δ is negative:
1. ΔOI × initial margin = margins leaving
2. ΔOI × ΔP = variation margin taken out
3. OI × ΔP = smaller variation transfer

Example:

ΔOI = –100 gold contracts
100 × ($400 × 100 oz.) × 10% = $400,000 margin leaving
ΔP = $10
100 × ($10 × 100 oz.) = $100,000 in variation margin is transferred or leaves

Three margin components make up the accumulation process—initial, variation (amount transferring from losers to winners) and new initial and variation margins resulting from increases in open interest. Distribution is the net process of liquidation of this money, signaling the end of a trend.

with the abandoned traders is rapidly replaced in the opposite direction. In theory, the money that pushed prices to the head is sufficient to reverse prices through the "neckline" by an equal distance.

The assumption is that the Price = Money × Velocity formula works equally in both directions. Therefore, the first objective after a neckline is penetrated is measured as the distance from the neckline to the head in the opposite direction.

The September 1994 S&P 500 chart illustrates a head and shoulders. (See Figure 4-11.) The head is particularly significant because it is formed by a series of erratic gaps that confirm the trend is exhausted. Volume was weak while the head was forming. This indicates that fewer traders participated at this peak. As the right shoulder formed, volume picked up. Once the neckline was significantly penetrated, prices collapsed on high volume. Open interest confirmed a potential reversal.

If the head is formed by an exhaustion formation (gaps on weak volume or declining open interest), the head and shoulders pattern is more likely to

Figure 4-11

SP1994U Daily   12/21/93 - 09/15/94 High = 485.2 Low = 436.75 Last = 473.75

be real. Understand that there are many instances where the pattern seems to exist without the expected subsequent action.

Even in the case of the S&P 500 illustration, some might argue that the brief rally after the neckline was clearly penetrated negated the head and shoulders. This is a subjective debate. TechnoFundamentals would weigh the exhaustion apparent in the head formation more heavily than the subsequent rally that failed to fully materialize.

There are proprietary studies that claim to have correlated cash flows with price projections. By measuring the amount of cash that builds during a trend and the amount that leaves prior to a reversal, some models claim to predict the size of the reversal. You can construct such a study by using the formulas for measuring money previously described.

Many chart advocates insist that technical analysis is simply an art form. Some individuals have a "sixth sense" about plotted price action. Yet even for those of us lacking artistry or extrasensory perception, linking price action to our fundamental discussion can accomplish equally impressive results.

CHAPTER 5

A KEY TO TECHNOFUNDAMENTALS: SUPPLY

Our review of past commodity trends illustrates the critical causal role played by supply in initiating major price trends. In general, supply is more susceptible to rapid change than demand. Therefore, it is usually the primary focus of any TechnoFundamental evaluation.

A crop failure can disrupt supply. A strike among mine workers may suddenly shut down production. An oil embargo limits energy resources. These events elicit immediate price reactions may be the primary reasons for economic dislocation.

How to Construct the Supply Picture

There are three supply considerations: what supply has been, what it is, and what it will be. A perspective is drawn from previous supply and its impact upon prices. At some point, supply must be considered in relation to demand. Yet it is important to examine supply alone to understand how it can be technically and fundamentally evaluated.

Again, the exact line between technical and fundamental analysis is not distinct. Is a statistical study of supply in relation to price a fundamental exercise? If a computer model extrapolates price based upon supply, are we using fundamentals?

Most traders agree supply is a fundamental consideration. However, TechnoFundamental analysis looks for technical patterns in supply statistics.

For example, supply charts can form consolidations, breakouts, gaps, reversals, and even head and shoulders. (See Figure 5-1.) These formations and patterns are helpful in predicting future supply statistics and potential effects upon demand.

Figure 5-1
Silver Consumption World Total

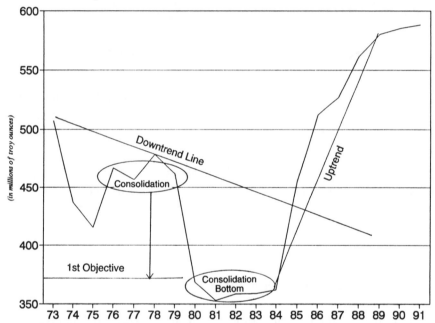

Technically, silver consumption was in a downtrend before the explosive uptrend of 1979/80. The enormous surge in prices caused a powerful decline in usage which consolidated between 1980 and 1983.

The 1976/79 consolidation marked a halfway point with a projected downside of 75 million ounces from approximately 450 million ounces.

Supply was the dominant price determining factor through 1993/94; however, we can see how usage conforms to technical patterns. Once a consumption trend is in place, we can identify momentum and potential objectives.

These patterns can be correlated to supply to establish crossovers where usage can overtake supply or vice versa. This allows us to predict pivotal years for price.

The technical term "overbought" relates to the fundamental term "under-supply" while "oversold" pertains to "oversupply." Analysis becomes challenging because statistics reflect past, present, and predicted supply. We must juxtapose these three components to determine a potential impact upon demand and price.

If we face a present oversupply, should you assume supply will taper off? Isn't oversupply a function of demand? Can supply stand alone? These questions increase the fascination in using TechnoFundamental analysis.

Some of the most perplexing historical events demonstrate supply's illogical behavior. Why do supply trends frequently seem to ignore price and demand? Part of the answer is found in the theory of *supply momentum.*

For example, building capacity often carries a certain momentum which is not easily controlled. A new factory is built, labor is hired, machinery is financed, materials are purchased. Once the factory is in full production, a decrease in output requires layoffs, reduced machine time and raw material purchases. Layoffs might not lower costs because labor contracts could foreclose any immediate saving. Trimming labor could force overtime at more expensive wages. Reducing machine time does not decrease carrying costs associated with financing, lighting, rent, and other environmental variables. Dropping purchase orders for raw materials might increase costs due to lost volume discounts.

These considerations can prevent or delay output reductions. In other words, the new factory has added momentum to supply.

By the same token, once a supply reduction is underway, it can gather momentum. If a factory is shut, rebuilding capacity (if required by demand) takes time. A new facility must be constructed, staffed, equipped, and debugged. Momentum in either direction creates supply trends and cycles.

Supply also experiences seasonal variations, as previously mentioned. When you technically measure supply, your conclusion can be fundamental. Is momentum increasing? Is the increase due to temporary conditions or structural change?

After a drought or other conditions that decrease crop output, we are likely to see prices rise. Higher prices are an incentive to increase production. Once production is expanded, we can assume prices will adjust to greater supplies. All this assumes no change in demand.

Logically, we associate the change in supply with a temporary event. Suppose a new seed were developed which increased crop yield by 30%. This technological advance would permanently affect supply. If the 30% increase required no additional farm inputs like fertilizer, pesticides, irrigation, land preparation, and care, we might see an overall increase in production. Would prices come down? Probably. Would demand rise? Not necessarily.

Technically, weather's influence upon grain supply usually appears as a downward line followed by a bottom and a rising line. The new seed may create a different pattern. The downward line would probably gain momentum as more farmers employed the new strain. A secular downtrend in supply would result from a structural change that improved production.

Such changes are becoming increasingly important. Genetically altered plants are likely to increase crop yields, disease resistance, insect resistance, quality, weather adaptability, and a host of other production/cost components.

As these developments enter the market, you must be able to recognize technical and fundamental impacts. Yield enhancement experiments show plants are responsive to light filters, air quality, methanol exposure, and even color backgrounds sprayed onto soil. There is little doubt there will be changes in agricultural supply over the next several decades.

The Changing Gold Supply

Industrial commodities are equally likely to undergo supply changes. The boom in gold stocks (equities) from the mid-1980s through the early 1990s was a result of decreasing mining costs as much as rising gold prices. In fact, technological advances in gold extraction from low grade ores lowered some production costs by as much as 33% over a five-year period when gold's price remained remarkably static relative to currency volatility. From 1980 to 1990, U.S. gold production increased tenfold. From a net importer of gold, the U.S. became a major exporter.

Gold's supply paints an interesting TechnoFundamental picture that explains sluggish performance through the 1980s and early 1990s. Even with 15 years of moderate inflation, gold remained steady to substantially lower because supply outpaced requirements.

The creation of new financial vehicles like currency and interest rate futures and options also had a strong influence upon gold. However, the trends in supply provided a TechnoFundamental indication prices would trend lower.

Examine the plot for gold supplies from 1969 through 1992. (See Figure 5-2.) In typical "technical" fashion, new supplies began declining in 1971. The gold window was closed and mining incentives were curtailed by high production costs and low prices.

Supplies formed a "consolidation base" just above 1.2 million kilos from 1975 through 1980. Fundamentally, 1975 was the first year U.S. citizens were allowed to legally own gold since it was removed from circulation during the Roosevelt Administration. The "Gold Rush" that was supposed to develop after lifting the U.S. restriction did not materialize until 1979/80. (See Figure 5-3.)

The trend toward tight supplies was clearly in place from 1969 forward. Supply/demand equilibrium relative to price lasted from 1975 through 1979. The price chart and supply chart reveal a five-year "trendless" period. (See Figure 5-4.)

Figure 5-2
Global Gold Supplies 1969–1992

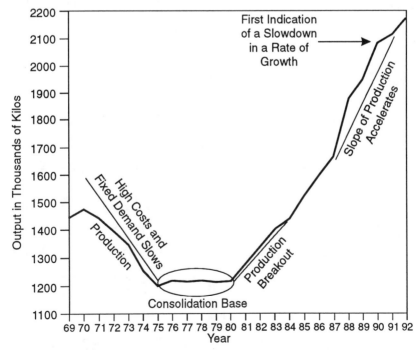

Figure 5-3
World Production of Gold (Mine Output) in Thousands of Fine Ounces (Troy Ounces)

Year	Australia	Zaire (Congo)	Canada	Colombia	Ghana	India	Japan	Mexico	Nicaragua	Philippines	Rhodesia	South Africa	United States	U.S.S.R. (1)	Total World (1)
1969	722	176	2,545	219	707	109	246	181	120	571	480	31,276	1,733	6,250	46,612
1970	620	181	2,409	202	708	104	255	198	115	603	500	32,164	1,743	6,500	47,522
1971	672	172	2,243	189	698	119	255	151	121	637	502	31,389	1,495	6,700	46,495
1972	755	141	2,079	188	724	106	243	146	112	607	502	29,245	1,450	6,900	44,843
1973	554	134	1,954	216	723	105	188	133	85	572	800	27,495	1,176	7,100	43,297
1974	513	131	1,698	265	614	101	140	134	83	538	800	24,388	1,127	7,300	40,124
1975	527	103	1,654	309	524	91	144	145	70	503	600	22,938	1,052	7,500	38,476
1976	503	91	1,692	300	532	101	138	163	76	501	600	22,936	1,048	7,700	39,234
1977	630	80	1,734	263	481	97	149	213	66	558	600	22,502	1,100	7,850	39,121
1978 (2)	648	76	1,735	258	402	88	145	202	66	587	640	22,649	999	8,000	39,304
1979 (1)	588	75	1,581	290	482	85	133	188	60	547	700	22,617	970	8,160	39,000
1980 (1)			1,600									21,500	930		38,200

World Mine Production of Gold in Thousands of Kilograms (1 Kilogram - 32.1507 Troy Oz.)

Year	Australia	Brazil	Canada	China	Colombia	Ghana	India	Japan	Mexico	Malaysia	Papua N. Guinea	Philippines	Zimbabwe	South Africa	United States	Former USSR(1)	Total World
1980	17.0	40.4	50.6	70.0	15.9	11.0	2.4	3.2	5.5	1.2	14.0	20.0	11.4	674.0	30.1	258.2	1,219
1981	18.4	37.3	52.0	52.9	16.5	10.6	2.5	3.1	6.2	1.8	16.8	23.4	11.5	656.9	42.9	262.0	1,283
1982	27.0	46.7	64.7	56.0	14.7	10.3	2.2	3.2	6.5	1.8	17.5	26.0	13.3	664.2	45.6	265.9	1,340
1983	30.6	54.4	73.5	57.5	13.6	8.7	2.2	3.1	6.2	1.8	18.1	25.3	14.1	679.5	60.8	267.5	1,396
1984	37.3	54.4	81.3	59.1	22.9	8.1	2.1	3.2	6.4	1.9	26.0	24.0	14.6	681.3	64.0	269.0	1,432
1985	58.5	72.2	87.6	61.0	35.5	9.3	1.8	5.3	8.3	2.8	36.9	33.1	14.7	670.8	75.5	270.0	1,532
1986	75.1	67.5	102.9	66.0	40.0	8.9	1.9	10.3	7.8	2.7	35.1	40.3	14.9	638.0	116.3	275.0	1,602
1987	100.7	83.7	115.8	72.0	26.6	10.2	1.9	8.6	8.0	3.5	33.3	32.6	14.7	596.5	153.9	275.0	1,658
1988	157.0	108.5	128.0	87.0	29.0	12.0	2.1	7.3	9.1	3.0	32.8	30.5	14.8	617.8	205.3	295.5	1,862
1989	202.9	97.0	158.4	87.0	30.0	12.8	2.0	6.1	9.7	2.9	33.7	30.6	16.0	606.2	259.1	289.2	1,940
1990	208.0	107.0	171.5	93.0	30.6	17.8	2.2	6.1	8.4	2.9	42.6	33.0	16.0	605.9	300.5	299.0	2,083
1991 (2)	234.0	89.0	172.0	120.0	27.9	17.5	2.6	6.9	8.4	3.0	50.0	35.8	14.8	601.0	290.0	240.3	2,110
1992 (2)	240.0	90.0	170.0	140.0										600.0	320.0	230.0	2,170

(1) Estimated. (2) Preliminary.

Source: U.S. Bureau of Mines. Table provided through Knight-Ridder CRB InfoTech™ CD-ROM.

Gold's spectacular price breakout in 1979 was accompanied by surging new supplies. The immediate and accelerating response by producers represented a "technical breakout" from the consolidation pattern that plagued gold during the previous five years. The breakout provides the first hint that gold supplies were moving into an uptrend. Thus, even without knowing specific fundamentals behind rising output, it is possible to identify growth and momentum. (See Figure 5-5.)

This TechnoFundamental approach contrasts with traditional fundamentals which might examine specific mine output, plans for capital improvement or expansion, new gold fields, ventures, and economic conditions in producing countries. It is enough to simply identify a change in statistics as it appears on the chart.

Gold presents an interesting picture because its specific price phases are wonderfully uniform and easily identified. Other commodities do not provide such clear indications. The slopes of gold's downtrend, consolidation, and uptrend for new production are nearly constant.

Figure 5-4
Global Gold Supplies 1969–1979

Figure 5-5

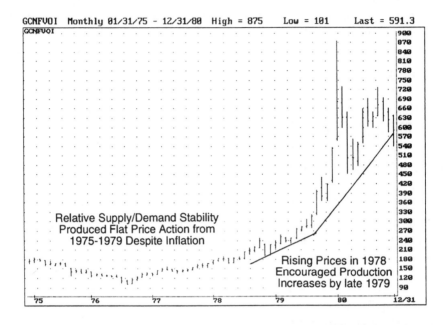

GCNFVOI Monthly 01/31/75 - 12/31/80   High = 875   Low = 101   Last = 591.3

TechnoFundamental analysis was important when considering information released from 1983 through 1990. Various associations including the Gold Institute reported declining deep shaft mining. Since the majority of gold was produced from deep shaft mines prior to 1980, many investors assumed supplies would be declining. In addition, forecasts for production costs called for significant increases associated with developing new deep shaft facilities.

However, we now know that decline in deep shaft production was replaced by surface mining and the reprocessing of tailing waste from copper, zinc, silver, lead, nickel, and other metal mines using heap leaching and solvent extraction technologies. The price boom of 1979/80 caused a surge in new mining and processing methods for gold, silver, and other metals. (See Figure 5-6.)

This new "technological trend" was so significant that it transformed nonproducing states like South Carolina into significant gold producers. From 1982 to 1992, South Carolina became the ninth-largest gold mining state in the U.S. Countries like Greenland were transformed into sizable contributors

Figure 5-6
Global Gold Supplies

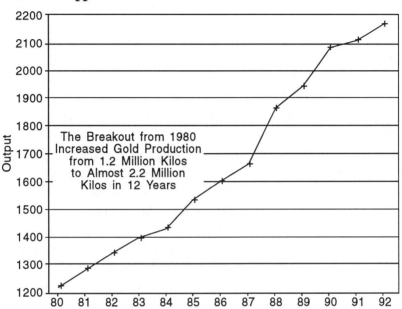

to new gold inventories. All of this serves to explain fundamentally why annual gold output increased 1,000% over a 10-year period.

Are the specific facts important? Certainly: when evaluating potential future supplies, you might want to look at specific fundamentals.

On the other hand, you can apply TechnoFundamental analysis to determine if a supply trend is in place, accelerating or losing momentum, if a top or bottom is forming, or if production is static. Isolating the technical trend in supply fundamentals lets you screen out self-serving misinformation that may be released by mining interest groups, farmers, oil producing countries, coffee growers, and others.

The decline in deep shaft mining contrasts with the technical supply picture for gold. In 1993, the senior metals analyst for Prudential Bache predicted gold would exceed $400 before the year ended. The forecast was based upon a fundamental analysis of the world's two largest producers: the former Soviet Union and South Africa.

South Africa's transition to majority rule was considered destabilizing. The tremendous amount of cash required to keep precious metal mines operational while building new prosperity for the black population was believed to be more than the economy could sustain. By the same analysis, the Commonwealth of Independent States would be forced to divert funds away from mining operations to support social programs.

Bold prognostications of a near collapse in gold, platinum, and palladium production generated price expectations of $450 to $500 an ounce for gold and from $6.50 to $7.50 an ounce for silver. Absent from these predictions were inflation, interest rate, and economic considerations. Added together, there seemed to be little fundamental doubt that precious metals had reached bottoms in 1993.

These conclusions were extremely well founded. Examining major producing regions of the new Commonwealth clearly showed mines in disrepair with insufficient resources to bring back capacity. South Africa did not lose ground as anticipated after Mandela assumed the presidency. However, output in 1993/94 was static and capital accumulation did in fact go negative.

TechnoFundamentals revealed this focus was misplaced. Despite the pessimistic outlook for Russia and South Africa, the supply chart showed no loss in upward momentum. Understand that an uptrend of this nature foretells ever increasing production. This means that demand must increase at a proportionately greater rate to induce a rising price trend in a "constant dollar" economic environment.

Only after tediously putting together bits and pieces of a supply puzzle could you have seen how gold's reality contrasted sharply with perception. Regardless of potential problems in South Africa and the former Soviet Union, corporate producers were rapidly adding capacity based upon modern technology. The decline in U.S. dollar denominated gold values was more than offset by decreasing average production costs relative to increasing output. The cashflow equation remained positive. As long as this is the case, prices can decline without adversely affecting a producer's bottom line. In fact, if lower prices stimulate demand, producers actually make more net revenue after costs.

If the supply trendline slope decreased, we could have accepted the possibility of gold's breakout above $400 within the first half of 1994. This analysis would have required adding demand TechnoFundamentals to see if the supply/demand equation was destined to change within the prescribed period. Again, we know time is necessary to slow momentum for supply and demand.

Closeup on Silver

In the case of gold, demand has a much faster reaction time because gold remains a monetary commodity rather than a consumable. Silver is valued based upon industrial and monetary demand. Unlike gold, more than 50% of annual silver production is consumed by one process: photographic imaging. (See Figure 5-7.) Another 20% is used by other industrial processes. Thus, silver has a more significant industrial role than gold.

Having been used as a monetary instrument for ages, silver's main identity as a form of exchange remains. However, silver's role as coinage has virtually disappeared and the world's capacity to hoard silver is severely limited relative to growing production. As with gold, the tremendous price increase between 1979 and 1980 changed production and consumption economics.

Silver was actually the catalyst for rethinking how global monetary systems should work. Without revisiting particulars, the famous Hunt Brothers' plan to move the free world onto a silver monetary standard created a precious metals panic. Excessive currency instability eroded confidence in governmental credit. The floating exchange rate was being challenged.

Unlike the case with gold, U.S. citizens were never prevented from owning silver. Plans put forth by the Johnson Administration for the Great Society came on the heels of an accelerated military buildup and the funding of the Vietnam War. Silver represented a "poor man's gold" and was the only hard asset metal available in the United States. Therefore, demand for silver stimulated a build-up of production capacity several years in advance of gold.

The most significant monetary event for silver came when its dollar-denominated value climbed well above $1 per ounce. Suddenly, silver coinage was worth more in silver content than its face value. Between 1967 and 1972, profit margins were sufficient to stimulate production. However, as inflation heated up in concert with the Arab Oil Embargo, shrinking margins hindered production expansion. Even with record prices as high as $6 in 1974, we can see production remained flat. (See Figure 5-8.)

By 1975, silver forecasts called for prices above $7 per ounce. First, silver was supposed to move with gold. Then the recovery from the 1974 recession was viewed as bullish. But TechnoFundamental analysis of silver output showed a double bottom formation between 1971 and 1974 with a breakout above a double top made in 1970 and 1973. While growth in silver output

Figure 5-7
Silver Demand 1992

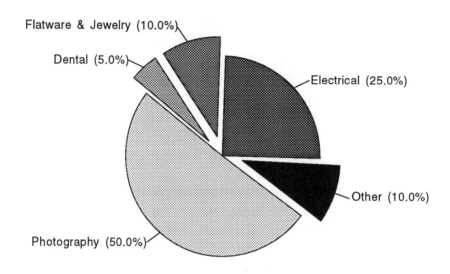

Approximately half of all silver is used by photographic processes. The rapid growth in video camcorders is an indication of how vulnerable photographic usage is to technological change. While "filmless photography" was not a factor in 1992, long-term fundamental analysis would call for careful evaluation of the potential.

Technically, any deterioration in photographic usage would show up in the consumption chart pattern. A long-term downtrend would be apparent.

was accelerating from 1974 to 1978, the TechnoFundamental outlook called for price containment.

Silver did not show signs of slowing production until 1978/79. Economic problems in producing countries like Chile and Peru, coupled with rapidly rising mining costs, held silver supplies in check for the first time in four years. This drop coincided with the Hunt Brothers' attempt to corner the market and require payments for oil using silver-backed certificates.

It is likely that TechnoFundamentals would have been deficient in catching the beginning of silver's price surge. By the time statistics revealed supplies were static, prices had already moved up more than 200%. What supply

Figure 5-8
Global Silver Output (Millions of Troy Ounces)

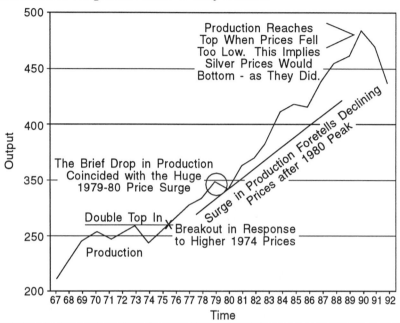

analysis reveals is the rapid recovery in primary production from 1980 forward. TechnoFundamentals suggested the bull market was over and a return to pre-1979 prices was possible. Production flattened from 1984 to 1986. Here again, TechnoFundamental supply analysis is late relative to price movement. (See Figures 5-9a and 5-9b.)

Between 1982 and 1984, silver prices spiked higher. The correct conclusion was that silver output would be encouraged by the high prices. However, this represents trading after the fact. Viewing the whole picture, you could make the argument that silver was destined to return to 1969 price levels after inflation adjustment. Indeed, in 1987, TechnoFundamentals provided a forecast for a price decline through the end of the '80s.

From 1989 through 1994, this author relied upon TechnoFundamental analysis while acting as a guest commentator on the Cable News and Business Channel (CNBC) and the Financial News Network (FNN) television stations. My analysis challenged the Platinum Guild, Gold Institute, Silver Institute, and dozens of professional metals analysts. Each time, TechnoFundamentals

Figure 5-9a
Silver Prices 1967–1993

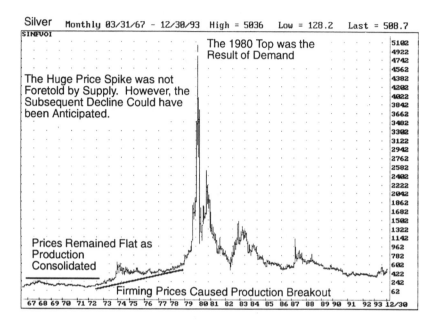

Silver   Monthly 03/31/67 - 12/30/93   High = 5036   Low = 128.2   Last = 508.7

The 1980 Top was the Result of Demand

The Huge Price Spike was not Foretold by Supply. However, the Subsequent Decline Could have been Anticipated.

Prices Remained Flat as Production Consolidated

Firming Prices Caused Production Breakout

indicated oversupply with static demand. Gold and silver simply did not break out into new bull trends.

Finding the (Supply) Trend That's Your Friend

Commodities like gold, silver, copper, platinum, palladium, and energy products are particularly well suited to TechnoFundamental analysis because supply and demand trends frequently build or decline at constant rates. The "infrastructure" required to produce these commodities creates momentum as previously explained. It is a difficult and lengthy process to open a new mine or drill a new well. Once in place, the decision to close a mine, oil well, or refinery is equally problematic.

To an extent, commodities like coffee, orange juice, cattle, and hogs gather momentum because production depends upon established bases that have lead times or cycles. For example, coffee trees take three to five years to

Figure 5-9b
World Mine Production of Silver, by Selected Countries, in Metric Tons (4) (2,204.6 lbs.)

Year	Argen-tina	Aus-tralia	Boli-via (1)	Canada	Germany	Hon-duras	Japan	Mexico	Mo-rocco	Peru	Poland	United States	Former USSR(2)	Yugo-slavia	Zaire (Congo)	World Total (2)
1979	2.21	26.76	5.74	36.87	1.04	2.43	8.68	52.17	3.28	39.25	22.6	37.90	46.0	5.21	3.89	348.1
1980	2.36	24.65	6.10	33.34	1.06	1.77	8.60	50.05	3.15	44.42	24.63	32.33	46.0	4.79	2.73	342.8
1981	2.52	23.91	6.39	36.30	1.13	1.82	9.01	52.92	2.12	46.94	20.58	40.68	46.5	4.44	2.58	361.6
1982	2.68	29.16	5.47	42.25	1.28	2.10	9.84	59.18	2.64	41.96	21.12	40.25	46.9	3.34	1.75	371.2
1983	2.50	33.21	6.03	35.56	1.17	2.59	9.88	63.61	2.85	50.48	21.80	43.43	47.2	3.99	1.29	387.7
1984	1.98	31.26	4.56	42.66	1.23	2.70	10.40	75.34	2.41	53.08	23.92	44.59	47.4	4.05	1.23	413.9
1985 (4)	68	1,086	111	1,197	38	86	339	2,153	85	1,811	831	1,227	1,490	156	43	13,051
1986	66	1,023	95	1,088	28	54	351	2,303	49	1,926	829	1,074	1,500	177	34	12,970
1987	60	1,119	142	1,375	91	23	281	2,415	44	2,054	831	1,241	1,510	165	37	13,757
1988	79	1,118	232	1,443	80	58	252	2,359	226	1,552	1,063	1,661	1,520	139	74	14,167
1989	83	1,075	267	1,262	69	50	156	2,306	237	1,840	1,003	2,007	1,520	127	70	14,452
1990	83	1,138	311	1,400	28	19	150	2,346	241	1,725	832	2,125	1,400	105	84	15,106
1991 (2)	56	1,180	337	1,400	22	20	171	2,196	200	1,770	870	1,848	1,300	94	80	14,723
1992 (3)				1,200				2,000		1,500		1,800	1,200			13,700

World Production of Silver, by Selected Countries, in Millions of Fine Ounces (Troy Ounces)

Year	Argen-tina	Aus-tralia	Zaire (Congo)	Boli-via (1)	Canada	Mo-rocco	W. Ger-many	Hon-duras	USSR(2)	Japan	Mexico	Peru	United States	Yugo-slavia	World Total (2)
1967	2.58	19.84	1.84	4.52	37.21	.77	2.04	4.01	35.0	10.80	38.27	32.11	32.12	3.08	258.2
1968	2.42	21.39	2.14	5.18	45.01	.92	1.77	4.40	35.0	10.69	40.03	36.36	32.73	3.02	275.3
1969	3.11	24.46	1.90	6.01	43.53	.86	1.68	3.91	37.0	10.81	42.90	35.89	41.91	3.82	295.7
1970	2.05	25.99	1.71	6.82	44.25	.68	1.80	3.82	38.0	10.80	42.84	39.84	45.01	3.42	303.9
1971	3.18	21.70	1.47	5.37	46.02	2.94	1.80	3.64	39.0	11.29	36.66	40.19	41.56	3.35	294.7
1972	3.27	21.89	2.08	5.58	44.79	3.38	1.74	3.60	40.0	10.05	37.48	42.02	37.23	3.58	301.5
1973	2.44	22.42	2.00	5.80	47.49	3.06	1.45	3.15	41.0	8.55	38.79	34.89	37.83	4.30	307.9
1974	3.10	21.54	1.65	5.39	42.81	3.04	1.24	3.66	42.0	7.31	37.55	37.53	33.76	4.70	292.2
1975	2.28	23.35	2.29	5.47	39.70	2.05	1.08	3.80	43.0	8.73	38.03	35.58	34.94	5.41	303.1
1976	1.75	25.07	2.47	5.09	41.20	2.24	1.03	2.96	44.0	9.30	42.64	30.10	34.33	4.63	312.2
1977 (3)	1.80	27.42	2.73	5.89	42.76		.97	3.21	45.0	9.65	47.03		38.17	4.69	325.5
1978 (2)		24.9			40.9					9.3	50.8	38.6	39.4		333.7
1979 (2)		22.9			40.0		1.10				58.0	40.0	38.3		351.3

(1) Exports. (2) Estimate. (3) Preliminary. (4) Data prior to 1985 are in millions of troy ounces.

Source: Bureau of Mines. Table provided through Knight-Ridder CRB InfoTech™ CD-ROM.

reach production maturity. Therefore, a destructive freeze implies a multi-season shortage.

Cattle and hog inventories grow in relation to the number of breeders held. Growth in the breeding stock causes a cyclical expansion. If breeders are slaughtered, it takes time to rebuild capacity.

Livestock provides an example of cyclical expansion and contraction that is worth examining. Beef production is a function of four main processes. First, cow and calf operations generate animals that begin the cycle. Since the size of any calf crop depends upon the number of breeding cows, any future expansion or contraction of beef supplies will depend upon the number of calves that can be put into the cycle. The majority of the calf crop is placed on feed to be fattened for slaughter. Ranchers and vertically integrated operators manage their inventories and cycles by retaining heifers (young cows) for eventual breeding or dairy production or culling their herds. The culling rate affects immediate beef supplies while retention projects potential output. You will encounter statistics for cow numbers and an approximate calving rate. The combination of cows and calving rates provides a way to calculate eventual supplies. Cows go into heat in three-week periods and gestation is nine months. Unless there is an unusual biological breakthrough, these cycles are fixed. Thus, when constructing your analysis, keep in mind that the cow herd takes nine months to produce calves.

Dairies play an important role in determining beef supplies because the cow slaughter accounts for a significant addition to dressed beef. Culling and retention plans can significantly alter the amount of beef on retailer shelves. In 1983, government milk price supports were lowered, which resulted in the liquidation of dairy cows. The result was a surge in available beef supplies that drove prices from highs near 7400 to lows below 5600. Once the supply of dairy beef was absorbed, prices promptly surged back above 7000. (See Figure 5-10.)

Understand that each production stage adds to the beef "pipeline." Slaughtered animals consist of cows, bulls, nonfed bulls/steers, and fed steers. When you read cattle reports, you will encounter statistics and opinions about calves, heifers, yearlings, bulls, and steers. Each represents a unique stage within the production pipeline as follows:

CALF—new born
YEARLING—one-year old
HEIFER— young cow after birthing first calf

Figure 5-10

LCNFVOI Weekly 01/15/82 - 12/28/84 High = 74   Low = 55.35 Last = 66.6

From a high of 74, cattle dropped below 5600.

BULL—male used for breeding
STEER—castrated male being fattened for slaughter
FEEDERS—animals on feed from 500 pounds to slaughter weight
BEEF—slaughtered and dressed carcasses
STEAK—food to be eaten rare and rarely according to some experts

By knowing these distinctions, you can approximate the flow of finished beef to the market. (See Figure 5-11.) In total, the process from birth to market takes between two and two-and-one-half years. The average cycle was two-and-one-half years in 1980 and has accelerated to approximately two years due to more effective feeds, feeding procedures, food supplements, and care. Today's birth weights are between 70 and 100 pounds. It takes one-and-one-quarter to one-and-one-half years to grow an animal into a feeder at about 500 pounds. Finished weights are between 900 and 1,100 pounds and take about six to eight months. Why is this information important?

There are many factors that influence cattle producers. A dramatic change in feed costs will have different effects depending upon where the bulk of

Figure 5-11

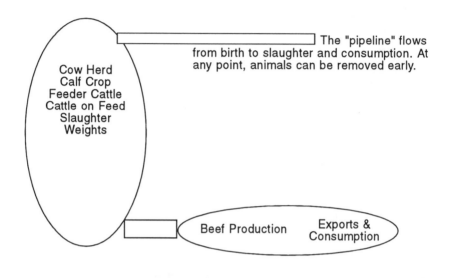

Cow Herd
Calf Crop
Feeder Cattle
Cattle on Feed
Slaughter
Weights

The "pipeline" flows from birth to slaughter and consumption. At any point, animals can be removed early.

Beef Production   Exports & Consumption

cattle is in the pipeline. If there is a large number of feeders, high grain prices could force early liquidations and change the phase of the cattle cycle. Recall the previous discussion of "phase shift." When you know the probable causes of phase shift, you can prepare an appropriate trading strategy to avoid unnecessary exposure. Anticipation is marvelous protection under such circumstances.

You may be interested in the "gain" associated with grazing in comparison with feedlots. Generally, range fed cattle gain one to two-and-one-half pounds per day while feedlot animals grow two-and-one-quarter to three-and-three-quarters pounds per day. Range cattle are more susceptible to adverse weather which includes very hot weather (leading to lethargy and weight loss), extreme cold (causing weight loss and sickness), excessive rain (muddy conditions), and drought (loss of grass). In other words, extremes are not good. Slaughter ratios also are helpful for rounding out your analysis. Cows account for between 15% and 30%, nonfed steers and heifers range from 5% to 15%, bulls are less than 3%, and fed cattle account for 50% to 75%.

Now you are armed with the basic information you need to understand and analyze cattle supplies, capacity, cycles, and external influences. Each component of the pipeline will exhibit technical patterns that are linked to fundamental developments. A top formation in the cow herd is a leading indicator of total beef production. Charts of the pipeline supply components paint a picture of developing cycles and opportunities. The long-term chart illustrates regular cattle seasonals, cycles, and a secular uptrend extending from 1986 through 1991 on the chart. (See Figure 5-12.) Notice how seasonal and cyclical patterns remain intact despite the fact that the trendline shifts upward from the double bottom made in 1985/86. Referring to Chapter 3, you can see all of the time series components displayed by cattle. Although it may not be as obvious, the same patterns are inherent in all commodity contracts and most financial instruments.

One of the most significant events of the 1970s was the oil embargo OPEC nations imposed upon the United States in retaliation for supporting Israel. This one development caused a devastating "cost-push" price spiral that spread to virtually all economic sectors. The cost of energy is basic to almost all production. From lighting, heating, and cooling, to running machinery and processes, from transportation to chemical feedstocks to fertilizers, oil plays the dominant role. There is little wonder inflation heated up subsequent to the embargo.

Rising oil prices precipitated supply trends in other commodities. In addition, the use of embargo as a political and economic weapon was briefly popularized by OPEC's bold move. Later in the 1970s, President Carter attempted the same strategy by imposing a grain embargo against the Soviet Union. Unfortunately, the policy backfired when the European Community, South America, Australia, and Canada gladly stepped in to fill the gap left by the U.S.

As we will see, President Carter's action created an opportunity for other nations to expand their grain output at the expense of the U.S. farmer. This caused an uptrend in global supply that held grain prices in check despite an overall inflation.

The chart of corn production (see Figures 5-13 and 5-14) illustrates how TechnoFundamentals provide a foundation for forming a market bias. From the 1980/81 crop year through 1992/93, world corn output increased from 406.7 to 524.1 million metric tons. Unlike gold's steady rise in supply, grains

Figure 5-12

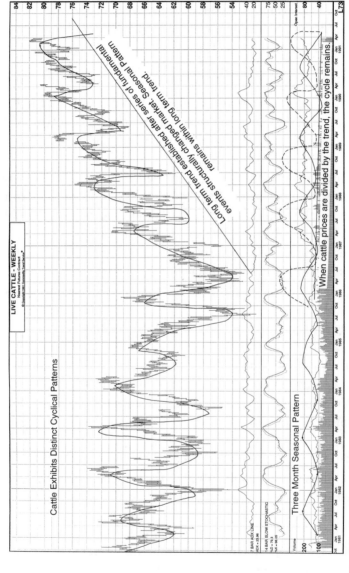

are a seasonal commodity subject to dramatic changes in weather and planting conditions from year to year. Supplies are consumed and must be replenished. Each year's production is independent of the previous growing season. Yet the effects of each harvest are cumulative to the extent that some supplies are carried over from season to season.

Interruptions in expanding production were clearly the result of identifiable fundamental events. The drought of 1983 reduced the 1983/84 crop yield by more than 20%. While there was an immediate rebound in the following crop year, the 1983 drought established a "bottom" from which supplies recovered. Production peaked in 1985/86 at 480 million metric tons. This production "spike" took place within two years and has been explained as a response to the 1983/84 price surge. From a fundamental standpoint, we can identify a cyclical "causal correlation" where high prices stimulate production while low prices discourage adding acreage. Even with this in mind, there was a secular trend toward greater global output.

Figure 5-13
Corn Production

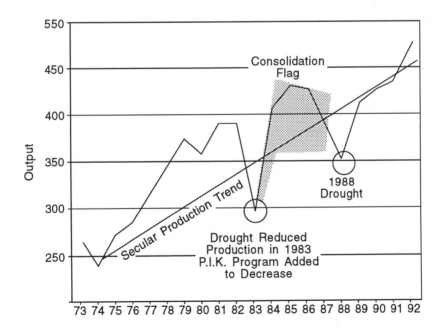

Figure 5-14
World Production of Corn or Maize (in Millions of Metric Tons)

Crop Year	Argentina	Brazil	Canada	China	France	Hungary	India	Indonesia	Italy	Mexico	Romania	South Africa	Thailand	United States	Former USSR	Yugoslavia	World Total
1980-1	12.9	22.6	5.4	62.6	9.2	6.5	7.0	4.0	6.4	12.5	10.3	14.6	3.2	168.8	9.5	9.3	406.7
1981-2	9.6	22.9	6.7	59.2	9.0	7.0	7.0	4.5	8.2	12.5	11.9	8.4	4.5	208.3	8.0	9.8	441.2
1982-3	9.0	19.5	6.5	60.3	10.4	7.8	6.3	3.2	6.8	7.0	12.6	4.1	3.5	212.3	13.5	11.1	440.4
1983-4	9.4	20.5	5.9	66.3	10.1	6.4	6.8	5.0	6.6	9.3	11.1	4.1	4.0	106.8	16.2	10.7	344.1
1984-5	11.5	22.0	7.0	73.4	10.4	6.7	8.4	5.3	6.8	9.9	13.3	7.8	4.4	194.9	12.5	11.3	457.0
1985-6	13.0	19.0	7.4	64.0	12.3	6.5	7.8	4.6	6.4	10.0	14.0	8.5	5.2	225.2	13.5	9.9	480.0
1986-7	9.5	26.5	6.7	69.0	11.3	7.0	7.2	5.4	6.5	10.0	15.5	8.5	4.1	209.6	12.5	12.5	477.2
1987-8	9.0	23.0	7.0	76.0	12.3	7.0	5.5	4.8	5.6	9.9	10.5	7.5	2.7	179.4	14.8	8.8	439.3
1988-9	5.0	26.1	5.4	77.4	14.6	6.0	8.3	5.2	6.3	10.1	10.0	12.4	4.2	125.2	16.0	7.7	400.7
1989-90	5.2	21.8	6.4	78.9	13.4	6.7	9.4	5.0	6.4	9.8	9.0	8.9	4.1	191.2	15.3	9.4	462.5
1990-1	7.6	23.7	7.4	96.8	9.5	4.5	9.0	5.2	5.7	14.1	6.8	8.3	3.8	201.6	9.8	6.7	477.2
1991-2 (1)	10.6	28.5	7.4	98.8	12.9		8.0	5.3	6.2	14.5	10.5	3.3	3.6	190.2	9.3	11.6	484.6
1992-3 (2)	10.0	25.0	5.3	93.0	13.6		9.4	5.3	7.6	15.0	8.5	8.0	3.6	240.8	9.1	7.1	524.1

Crop Year	United States	Argentina	Brazil	Mexico	South Africa	France	China	India	Italy	Bulgaria	Hungary	Yugoslavia	Romania	Indonesia	USSR	World Total
1970-1	105.5	9.9	13.5	8.7	8.6	7.6	26.4	7.5	4.8	2.4	4.0	6.9	6.5	2.9	7.8	255.1
1971-2	143.3	5.9	12.9	9.1	9.4	8.8	25.3	5.1	4.5	2.5	4.7	7.4	7.9	2.6	8.6	292.1
1972-3	141.6	9.0	13.8	8.1	4.2	8.2	22.0	6.2	4.8	2.9	5.5	7.9	9.5	2.0	9.8	286.3
1973-4	143.4	9.9	15.0	9.0	11.1	10.7	28.0	5.8	5.1	2.6	5.9	8.3	7.4	2.9	13.2	314.7
1974-5	118.5	7.7	16.4	7.8	9.1	8.7	30.7	5.6	5.0	1.6	6.2	8.0	7.4	3.0	12.1	286.5
1975-6	147.3	5.9	17.9	9.2	7.3	8.2	32.0	7.0	5.3	3.0	7.1	9.4	9.2	2.6	7.3	321.6
1976-7	157.9	8.3	18.8	9.6	9.7	5.5	31.4	6.3	5.3	3.0	5.2	9.1	11.6	2.6	10.1	336.3
1977-8	161.8	9.7	13.6	9.7	10.2	8.6	49.5	5.9	6.4	2.6	6.0	9.9	10.1	3.0	11.0	364.9
1978-9	184.6	9.0	16.3	10.2	8.3	9.5	55.9	6.2	6.2	2.2	6.7	7.6	10.2	4.0	9.0	390.9
1979-80	201.7	6.4	20.2	9.2	10.8	10.4	60.0	5.6	6.2	3.2	7.3	10.1	12.4	3.6	8.4	423.7
1980-1	168.8	12.9	22.6	10.4	14.6	9.4	62.6	6.8	6.4	2.2	6.4	9.3	11.2	4.0	9.5	406.7
1981-2 (1)	208.3	9.6	22.9	12.5	8.4	9.0	59.2	6.0	7.7	2.3	6.8	9.8	10.5	4.3	8.0	437.4
1982-3 (2)	213.3	7.5	23.5	7.5	4.7		62.5								13.5	443.1
1983-4																

(1) Preliminary. (2) Estimate.

Source: Foreign Agricultural Service, U.S.D.A. Table provided through Knight-Ridder CRB InfoTech™ CD-ROM.

It stands to reason that you would see increasing crop sizes based upon rising populations, world prosperity, industrialization, and changing diets. A technical evaluation of corn supports this fundamental perspective with an interesting twist.

The 1983/84 drought set up a "consolidation flag." Based upon previous patterns, this consolidation suggests a continuation in growth with an approximate 680 to 690 million metric ton production ceiling expected between 1996 and 1999. By any estimate, this is a bold prediction to make in 1984.

However, using technical assumptions after the 1983 drought, the first objective for the following season's production was approximately 441 million tons—the most recent previous high. When the 1984/85 crop broke through this objective, the uptrend was reconfirmed.

Using this information alone, TechnoFundamentals strongly suggested price support at approximately $2.20 per bushel would be broken within the next two crop years. Indeed, despite assertions that corn had a "cost based" bottom above $2.15, prices crashed between 1986 and 1988 to lows around $1.50. For some farmers, this was below cost. However, government support mechanisms made up for this "deficit" under most circumstances.

Even with plummeting prices, 1988 planting intentions and final acreage confirmed the trend toward greater overall output. Another weather incident changed the course of production. The 1988 drought reduced U.S. yields and eventually pushed prices to four-year highs.

The TechnoFundamental perspective warns that prices remain vulnerable to a test as low as $1.50 per bushel. Any potential for global output in excess of 480 million metric tons would be a catalyst for revisiting a $1.50 bottom, assuming no extraordinary government intervention or global political movement. Since grains find price supports in the form of targets and guaranteed loans as well as government purchasing programs, there is always a possibility prices could be artificially prevented from returning to predicted lows. Under such circumstances, a logical interpretation of fundamentals would temper our expectations.

Getting Technical about Supply

The question arises, "Is this long-range TechnoFundamental analysis really helpful in day-to-day trading?" After all, few traders hold positions from crop year to crop year.

Certainly, those involved in farming, agricultural policy, food processing, and animal production should have an interest in TechnoFundamental considerations. The trader also gains important insights. The most critical decisions are made when markets reach new "interim" highs or lows. At these times, you must determine whether a market can, in fact, move further in either direction.

Equally important are times when markets are making all-time highs or new historical lows. We face the question, "How high is too high?" or "Can prices go any lower?" Tracking technical "breakouts" in production can give a reference point for drawing an accurate conclusion.

In the beginning of this chapter, we touched upon three supply factors: where supply has been, where it is, and where it is going. Technical analysis of price uses the same factors and attempts to make the same type of forecast. Our technical analysis theories remain consistent.

First, we are measuring momentum that can drive supplies higher or lower. Then we seek out formations and patterns that indicate the propensity for increasing, decreasing, or static production.

Our aim with TechnoFundamentals is to combine the two major market approaches. If you recall our earlier discussion of price theory, you'll remember that prices move higher because buyers continue to be willing to buy at ever-increasing prices while sellers are only willing to sell if offered better prices.

A similar theory can be applied to supply. Supplies rise when producers are willing to increase output to take advantage of perceived or actual selling opportunities. Capacity builds as producers continue to be willing to expand despite increasing aggregate output. Further, producers may be forced to increase production to compensate for decreasing selling prices. In short, our assumption is that market components adhere to the same rules.

This assumption is logical when we consider that price, supply, and demand are, by definition, related concepts. While seasonally dependent commodities like crops are subject to more volatile production than industrial commodities like copper, agricultural capacity operates according to the same principles. Available farmland determines gross capacity. Certainly, set-aside programs and planting incentives dictate how much capacity is used in any season. Thereafter, Mother Nature determines yields. In combination, capacity utilization and weather determine the end harvest.

But we must keep in mind that fields, whether planted or lying fallow, represent an ability to produce. Once cultivated, farmland creates supply momentum. In addition to annual harvests, agricultural commodities have "cumulative supplies" commonly referred to as "carryovers." This brings us to another analytical plane which takes cumulative supplies into consideration.

You may have already raised the question in your mind about cumulative industrial supplies. After all, copper inventories can have as much of a price impact as copper production. There is a lead/lag relationship between available stocks and anticipated production that often plays upon immediate price levels. This correlation helps us refine analysis using additional TechnoFundamental applications.

However, industrial commodities tend to experience smoother cycles because seasonality is far less intense. Moreover, carryover analysis often requires some subjective logic.

For example, gold inventories are forever growing because it is held as a "store of value." Nonetheless, one of the most significant fears gold investors shared during the early 1990s was the possibility of gold abandonment. With more than 42,000 metric tons of gold held as central bank assets, any move toward liquidating this enormous hoard would spell disaster for gold prices.

However, abandonment implies a total philosophical and structural change for gold and central banking practices. More practical analysis calls for assuming the status quo—gold will be accumulated and hoarded.

When information is available, carryovers can be plotted in relation to new supplies. Generally, a build-up in inventory leads a production slowdown. This is frequently called the "inherent business cycle."

It is important, however, not to rely too much upon generalities. Recently, there have been as many exceptions to the "inherent business cycle" rule as adherences. On a global basis, growing inventories did not discourage capacity build-ups in coarse grains, gold, base metals, and fossil fuels. To the contrary, the expansion pattern has stayed in place for these commodities.

On the local level, inventory build-ups have been intercepted by government policy to temporarily adjust output. For example, a massive global accumulation of grain from 1980 through 1982 led to the U.S. "Payment in Kind" (PIK) program. Farmers were paid in the form of U.S. grain in return for not planting. The double objective was to reduce government inventories while lowering output. At best, the plan would only reduce supplies momentarily. At worst, the program would deplete buffer stocks while supplementing a poor harvest. As you might have guessed, the worst happened when the U.S. experienced the 1983 summer droughts.

The possibility for such artificial intervention must always be considered. Under such circumstances, the affected market takes on a bias which can be contrary to the underlying production trend. In the case of grains, a crop reduction program predisposes markets to shortages and higher prices. The fundamental price reference point can be derived from the previous season's low. Since we know supplies are going to be negatively affected by policy, the crop should be no larger than the last harvest. If the program is effective, the crop reduction should be sufficient to support prices over the past season's lows.

Other commodities are susceptible to interventions which include environmental restrictions, trade embargoes, technological changes, and political influences. If lead is no longer allowed as a component of gasoline, demand will be legally altered and supply patterns will follow. If strip mining is forbidden, supplies from these sources will be eliminated. An oil or grain embargo politically restricts supplies. If solvent extraction of minerals enhances efficiency, more product can be refined at higher rates at lower costs.

You must keep a watchful eye for developments that can influence technical patterns identified in your supply analysis. This will be examined in greater detail in our discussion of "structural change." Our examples of TechnoFundamental supply analysis have used annual data to illustrate long-term trends.

Just as technical price analysis can be viewed monthly, weekly, daily, or even minute by minute, so can fundamental data be analyzed within different time frames.

Government reports include planting intentions, crop conditions, and yield predictions. Taken individually and as a whole, this information can depict near-term supplies. There are interim projections for gold, silver, platinum, and palladium output published by metals processors like Johnson Matthey, brokerage firms, and industry groups like the Platinum Guild, Gold Institute, and Silver Institute. Information is also available from commodity exchanges, private forecasters, and producers.

The Importance of Converting Apples to Apples

Whether your interests are precious metals, grains, meats, currencies, or other commodities, there are numerous sources for technical and fundamental data. Unfortunately, supply statistics are not always uniform and easily digested. A data translation exercise is usually required to create "comparative sets." This is true for demand statistics as well as supply. However, it is appropriate to review this data translation process in this chapter to broaden TechnoFundamental applications.

Pick up any precious metals report and you will discover statistics are quoted in troy ounces, kilos, or metric tons. Frequently, these different units of measure will vary throughout the same document.

Look at various U.S.D.A. reports on grains and you will find planting intentions projected in acres, exports reported in millions of tons or bushels, and yields in bushels per acre.

The Brazilian Coffee Institute refers to yields per tree and "kilos available for export." You may also be confronted with total kilos produced, bags produced, bags available for export, and so on.

Cattle on feed reports and slaughter statistics give you the number of animals on feed or slaughtered for dressing. Yet futures contracts are quoted and delivered in pounds for live cattle, feeder cattle, hogs, and pork bellies. Since the early 1970s, advances in breeding and feeding have generated significantly more meat per animal. Therefore, a chart of the number of animals produced will not necessarily reflect pounds of meat unless a conversion formula is incorporated into the analysis.

There are also subtle differences between general fundamental information and commodity contract correlations. Perhaps the most frequently overlooked difference between gross statistics and significant figures is the *quality* that is deliverable against the futures contract.

For example, pork bellies are frequently exposed to long-side expiration "squeezes" because the futures contract requires delivery of a high grade belly. In the trade, a large amount of each year's belly production is "no grade"—i.e., not deliverable against the contract. Unsuspecting traders might believe an abundance of pork bellies exists based upon cold storage reports, only to find that a very small portion can qualify for delivery. The result is usually a rising price in the face of apparent large supplies.

Just such a situation developed in 1971 and 1989. In fact, the manipulation of prices based upon the discrepancies between gross statistics and deliverable supplies prompted the Chicago Mercantile Exchange to investigate making pork bellies a "cash delivery." This means that the contract would be settled in cash rather than actual pork bellies.

Commercial interests vigorously opposed this move because it would limit their true hedge protection in the event actual high-grade bellies were required to fulfill secondary contract obligations. Between the time a contract would be settled in cash and the time the hedger would need to find real pork bellies, serious financial damage could occur. Thus, the speculator must be careful to consider supplies of deliverable product as opposed to total supplies. Even delivery points are important. In 1995, the live cattle delivery was liberalized by providing more delivery locations. This lowered prices on contracts with the new specification.

This holds true for many commodities. In 1992, the New York Mercantile Exchange changed the delivery requirements for palladium from .995 fine to .9995. This pushed prices in the transition delivery higher because traders had to find the higher quality palladium or deliver at a discount to the market.

The copper contract on the New York Commodity Exchange Incorporated was similarly changed to a higher grade. Coffee supplies are usually quoted in gross supplies (total supplies) and "exportable supplies" (exportable total). This is important because nonexportable coffee is consumed within the country of origin. Internal consumption can distort figures for available world inventories.

The list of cautions of this type is far too extensive to cover in detail here. The key is to be aware that, in evaluating supply, things are not always as they seem.

Know What You Are Trading

In a year of drought, early freezes, or floods, crop quality is likely to be adversely affected as well as crop yield. When this happens, commercial interests will place a premium on "old crop" supplies in storage or "new" new crop productions. Thus, the tightness from a poor season can carry into a new season even if the new season experiences excellent growing conditions. Commercial grain processors and users will always want higher quality supplies on a price parity basis.

Price parity takes into consideration price difference relative to quality difference. Certainly, if low quality grain becomes cheap enough relative to higher qualities, it will be attractive. All of these relationships explain why you will frequently observe spread differentials between old and new crops.

Those trading financial contracts are not immune to the challenge of multiple statistics. For example, interest rate contracts can be indices derived from cash instruments. Exact correlations to specific instruments are elusive because T-Bond futures prices represent "cheapest to deliver."

Currencies traded on the International Monetary Market (IMM) are quoted in U.S. Dollar parity while Interbank and cash quotes are the inverse. Not all stock index futures move alike. The S&P 500 represents a different domain than the Value Line Index or the New York Futures Exchange Index (NYFE). "Small cap" stocks trend to a different drummer than the Dow industrials or utilities.

The rule is, "Know what you are trading." Don't automatically conclude that a pork belly is a pork belly or a soybean is a soybean. The very difference between actual commodities and their futures and options counterparts is called "basis." The extent to which cash and futures can vary in price is called "basis risk" or "basis exposure."

In addition to following this first rule, you must truly understand fundamental statistics. Otherwise, you will be subject to the "garbage-in/garbage-out" theory.

Consider the statement, "U.S. farmers plant a record 10 million acres . . . " Suppose the yield is 25 bushels per acre. The end result would be a crop of 250 million bushels. If the yield turned out to be 32 bushels per acre, the end result would be 320 million bushels. Thus, acreage must be correlated to yield.

You are likely to encounter fundamentals like, "Private forecaster expects harvest of 7.5 million tons . . . " If the crop report is given in bushels, you must convert bushels to tons or tons to bushels to make a comparison. The important question arises, "How many pounds are in a bushel?" An international report may say, "French farmers expected to plant 16 million square rods . . . " How many square rods are in an acre? What is the prospective yield per square rod?

Translating statistics into meaningful information requires knowledge of various conversion tables. Obviously, any fundamental study must compare apples to apples.

A primary reason many traders choose technical analysis over fundamentals is a fear of complexity. It is a common view that it's easier to remember a few chart patterns and formations or have the computer calculate some moving averages than to know and understand relationships of various measurements and reporting standards. In a diversified commodity trading program, comparing oranges to oranges becomes tedious when you have to remember exactly how many pounds are in a box!

CHAPTER **6**

HOW TO LOOK AT DEMAND TECHNOFUNDAMENTALLY

It stands to reason that if supply can exhibit technical tendencies, so can demand. Forces governing demand are substantially different from those influencing supply because the need for a commodity is based upon *human requirements* rather than natural phenomenon.

Demand can be governed by economic and political systems as well as technological and social developments. Those familiar with monetary policy tools are aware that manipulating the money supply can influence demand. Political sanctions and bans can immediately curb demand or force the use of a black market. Technology can displace the need for a particular commodity. Social patterns like changing diet, population aging, and general demographics can alter demand. While demand is considerably less responsive to acts of nature, hurricanes, floods, and fires can create a temporary need for specific commodities.

The link between money supply and demand is unique. It has been stated that the Federal Reserve is not capable of performing a rain dance in a drought. That is, a natural disaster cannot be avoided by using monetary policy. A disaster may affect supply, but it can also alter demand.

When hurricanes like Bob, Andrew, and Hugo rip through communities, demand for building supplies such as lumber and copper will temporarily increase. This event will show up on a chart as a spike pattern, since a surge in demand will impact prices and could also stimulate an increase in supply. Depending upon the magnitude of the disaster, even financial markets like

T-Bills, Eurodollars, and T-Bonds can be affected by insurance company port-folio adjustments.

It is true that the Fed's monetary policy can combat rising prices by limiting available money. Nonetheless, techniques like interest rate manipu-lation, open market operations, and changing reserve requirements are almost like fighting cancer with chemotherapy. The drugs affect the entire body while we hope the cancer will die first. Similarly, this lack of precision simply does not permit the Federal Reserve to control prices within specific sectors.

Political actions can have a more targeted effect. Mandated catalytic convert-ers will increase demand for platinum and palladium. Removing or adjusting government price supports can change pricing and influence demand for grains, dairy products, peanuts, tobacco, cotton, and other agriculturals.

Creating new environmental standards can force the use of some com-modities and the abandonment of others. Over the next 20 years, new laws might require us to drive electric vehicles in order to meet a zero emission standard. The workday might be staggered by law. Car pooling could be regulated. Obviously, such rules and regulations would have a profound impact upon energy consumption.

The list of government tools that can alter demand is extensive. The object of a TechnoFundamental approach is to measure the actual impact or pattern caused by intervention and policy.

No discussion of demand would be complete without considering busi-ness cycles. While it may be argued that the business cycle is inherent in government policy, we have touched upon the natural tendency for commod-ity prices to rise and fall relative to cyclical growing patterns. It takes time to build capacity and it takes time for demand to respond to the availability of goods. When raw materials are cheap and plentiful, manufacturing expands, the expansion increases demand which, in turn, depletes supply. As prices rise, raw materials are not as cheap and plentiful. As higher costs begin affecting demand, manufacturers seek to trim production and the downward phase is established.

Riding a Cycle

Business cycles follow different phases. The cycle in durable goods could be different from the housing cycle. Retailing cycles might be negatively corre-lated with the machine tool cycle. Without seeking specific reasons for each cycle, experience tells us that phases can gradually move toward each other to cause a more comprehensive economic cycle, often called the "Grand Cycle."

As a practical matter, the Grand Cycle makes little difference in day-to-day trading. It is useful to know if we are experiencing a general expansion or contraction when planning a long-range forecast.

Yet we can see that within the comprehensive movement of any Grand Cycle, there are countercycles that more immediately impact supply, demand, and price.

Some analysts insist that the Grand Cycle must be used to assess the potential extent of specific price movements. A gold trend might be intensified by the upward or downward thrust of the Grand Cycle.

From a TechnoFundamental perspective, any such influence should be apparent in supply or demand patterns. It is interesting to note that many predictions based upon Grand Cycle assumptions have proven false. During the 1960s and 1970s, there was a consensus that the world would "run out of fuel" by the year 2000. This was based upon an examination of consumption trends in conjunction with the perceived position within the Grand Cycle. The same logic was used to warn of explosive population growth that would be the direct result of global industrialization.

Conservation and exploration contradicted the forecast for depleted fossil fuels. Industrialized nations moved toward negative population growth while China actually forced a limit upon family size. As of 1995, the prediction for global population was clouded by the tragic spread of AIDS through Africa, Haiti, and other Third World countries. Initial estimates called for infection rates as high as 7% to 15% of Africa's total black population. It is terrifying to know that such estimates may be far short of reality. According to some studies, as many as 50 million people were presumed infected by 1994.

There is no question that a pandemic of such proportions could alter global consumption patterns within a decade. Even with a cure or vaccine, the AIDS virus will stall population expansion in several regions. Birth rates in India and Latin America may offset this population decline.

You can see the importance of demographics when you consider that gold has religious significance in India. From the poorest in the caste system to the most elite, almost all Indians own some token in gold. From a ring to a nose pin, gold is practically essential. Individual ownership by the masses may be small, yet the population size and growth curve imply a healthy gold appetite will exist into the future.

Some may argue that gold plays as significant a role in China. The declining Chinese population could offset the rising Indian population. What is intriguing is the focus in both societies on the same market—gold. We see that tangential considerations like demographics can be as significant as plans for mining facilities, economic growth, and inflation.

This brings us to an all-important question: "Who consumes what?" Until recently, the answer for most commodities was usually static and unchanging, since consumption was easily identified. Today, consumption patterns quickly change in response to specific events or from structural developments.

In Chapter 2 we reviewed sugar's bull move of 1974 when prices soared over 60 cents—and the original incentive to use high fructose corn syrup (HFCS) was born. This introduced a competitive product to cane and beet sugar which could offset rising sugar prices: demand for white sugar could be tempered by HFCS supplies. While many may argue that HFCS changed the supply equation, we must understand that white sugar can be displaced only for certain processes.

Therefore, it is more appropriate to identify HFCS as a "demand event." While the supply of sweeteners was expanded by HFCS, the supply of cane and beet sugar was not affected.

Demand for white sugar by food companies that could use HFCS in place of white sugar was changed—and in a subtle way. In addition to watching the primary correlation between white sugar and HFCS, traders had also to consider relative prices for corn to determine the efficacy of substituting HFCS.

That meant the supply and demand for corn became a factor in determining the limits on white sugar price movement. In answering the question, "Who consumes what," HFCS represented new demand for corn. The intricacies of these relationships are even more intriguing when you consider that processing HFCS does not materially reduce corn feed. Thus there is independence between corn feed and HFCS demand which does not influence supply.

Traditional fundamental analysis analyzes demand components and evaluates their independent and interdependent influences. Copper is consumed by housing, electric, electronics, communications, automotive, chemical, and brass industries as well as by the U.S. Treasury for stamping pennies.

Each category can be plugged into an equation to forecast consumption patterns. This requires an analysis of trends in housing, automobiles, electronics, etc. From the analysis, we try to extrapolate a total demand picture.

The study could take into consideration the impact of fiber optic cable upon copper communications wire or the use of plastic pipe as a substitute for copper. With each consideration, the forecast becomes more complex. Even with the most accurate information, there is always uncertainty over when fundamental influences will translate into price movements.

Demand is an intriguing study. In reality, we are examining human behavior in its totality. A change in Western diet affects demand for beef. An upgrade of diet in China, Japan, and the Commonwealth of Independent States could offset the consumer shift away from beef in the U.S.

Economic conditions influence consumption of "luxury" commodities like cocoa. Coffee may slowly encroach upon tea. Plastics may supplant woods as nations seek to preserve forest resources. Natural fibers like cotton and silk must maintain a perceived advantage over modern synthetics.

Each of these shifts in demand reflects human response. This is not to say that external forces do not play a role in demand. As mentioned, technology can decrease a commodity's usefulness. Since the behavioral sciences are inexact, it's not hard to understand why so many incorrect conclusions have been drawn about demand.

In 1992, approximately 40% of U.S. copper demand came from building and related trades. (See Figure 6-1.) Top forecasters called for growth in this sector resulting from low interest rates. However, interest rates turned higher and housing lower. Copper prices recoiled as demand slackened. (See Figures 6-2 and 6-3.)

The graph of U.S. copper consumption from 1982 through 1990 shows an uptrend existed from the beginning to the middle of the decade. (See Figure 6-4.) The consolidation in consumption in 1985 was primarily a response to a construction slowdown. This was brought on by changes in tax law rather than high interest rates.

The beginning of the real estate crisis was reflected in changing copper consumption. Within two years, copper consumption resumed its uptrend, which helped push prices to new highs.

However, a correlation with supply statistics is necessary to derive a complete picture of the supply/demand imbalance here. Moving forward from 1990, U.S. copper consumption consolidated into a trading range from 2.1 million metric tons to 2.21 million. Extreme prices from 1989 forward coupled with weak economic conditions contributed to the lack of demand. The consolidation in consumption from 1988 forward gave a clear indication

Figure 6-1

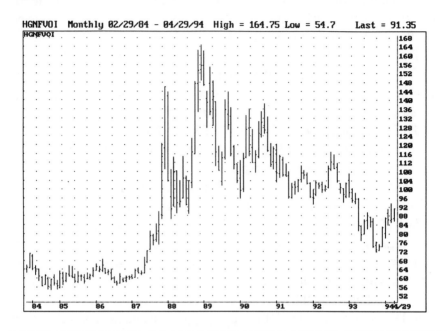

HGNFVOI Monthly 02/29/84 - 04/29/94 High = 164.75 Low = 54.7   Last = 91.35

prices could decline. When combined with increasing supplies, this interpretation was confirmed by a more comprehensive TechnoFundamental forecast.

As of 1991, copper's consumption pattern hinted at a head and shoulders top. Penetration below 2.1 million metric tons would suggest an objective of approximately 2.0 million. On an inflation adjusted basis, copper had the potential to retreat more than 50% from 1989 highs by 1993/94 to approximately 70 cents. This, in fact, took place.

After 1995, China and the Commonwealth of Independent States would represent demand wild cards. Major capital rebuilding by these two powers threatened to upstage any consumption decline in North America and Western Europe. From a TechnoFundamental view, any change in consumption would appear as a trend reversal. Changing demand would be compared with supply to determine which would exert greater price influence.

Copper represents a particularly good subject because smelting facilities were undergoing a technological transition from 1980 forward. Solvent extraction processes were being employed in old and new smelting plants with greater efficiencies and lower costs. This raises the TechnoFundamental ques-

Figure 6-2
Copper Consumption

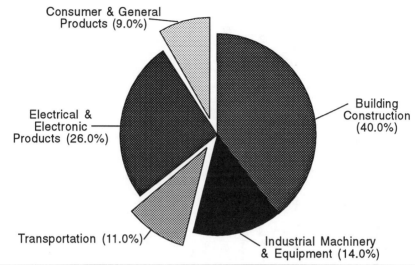

tion whether supplies can keep pace with demand from China and Russia. (The answer will emerge after the publication date for this book.)

How to Measure Demand

TechnoFundamental demand analysis is not unique to physical commodities. Even financial contracts provide a myriad of demand factors ranging from interest rates to public confidence. There have been hundreds of models designed to estimate potential demand for short-term and long-term government debt. The most powerful financial institutions in the world dedicate tens of millions in dollars, Deutschmarks, Japanese yen, and British pounds in search of even modestly accurate predictors. Newspaper headlines attest to predominant failures as we read about "derivatives strategies" gone awry and losses in institutional bond trading operations.

If such well-funded and well-staffed institutions cannot beat the odds, how can we take up the challenge as individuals? Can TechnoFundamentals provide an accurate assessment of demand upon which we can confidently trade? I believe the answer is a definite "Yes."

Figure 6-3
Consumption of Refined Copper (2) in the United States in Thousands of Metric Tons

Year	By-Products						By Class of Consumer						
	Cathodes	Wire Bars	Ingot & Ingot Bars	Cakes & Slabs	Billets	Other	Wire Mills	Brass Mills	Chemical Plants	Ingot Makers	Foundries	Miscellaneous	Total Consumption
1982	1,211.0	195.1	45.1	92.4	82.2	32.4	1,232.8	393.2	.4	4.4	7.6	19.7	1,658.1
1983	1,448.1	77.4	53.2	115.3	101.8	8.2	1,269.9	500.3	.6	3.2	11.3	18.8	1,803.9
1984	1,635.4	72.1	74.4	127.7	118.5	8.2	1,401.7	514.0	.7	5.3	19.8	34.6	1,976.0
1985	1,563.4	70.3	64.2	115.8	139.6	22.8	1,401.7	564.9	.9	1.4	20.6	22.9	2,101.5
1986	1,717.7	52.5	105.9	81.6	127.9	16.9	1,491.9	564.9	.9	1.4	20.6	22.9	2,102.6
1987	1,849.2	14.4	113.3	68.4	86.5	20.0	1,595.6	514.5	1.2	1.4	16.6	22.5	2,151.8
1988 (1)	1,967.4	14.0	54.2	63.0	99.0	12.7	1,667.2	493.2	1.0	2.6	14.5	31.9	2,210.4
1989 (1)	1,981.6	6.1	34.4	64.9	104.9	11.2	1,698.4	461.0	.9	1.3	14.9	26.6	2,203.1
1990 (3)							1,653	445					2,143

(1) Preliminary. (2) Primary and secondary. (3) Estimate.

Source: Bureau of Mines. Table provided through Knight-Ridder CRB InfoTech™ CD-ROM.

Figure 6-4
Total U.S. Copper Consumption

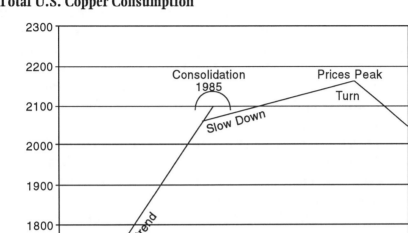

U.S. copper consumption patterns show why prices enjoyed a price spike in 1989. Obviously, high prices slowed and reversed U.S. consumption.

A fundamental question arises as to the structure of copper usage. Wire and electronic applications showed particular sensitivity to price.

The pie chart illustrates "who uses what." The two most significant areas as of 1992 were electrical/electronic and construction. Therefore, further analysis could be conducted on trends in these industries.

Following the October 1987 market crash, the Federal Reserve was forced to pump money into the banking system to maintain liquidity. Despite massive infusions, the economy remained sluggish because the system was overextended. An incredible amount of stock market wealth evaporated in less than a month. At the same time, S&Ls were scrambling to shore up sour real estate transactions.

In retrospect, the U.S. financial system came dangerously close to meltdown. In the process, government interest rates plunged as investors raced toward quality. Many analysts believe tight monetary policy was the precursor and cause of the crash. The Federal Reserve tightened throughout 1987 until investment ground to a halt. The final outcome was one of the worst "double-dip" recessions in modern U.S. history.

Liquidity was the gauge of economic performance throughout the 1980s. The more money the Federal Reserve pumped into the system, the better the stock market performed. This caused a philosophical departure from the fundamental view that equity prices depend upon earnings. The 1980s brought about a stronger emphasis upon general conditions and longer-term anticipation. Thus, if the Fed pushed interest rates higher because the economy was doing well, investors sold stocks for fear of an eventual slowdown. If the Fed lowered interest rates to stimulate, investors bought stocks in anticipation of better performance.

When stability seemed to return in 1988, the Fed resumed its attack upon inflation before business was fully able to regain its footing. From 1988 through the first half of 1989, demand for funds drove short-term interest rates as represented by Eurodollars above 11%. Banks decided it was safer to lend money to the government at such rates rather than risk business or consumer loans. A substantial premium was placed on loans to offset the "risk factor."

As a result, commercial banks priced money out of reach. Although the economy suffered, commercial banking was rescued without a direct bailout. The private sector was sacrificed in favor of allowing banks to recover bad debt through their spreads. Rates offered to depositors were less than rates provided by the Treasury. The difference represented badly needed bank revenue.

The process employed by commercial banks created a surge in demand for government debt that lasted from the second half of 1989 through 1992.

While banks took advantage of spreads, the Treasury took advantage of refinancing opportunities. Plunging short-term rates allowed the readjustment of government debt. Long-term instruments were retired in favor of short-term financing. This process was reflected by demand for government instruments all along the yield curve.

Financial institutions, pension funds, and insurance companies rely upon a mix of various government instruments to achieve appropriate "time horizons" and yields. Large pools of capital cannot maneuver in and out of markets easily. Therefore, longer maturities like the 30-year bond extend the fixed income portfolio time horizon and limit excessive trading. There was a fear that 30-year bonds could become scarce if Uncle Sam retired these maturities in favor of shorter maturities.

Financial instruments present certain challenges because demand is not as easily quantified as with commodities. Demand can be a function of sales, transfers, or cash flow. Calculating demand is frequently referred to as creating "synthetic demand." You must be careful when hearing or using the term "synthetic" because it has different meanings in different contexts.

For the purpose of measuring demand, synthetic calculations construct a theoretical statistic that is based upon combinations of volume and open interest in the futures and options markets along with an assumed transfer rate in the cash instrument.

To simplify this concept, we can formulate the following synthetic model:

Demand = (Rate of Change in Open Interest) + (Rate of Change in Average Volume) + (Change in Price × Cash Volume).

This calculation can be "standardized" to create a "synthetic demand index."

When correlated with price, we find that rising demand is associated with falling interest rates and increasing principal values. Falling demand sees rising interest rates and decreasing principal values. Synthetic demand follows technical formations and patterns. (See Figures 6-5 and 6.6.) Like any time series, we are also likely to see seasonal and cyclical variations along with interim and long-term trends.

Thus, if the government is truly limiting the supply of long-term debt, we should see a relative increase in demand. Note the term "relative." Demand can be static while supplies decrease. This still implies rising demand relative to available supplies.

The statistic for outstanding government debt is readily available. However, taking into account only this cash market activity may overlook the multiplier effect of futures and options. These "derivatives" may add or subtract from implied supply and demand.

While an entity may not own T-Bonds, its commitment to T-Bond futures or options represents money dedicated to this market. From our earlier discussions, we know that money moves prices higher or lower. There is no doubt that a sizable futures transaction can influence cash prices. This has been referred to as the "tail wagging the dog." Whether you believe futures dominate cash or the opposite, the object is to measure the market as a whole.

Figure 6-5
Treasury Bonds

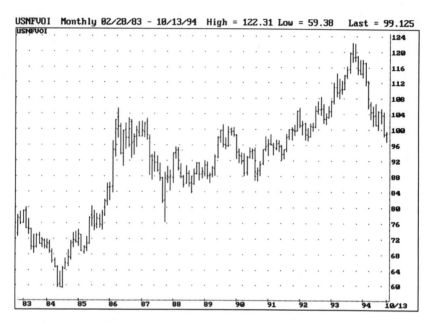

USNFVOI Monthly 02/28/83 - 10/13/94 High = 122.31 Low = 59.38 Last = 99.125

Bond prices track liquidity as a function of money supply and demand. Synthetic demand tracks price action using rates of change in futures and options open interest relative to price.

In 1987, 1990, and 1992, synthetic demand led price action. Notice how the 1988/89 price consolidation trading range was reflected by flat demand.

Since open interest corresponds to *supply,* the synthetic demand can be considered a hybrid indicator.

The 1992 downtrend in demand was premature relative to the turn in 1993. However, cash traders were warned that a top was near.

The Difference a Faster Chip Can Make

In our fast-moving technology age, we must be aware of the potential for structural changes that permanently alter demand. Implementing laws that require or ban the use of particular commodities are, in effect, structural changes. As I suggested above, mandated catalytic converters will, by nature, increase demand for platinum group metals (platinum, palladium, rhodium).

However, if engine technology is altered to eliminate the need for converters, we would experience an opposing structural change. As of this writing, just such a situation was developing. "Lean burn" automotive pollution tech-

Figure 6-6
U.S. Money Supply M2 (in 1982 Dollars)

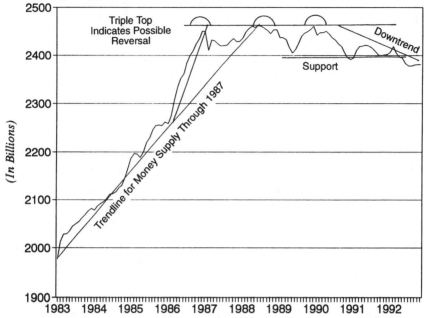

U.S. Money supply as reflected by M2 shows rapid growth into 1986. Topping action is clear and provides an explanation for the October 1987 stock market crash.

M2 correlates with the "synthetic supply" of U.S. Treasury debt. Notice how M2 correlates with U.S. 30-year bonds.

Technically, M2 consolidates from 1986 through 1990. The triple top leads to a penetration of support at 2400. Typical technical rules apply with lower highs within the trading range leading to the dip below support.

If the triple top consolidation fails to test 2300, a recovery would imply the consolidation was a halfway point in a longer-term uptrend.

M2 is considered the MONEY component of the equation

$$PRICE = MONEY \times VELOCITY$$

nology was rejected by the European Community (EC) in the early 1980s because precise computer controlled fuel injection and ignitions systems were too expensive compared with catalytic converters. The higher cost was due to the state of computer technology at the time the decision was made.

Obviously, no consideration was given to the exponential advancement in computer power and its associated decline in the price-to-power ratio.

When you consider that the computer aboard the first Apollo lunar module had less processing power that the first personal computer, you gain a perspective on just how fast this technology is moving forward. Today, a basic PC has enough computing power to guide a spaceship to any location within the solar system with plenty of computing capability to spare.

New automotive systems can control the exact mixture of fuel and air while timing ignition within millionths of a second. These same systems can incorporate high-density disk drives to record driving habits and conditions for referencing ideal fuel-to-air ratios and ignition timing.

As conditions change, the computer makes necessary adjustments for maximum power and fuel economy. All of this computing capability is presently available at a fraction of its cost just 10 years ago. Today's computer technology is within the same cost parameters as catalytic converters, implying that automobile manufacturers can move away from catalysts into lean burn engines. Aside from pollution control, computerizing engine functions increases horsepower and fuel efficiency. This is a government mandated requirement in the U.S. and is likely to be picked up by the EC as well.

Thus the long-range future of platinum and palladium demand was just beginning to be threatened by technology in 1994. Nissan and Toyota announced versions of lean burn cars for their 1994 model years. Although the new cars were not exported to the U.S. that year, the message was clear. A structural change in demand for platinum and palladium was on the horizon.

Interestingly, the Platinum Guild trade group played down the development of noncatalytic cars in a CNBC television debate in 1993. Their claim was that lean burn technology would never be advanced enough to completely eliminate catalytic converters. Time will be the ultimate arbitrator in the debate and "never" is a very long time.

The immediate question is, "When will lean burn technology make a difference in platinum and palladium prices?" This isolates a single demand factor and exposes us to analytical error. While 30% to 40% of the platinum group metals may have been dedicated to automotive applications in 1993, other technologies were emerging that could outpace any decline in consumption for catalytic converters. (See Figure 6-7.)

Most notably, platinum-based fuel cells were under rapid development in 1993/94. These devices used platinum to convert hydrogen and carbon-based fuels into energy. While still experimental at the time, the promise of a

Figure 6-7
Platinum Demand in the West

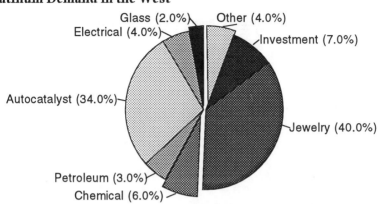

Glass (2.0%) Other (4.0%)
Electrical (4.0%) Investment (7.0%)
Autocatalyst (34.0%)
Jewelry (40.0%)
Petroleum (3.0%)
Chemical (6.0%)

Platinum demand was clearly dominated by automotive catalysts in 1992. By 1994 palladium cut into this area by 2% to 4%. This accounts for rising palladium prices and static platinum prices from 1991 through 1994.

The pie chart indicates the significance of lean burn engine development. One-third of platinum demand could disappear with the introduction of computerized combustion control.

high efficiency and low cost platinum fuel cell seemed well within reach by 1994. This suggested that any decline in automotive use could be offset by demand for fuel cells.

Using technical analysis of demand, we can measure the net effects of declining automotive use and rising fuel cell consumption. As of 1994, there was no indication that catalytic converters were being replaced by lean burn technology. Further, platinum consumption for experimental fuel cell applications was insignificant.

Demand statistics did show a rise in demand for palladium over platinum from 1992 forward. This was due to breakthroughs using palladium rather than platinum in converters for trucks and cars. Using this insight, this author recommended the purchase of palladium and sale of platinum as a "spread strategy." From 1992 through 1994, the price of platinum advanced from approximately $350 per ounce to $400 while palladium rose from $75 to $160. (See Figures 6-8 and 6-9.) The spread realized a profit of $3,500 over the two-year period on margin of just $400. This elementary strategy was completely based upon technical demand patterns reflecting the platinum/palladium situation.

**Figure 6-8
Platinum**

PLNFVOI   Weekly 01/12/90 - 10/13/94 High = 536.9 Low = 330   Last = 413.5

Platinum did not share palladium's prosperity. The move to substitute palladium for platinum catalytic converters held platinum prices in check from 1991 through the first half of 1994.

How to Trade Cold Fusion Technology

In March of 1989, two professors at the University of Utah called a press conference to make an astounding announcement. Doctors Pons and Fleischmann claimed they were able to produce a fusion reaction at room temperature using palladium cathodes, platinum wire, and heavy water (a form of water that is saturated with deuterium). The announcement rocketed palladium prices from $125 per ounce to $180 per ounce within a few short weeks. However, the process was almost immediately discredited and palladium prices sank to their lowest levels in 10 years by June 1992.

Yet the process known as "cold fusion" did not completely lose its following. A dedicated band of cold fusionists continued conducting experiments and writing papers about the phenomenon. By 1993, experimental palladium demand was estimated at more than 50,000 ounces. One year later, it had

Figure 6-9
Palladium

Use of palladium for catalytic converters and new demand for cold fusion experiments caused a demand-driven bull trend from June 1992 through 1994. Will demand take prices higher?

grown to an estimated 200,000 ounces. With total palladium output projected at four million ounces in 1994, experimental demand was just beginning to impact supplies. In an interim report, the large metals refiner, Johnson & Matthey, predicted a supply deficit of 150,000 to 200,000 ounces in 1994.

We see that emerging cold fusion technology was responsible for upsetting the supply/demand balance. Regardless of the eventual efficacy of cold fusion, it had an increasing impact upon palladium from 1992 forward.

This raises a question whose answer goes beyond the timeframe of this book. Will cold fusion become a reality? If so, will the technology demand substantial amounts of palladium?

The first question can only be answered as conjecture. As a concept, cold fusion could provide the world with unlimited clean and inexpensive energy. Assuming the technology were based upon palladium devices, the value of palladium would not be measurable within the price context up to 1995. There would be almost no upper limit to palladium's price until we could assess the quantity of palladium needed to satisfy the world's energy appetite.

As of the end of 1994, my estimate was that palladium could achieve a value of more than $5,000 per ounce before sufficient new supplies were brought to bear on the market. Fundamental research revealed that other metals also show signs of producing a cold fusion reaction. Most significant were announcements that ordinary nickel could be used to replicate cold fusion results. Thus, palladium could be challenged by a far more abundant and less expensive metal.

Of course, as of 1995, we could not discount the overwhelming consensus within the scientific community that cold fusion was an experimental error. According to the known laws of physics in 1994, cold fusion was simply "not possible."

This returns us to the use of TechnoFundamentals as a means for discovering who is right and who is wrong relative to the market. As traders, we do not care whether cold fusion takes palladium to new highs or lean burn technology drops prices to new lows. We are only concerned with detecting trends and measuring reactions. Knowledge of fundamental developments that drive technical demand patterns is extremely helpful because it provides an overview for our decision process.

Certainly, palladium never reached anywhere near $5,000 per ounce prior to 1994. On its face, such a prediction appears ludicrous. Just as the Midwest experienced floods "beyond the realm of possibility" in the summer of 1993, so too can cold fusion surprise us by pushing palladium prices beyond present-day reason. Certainly, if an ounce of palladium can be made to fuel indefinitely an entire factory or even a single-family home, an ounce of it could easily become worth $5,000.

Cold fusion is an extremely good example of potential structural change because it reaches well beyond its own fundamentals. We are dealing with an entire metamorphosis in the way the world would produce and consume energy. Depending upon the pace of cold fusion technology, the price of oil would plunge along with other energy costs. Electric utilities would change the way they produce or deliver power. If cold fusion devices became feasible as home units, electric utilities could become extinct.

This, in turn, would render billions of dollars of electric utility infrastructure worthless. Millions of jobs would be threatened around the globe. Entire oil-dependent economies would be destroyed. The internal combustion engine and related technologies would be relegated to the junk heap. Oil would be used solely as a feed stock for chemicals and plastics. In the near term, cold fusion could represent one of the greatest economic destabilizers of modern time. There is little wonder why governments of the United States and Europe remained cold to cold fusion after the 1989 press conference. Political and economic interests were far from the ideals of limitless clean and inexpensive energy.

The single technological development of cold fusion would have implications for investments in crude oil, energy company stocks, transportation stocks, and mining stocks. Palladium would become a primary target while other precious metals would become by-products. Price trends in virtually all commodities would be spectacular with secular patterns lasting several decades.

As an exercise, just try to list all the areas you believe would be affected by cold fusion. Jot down what you think the supply/demand impact would be. You'll be surprised by the enormous scope such a development would have upon global economics. Everything from the price of airfare to the cost of fertilizers and pesticides would be changed by cold fusion. It is a frightening as well as exciting prospect.

Cold fusion provides a forum for many speculative intellectual exercises. Until it becomes a reality or is properly discredited, it is unlikely we will profit from the cold fusion debate.

Subtle growth in palladium demand may be responsible for near-term bull trends. The more esoteric impacts are fun, but less valuable for immediate trading decisions.

Silver and the New Video Technology

However, there are technologies likely to cause more immediate and significant structural change to popular markets. In our chapter covering supply, we pointed out that silver's bear market through 1993 was about to change. Technical supply patterns showed the uptrend had been broken. Even with constant demand, TechnoFundamentals suggested silver could move above $6.00 per ounce before the end of 1995.

Without examining inflation prospects and other external influences, silver's TechnoFundamental supply picture appeared bright for the bulls as of the middle of 1994. On the other hand, demand was developing a dark side.

From 1982 forward, home videocamera prices fell within reach of the consumer market. Once the exclusive toy of the professional or the wealthy, the "camcorder" virtually eliminated the use of home movie cameras within the five years from 1981 through 1986. (See Figure 6-10.)

By 1994, the home video concept was being merged with "multi-media" computer technology at an unimagined pace. Computer imaging was supplanting analog video and the first consumer "still-shot" digital cameras were coming to market. Medical imaging from X-ray to sonograms to magnetic resonance imaging (MRI) were all implementing computer imaging. Even the

Figure 6-10
Camcorders (U.S.)

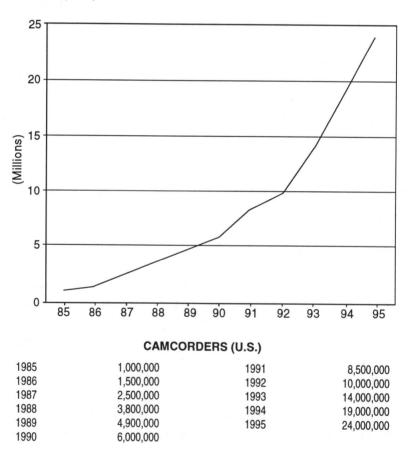

CAMCORDERS (U.S.)

1985	1,000,000	1991	8,500,000
1986	1,500,000	1992	10,000,000
1987	2,500,000	1993	14,000,000
1988	3,800,000	1994	19,000,000
1989	4,900,000	1995	24,000,000
1990	6,000,000		

printing industry was beginning to convert to "direct-to-plate" processes eliminating the use of film for making lithographic printing plates.

From the demand perspective, more than 50% of all silver consumption was for photographic processes in 1994. Thus, silver's primary use was being threatened by new computer imaging technology. Technology critics claimed that "filmless photography" was too expensive and crude for general public acceptance. The Silver Institute concurred.

However, by the 1994 Christmas season, several consumer digital cameras and print processors were introduced with prices of less than $500. This was considered the "threshold" for the consumer market. By comparison, recall that 15 years ago the music industry introduced the compact disc. This, too, was considered too expensive for the consumer market. Given the size of the installed base of turntable record players, most analysts believed compact discs would remain a high-end and insignificant component of music distribution media.

Within 10 years from that consensus, it has become almost impossible to buy conventional vinyl records. Even with the substantially higher price, consumers embraced new digital audio technology. By 1994, it appeared very likely digital picture technology would follow the same path. Solving the quality issue is usually a matter of time and the decrease in average prices for digital cameras and accessories was accelerating as of 1994.

State-of-the-art digital imaging actually exceeded all forms of film technology well before its introduction to the consumer market. Satellite pictures were known to be able to resolve license plates, faces, and other detailed images from hundreds of miles away. While many of the specific picture-taking and data compression techniques used to create high resolution pictures remained classified through the 1980s, consumer companies were rapidly catching up by 1994. Companies like Kodak and Apple Computer announced digital imaging projects. It was clear that the "filmless" age was dawning.

Understanding the potential impact of filmless photography requires some knowledge of "who uses what." Unless you know that photography accounts for more than 50% of silver consumption, the development of filmless photography has little significance.

Knowing demand fundamentals warns you that silver prices could decline as new technology begins reducing demand. TechnoFundamental analysis can indicate when the demand trend is turning and accelerating. This allows you to time fundamental trading more effectively.

Filmless photography and multi-media computers may cut silver consumption in half by 2005. All other factors remaining equal, silver's price could dip to the official U.S. price of $1.00 per ounce. Below this level, silver could become attractive as a monetary standard. How ironic it would be to see silver remonetized as coinage because of a price implosion.

A TechnoFundamental evaluation of silver coinage actually supports the theory that low prices encourage reestablishing monetary linkage. Notice how coinage increases in the consumption table over the past 10 years. (See Figure 6-11.) As silver prices declined, coinage increased. The surge in official government coinage illustrates strategies related to the use of metals as a monetary standard and profit center. Canada minted a one-ounce $5 Maple Leaf

Figure 6-11
Silver Consumption (Coinage)

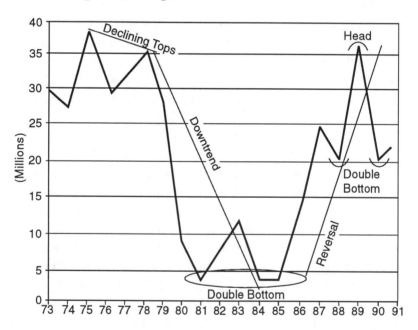

Silver coinage follows an opposite pattern relative to popular belief. As prices rise, coinage falls because profit margins shrink.

Falling prices can increase coinage demand. Notice how the double bottom comes following the price surge of 1979/80. Only after prices retreat do we see a return to minting.

As of 1992, there was a question whether a double bottom interim consolidation had formed or a head and shoulders top would develop. A head and shoulders would return coinage demand to 1981/85 lows.

while the U.S. issued a one-ounce silver dollar. Both coins sold at a premium to spot silver to provide an incentive for distributors and a profit for respective treasuries.

When silver fell below $5 per ounce, Canada faced an interesting paradox. Their coin's face value was greater than silver's price. An individual could receive $5 (Canadian) for a Maple Leaf when silver was selling below $4. Canada's treasury was exposed to a loss relative to current prices if the face value was honored.

The flip-side to this paradox is found in the treasury's ability to buy silver at less than face value and sell at the declared premium. Governments are the only market participants having this impressive power. Fixing value by fiat is an extremely important part of silver and gold's market structure. The two-tiered pricing available to government provides an ultimate safety mechanism that allows a government to realign currency through monetary linkage.

From the 1960s forward, gold and silver failed as monetary instruments because economic growth was on an exponential curve while metal production was static. The metals could not provide an expanding monetary base.

Growing industrial economies implied spiraling gold and silver prices if the cord between printed money and metal was not cut. While backing currency prevents the free running of government presses and thus prevents certain forms of inflation, it also restricts growth and can create a liquidity crisis. The stock market crash of 1929 and subsequent Great Depression proved the danger in not expanding the monetary base when gold was revalued. By raising gold's price in 1933, the U.S. government could increase dollars in circulation.

The initial result was a recovery. The secondary fallout was mild inflation. Today's economies would require an enormous amount of gold or silver to back currency. Values would be unrealistically high. By some estimates, assuming a gold standard would push prices to more than $50,000 per ounce. At such a level, gold would assume only symbolic value.

As an alternative, the massive amounts of silver that would be available if photographic use ceased might be sufficient to use as some standard. The value would need to be fixed in a way that allowed treasuries to buy at beneath face value. A sufficient margin would be required to prevent the cash value from exceeding face value.

Some may recall when copper prices moved above the face value of U.S. and Canadian pennies in 1974 and again in 1980. The result was hoarding, which created a severe penny shortage. When silver was marginally above the official U.S. government price, silver coinage became popular in $1,000 face value bags. The attractive selling feature was limited downside exposure: the bags could never fall below face value. Yet if the silver content appreciated, the bags could far exceed face value. This situation was similar to Canada's minting of the $5 face value silver Maple Leaf. If silver prices yield to growing inventories, the opportunity to recoin will be an option for government treasuries.

In the previous chapter we examined silver's supply. The pattern showed a trend reversal beginning in 1992. In contrast, we could assume that filmless photography would reduce demand. Obviously, supply and demand must be evaluated in tandem since each can cancel the other's price influence.

For example, we might see a drop in supply followed by decreasing demand. Depending upon the balance between the two forces, prices will be pushed higher or lower. Although this point may sound obvious, traders often focus solely upon supply or demand rather than correlating both.

This error is often apparent in the reactions to market news. Of the two, supply usually gets top billing. Demand is more elusive because assessment requires more intuitive analysis, since estimating demand is not a matter of going into the fields and counting corn stalks.

In some markets, demand has become easier to determine as users have consolidated. For example, vertical meat processors consolidated in the 1980s as difficult times took a toll. Esmark's Armour division was forced out of business by shrinking profit margins. Numerous small coffee roasters were replaced by a small number of giant processors. With consolidation we gain more concise demand data—simply because it is easier to analyze demand when there are only a few bidders.

An argument can be made for tracking technical industry consolidation patterns. Trends develop when there are changes in "economies of scale," i.e., efficiencies.

Economic theory supposes that there are ideal sizes for particular business entities beyond which efficiency is lost and below which efficiency is difficult to achieve. Economic viability is believed to be a function of scale or size. Hence, the expression, "economies of scale."

When a company has better economies of scale, it produces or processes more effectively and is able to reduce prices relative to competition. As competition heats up, the playing field shrinks.

These changes will be reflected in industry trends. If we compare the number of cattle operations today with 1972 statistics, we see a dramatic decline in the gross number of independent producers. (See Figure 6-12.) We also find the size of the cattle herd from 1972 to 1994 dramatically declined (Figure 6-13). This trend accelerated during the 1980s and prices increased into the 1990s as seen on the long-term chart presented in the previous chapter. You could have tracked trends in producer consolidations and herd reduction to see that the industry was consolidating.

At the same time, America's appetite for red meat faced a serious negative health campaign that included input from the American Heart Association, American Medical Association, American Cancer Society, and the U.S. Department of Agriculture. While Americans did not abandon their taste for beef, consumption growth on a per capita basis was flat.

This flat demand was not sufficient to offset tight supplies, however. By the mid-1990s, cattle prices were trading at the high end of a 10-year range.

A change in American or European diet would represent a structural change for the red meat complex. The number of vegetarians is rising in the U.S. and Canada. As of 1994, this number was still very small when compared with the total population. However, a trend is in place that could accelerate within the next generation. Many public and private schools offer programs encouraging healthful eating habits. The animal-rights movement adds to the popularity of a no-meat diet.

Will meat consumption decline in the U.S. and Western Europe? If so, what will take its place? As industrialized countries shun flesh, the Third World perceives meat as a desirable diet of affluent societies. Nonindustrialized countries are attempting to upgrade to meat.

With the exception of India and certain religious sects, poor nations believe they can make their citizens happier with steak. With the right data, these trends can be measured against each other to determine which might have the stronger price influence.

The statement, "We live in a changing world," may appear trite. Within the context of TechnoFundamental analysis, the phrase takes on new meaning. No market is immune to structural rearrangement.

When Western currencies were no longer pegged to gold or U.S. currency, a multi-billion dollar investment industry was born. Within a decade, currency trading or "investing" had created the single largest-volume cash mar-

Figure 6-12
Cattle Supply and Distribution in the United States (in Thousands of Head)

Year	Cattle & Calves on Farms Jan. 1	Imports	Calves Born	Total Supply	Federally Inspected	Other (2)	All Commercial	Farm	Total Slaughter	Deaths on Farms	Exports	Total Disappearance
1972	117,862	1,186	47,682	166,730	34,688	4,144	38,832	503	39,335	5,126	104	44,565
1973	121,539	1,039	49,194	171,772	32,329	3,607	35,936	570	36,506	6,487	273	43,266
1974	127,778	568	50,873	179,229	35,674	4,125	39,799	729	40,528	6,110	204	46,842
1975	132,028	389	50,183	182,600	40,798	5,322	46,120	750	46,870	6,992	196	54,058
1976	127,980	984	47,385	176,348	43,430	4,574	48,004	722	48,726	5,190	205	54,121
1977	122,810	1,133	45,931	169,974	43,413	3,960	47,373	700	48,073	6,000	107	54,180
1978	116,375	1,253	43,818	161,446	40,568	3,154	43,722	550	44,272	5,680	122	50,194
1979	110,864	732	42,603	154,199	34,342	2,473	36,502	430	36,932	5,600	66	42,598
1980	111,192	681	44,998	156,871	33,936	2,458	36,395	401	36,795	5,413	66	42,274
1981	114,321	659	44,776	159,756	35,273	2,478	37,751	399	38,150	4,902	88	43,144
1982 (1)	115,604	1,005	44,420	161,029	36,634	2,211	38,845	400	39,245	5,400	58	44,683
1983	115,001	921	43,885	159,807	37,614	2,112	39,726	410	40,136	5,494	56	45,686
1984	113,360	753	42,470	156,583	38,910	1,969	40,879	388	41,259	5,464	71	46,794
1985	109,582	836	41,050	151,468	37,933	1,745	39,678	370	40,048	5,046	125	45,219
1986	105,378	1,407	41,182	147,967	39,108	1,588	40,696	351	41,046	4,998	108	46,152
1987	102,118	1,200	40,152	143,470	37,147	1,315	38,462	330	38,792	4,800	131	43,723
1988	99,622	1,332	40,588	141,247	36,459	1,124	37,585	286	37,880	4,657	321	42,858
1989	98,065	1,459	40,142	139,626	35,110	979	36,089	287	36,329	4,452	169	40,950
1990	98,162	2,135	39,249	139,546	34,133				35,277	4,425	120	39,822
1991 (1)	98,896	1,939	39,256	140,091	33,226				34,375	4,400	311	39,086
1992 (1)	100,110	1,258									247	
1993 (3)												

(1) Preliminary. (2) Wholesale and Retail. (3) Forecast.

Source: Economic Research Service, U.S.D.A. Table provided through Knight-Ridder CRB InfoTech™ CD-ROM.

Figure 6-13
Live Cattle Production

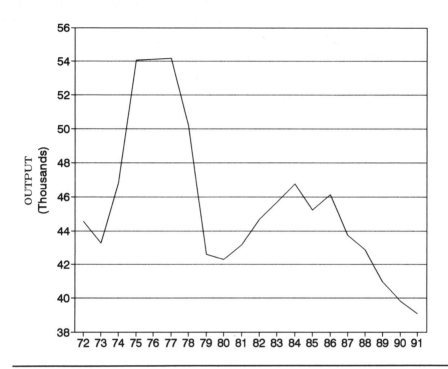

ket. Add futures and options, and this international currency trading boasted the largest net daily value of any freely traded investment vehicles.

This market was the direct result of structural change. However, as quickly as international currency trading grew, it could shrink. In the process of unifying Western Europe, EC members conceived the European Currency Unit (ECU) as a single means of exchange. The ECU would consolidate EC currencies into a single unit. Without free-floating individual currencies, however, much of the trading opportunity vanishes. Demand for individual European currencies would give way to a more narrowly defined demand for non-EC exchange. While currency trading would not disappear, it would certainly be altered.

Demand is partially a function of availability. In the absence of 30-year bonds, it is likely demand for these instruments would move toward 10-year notes or the next longest maturity. Demand for stocks is relative to returns available from other financial instruments. Demand for gold is sensitive to interest rates, inflation, currency parities, public confidence, and availability.

Events in the short term and long term can be technically measured. The fundamental analyst's traditional role involved subjective interpretations of supply, demand, and structural change. Today's multi-faceted markets are often too complex for this traditional approach.

TechnoFundamentals are a new alternative that preserves the intent of both of these "artful sciences."

CHAPTER 7

TECHNOFUNDAMENTAL REFERENCING

How high is up? How low is down? These are questions from which fortunes are made or lost.

If you ask any experienced investor about his or her experiences, the "megatrends" always seem to leave the greatest impression. Statistics, on the other hand, prove that the trader who is content to trade for interim movements invariably risks less and achieves more *by winning consistently.*

Yet the thrill of "making a killing" in the market seems to intrigue us all. Indeed, investing is a modern form of the hunt. I have often wondered why we call it making "a killing." Perhaps it is because financial prowess symbolizes the same things to modern man that skills with a bow and lance were for our ancestors.

Think about the inherent challenge in "stalking" a market. You wait for the right moment. You judge, you measure, you postulate, and then you pounce. If all goes well, you win. If you misjudge, you try to escape with only minor injuries.

As with sports records, each new achievement is there to be surpassed. In markets, each price extreme stands ready to be challenged. As investors, it is our challenge to determine which circumstances will force prices to extremes or beyond.

When will the highest high be taken out? Is there ever a point where prices cannot go any lower? The pitfalls of these questions should never be underestimated.

Figure 7-1
Sugar Monthly Prices

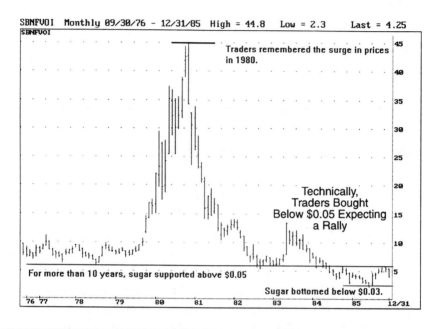

SBNFVOI Monthly 09/30/76 - 12/31/85 High = 44.8 Low = 2.3 Last = 4.25

Traders remembered the surge in prices in 1980.

Technically,
Traders Bought
Below $0.05 Expecting
a Rally

For more than 10 years, sugar supported above $0.05

Sugar bottomed below $0.03.

In 1985 sugar fell below 17-year lows (see Figure 7-1). At $.045 a pound, traders were anxiously awaiting a bottom. Just two years earlier, sugar had reached $0.13, while toward the end of 1980, prices had been more than $0.45. With such high/low mental reference points in mind, many jumped to the conclusion that anything under a nickel was too low.

This author shared this emotional point of view. However, market forces had a different idea. As Figure 7-2 illustrates, sugar was not at a bottom. In fact, sugar's decline accelerated after breaking below $0.045. Despite desperate attempts to pick a bottom at $0.040, $0.035, and even $0.030, sugar seemed to do the impossible by busting below three cents. For sugar lovers [i.e., sugar bulls?], this trend was their worst nightmare. On the surface, there appeared to be no logic behind a move that dropped prices to their lowest levels in almost two decades. How was this possible after so many years of inflation?

Figure 7-2

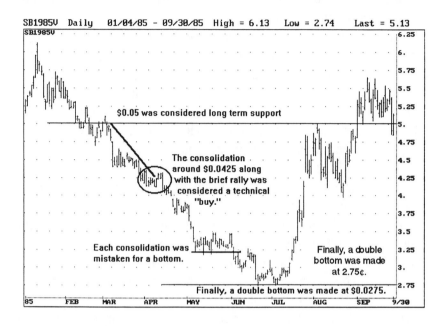

SB1985U Daily 01/04/85 - 09/30/85 High = 6.13 Low = 2.74 Last = 5.13

The Risks of Referencing the Market

The problem faced by many investors is frequently called "personalizing the market." In a more sophisticated sense, we subjectively "reference" a market. For example, a farmer in Nebraska who relies upon center pivot irrigation may look out over his fields and see a wonderful crop during a moderately dry season. His ability to irrigate lessens the impact of modest rainfall. His perception is that there is going to be a bountiful harvest and prices will surely fall. His inclination is to hedge his crop to preserve whatever profit margin exists.

This farmer uses his personal experience to extrapolate a universal picture. His "reference point" is limited to his own crop. However, in another region a different experience may emerge. Another farmer who does not have the luxury of plentiful ground water sees his crops suffering from a lack of rain. With his crop withering, he comes to the conclusion that the harvest will be poor and prices will rise. His course of action is not to hedge. He will wait for prices to rise before selling.

Take a moment to recall your own experiences. How often have you truly believed a market had made a top or bottom based upon a personal feeling rather than an objective evaluation?

Do you ever bend facts to fit the outcome you anticipated? Personalizing a market is an avoidable human response if you have the proper discipline. Unfortunately, such rigid discipline is beyond the reach of most personalities.

There are two solutions. You can allow a computer to conduct your trading or you can attempt to construct more objective references.

The farmer who judges an entire market based on observing his own fields is likely to fail. But suppose he evaluates conditions by viewing aerial photographs of 70% of U.S. crop lands. Then he would have a broad frame of reference from which he can draw a more objective conclusion. The picture is still incomplete, but getting clearer.

Prices can decline despite a poor crop. We must measure current production against existing supplies (carryovers). We should evaluate programs that could release government supplies if prices fall too low. If we know the average cost of a bushel of corn, we can use this as a reference point for picking a bottom. A price support could become a reference point.

Generally, these artificial levels represent extremes. However, there have been instances when prices have fallen below production costs and price supports. Such declines, by nature, do not last long.

However, in the world of futures, even a short-lived dip can spell disaster in a highly leveraged margin account. Without proximity to price supports or production costs, we need other methods for approximating tops and bottoms.

With technical analysis, we can seek "support" and "resistance" levels. In a sense, these are reference points based upon observed behavior. However, technical references are only good until they are violated. After support has been penetrated, we are faced with finding the next support. This process can be a hit or miss proposition. We may find a probable new support based upon chart formation. Then, in the next moment, we may be frustrated when these technical reference points fail to provide accurate predictions.

Look for the Patterns

TechnoFundamental referencing correlates patterns in supply, demand, and price. In its simplest form, we can reference current supply and demand against previous supply and demand to identify a price reference. The reference can be a specific high, low, or range.

For example, in 1992, a bountiful season produced a substantial corn crop. The harvest combined with carryover dropped prices under $2.10 a bushel. The following season, devastating floods reduced yields and rocketed prices above $3.00.

In 1994, farmers planted very large crops and weather was picture perfect. The U.S. Department of Agriculture predicted a record crop. Of course, prices tumbled. Based upon crop reports, the reference point for a potential 1994 bottom, derived from the 1992 low, seemed to be approximately $2.08 (see Figure 7-3).

But the supply fundamentals behind 1992's low were different than those of 1994. Even with a record crop, the harvest plus the carryover would not surpass 1992 ending stocks. As of September, 1994, domestic usage and exports appeared flat to slightly lower than the 1993 season.

With these fundamental references, a premium over the 1992 lows would be logical because total 1994 supplies would remain below those of 1992. Thus, with the 1992 low around $2.08, the 1994 low would be $2.08 plus a premium (see Figure 7-4).

This reference point became increasingly important as corn prices began declining in late June 1994. From highs over $2.65, prices plunged to $2.40. In back of many traders' minds was the possibility that weather could turn against the crop before the harvest. The downtrend abruptly stopped around $2.40 by mid-June. Was this the bottom?

Using U.S.D.A. estimates and careful weather tracking, it was clear corn could lose more ground. The TechnoFundamental target was somewhere above $2.08. Without an exact price, technical price patterns in the beginning of August suggested that the new bottom was above $2.15. Strategically, this was a signal for short sellers to cover positions while buyers could be more confident a base had been reached.

TechnoFundamental referencing does not, by itself, generate a buy or sell signal. As the name suggests, it gives a reference point for decisions. When prices are precipitously falling with no immediate end in sight, a TechnoFundamental goal yields an approximate objective with a safety factor.

From a purely technical standpoint, a trader might see $2.08 as a downside corn objective because that was the lowest previous bottom on the long-term chart and all previous interim supports on short-term charts had

Figure 7-3
Corn

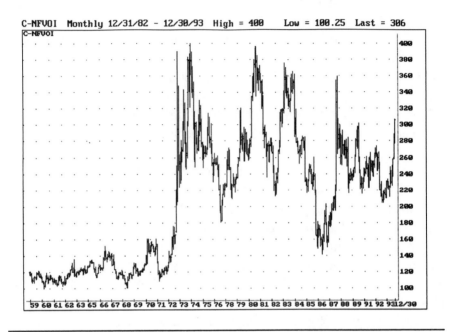

C-NFVOI   Monthly 12/31/82 - 12/30/93   High = 400   Low = 100.25   Last = 306

been taken out. Through September 1994, this would have been an elusive goal. By adding a 10 or 15 cent premium to the 1992 lows as compensation for fundamental patterns that revealed tighter supplies, the downside objective would have been met in August and sideways price action would have been avoided (see Figure 7-5).

Everybody's Getting Technical: RSI and Stochastics

During the 1980s, technical price analysis enjoyed exponential growth. Several price indicators became extremely popular. One well-known example was the calculation for a "Relative Strength Index" which is commonly referred to as the "RSI" (publicized in a book called *New Concepts in Technical Trading,* by J. Welles Wilder, Jr.).[*]

During the same period, differential measurements using stochastic formulas were also applied to prices to measure momentum and identify tops and

---

[*] Trend Research, ISBN 0-89459-027-8, © 1978 by J. Welles Wilder, Jr.

Figure 7-4
December Corn

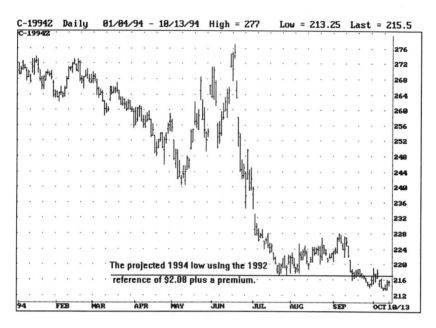

C-19942 Daily   01/04/94 - 10/13/94 High = 277   Low = 213.25 Last = 215.5

The projected 1994 low using the 1992 reference of $2.08 plus a premium.

bottoms. These popular indicators relied only upon price changes. They represented the purest modern technical distillation of consecutive price action.

Yet, by their construction, both techniques were extremely prone to false "overbought" and "oversold" signals in highly trending markets. This is because major bull and bear markets cause these indicators to reach their extremes well *in advance* of tops and bottoms.

For traders following loose rules associated with the RSI and stochastic, big price movements became serious problems. Once overbought or oversold conditions were signaled, there was no reference point if prices continued trending.

Copper, coffee, silver, lumber, 30-year bonds, and energy contracts were among those that made fortunes for traditional trend-followers—and generally spelled disaster for the advocates of RSI and stochastics.

There are always exceptions to general observations. Some traders may profess that they had a "special way" of applying the RSI or stochastic indicators. However, a review of account performance reveals the carnage associ-

Figure 7-5

C-19942 Daily 01/04/94 - 10/13/94 High = 277 Low = 213.25 Last = 215.5

ated with bucking trends because false tops and bottoms appeared to have been identified.

The common approach to constructing the RSI involves adding net changes for up and down trading sessions respectively and dividing by the number of days selected. A 10-day RSI, for example, examines the last 10 trading sessions. Each respective summation of net change is divided by the number of days.

For example:

$$(\text{Net Up Change} / 10) = \text{Net Up Average}$$
$$(\text{Net Down Change} / 10) = \text{Net Down Average}$$

The net up average is divided by the net down average and added to 1:

$$(\text{Net Up Average} / \text{Net Down Average}) + 1$$

The result is divided by 100 and then subtracted from 100 to produce the RSI. As a general rule, an RSI above 75 is overbought and below 25 is oversold.

However, it should be obvious that a strong market with consecutive limit sessions will cause the RSI to reach these levels quickly. Before an actual overbought or oversold condition exists, a trader following the RSI will not have sufficient information to make a trading decision.

The sensitivity of the RSI will depend upon the length of the series. (Mr. Wilder's book uses a nine-day RSI.)

The stochastic formula uses the rate of change (first difference) in the high, low, and close to create a standardized oscillator. In its popular application, there is a raw value and a smoothed value.

The raw value is calculated by taking the difference between the lowest low over a period and the current close and dividing the result by the highest high for the period minus the lowest low. This is multiplied by 100 to standardize the value.

Using 10 days we have:

$$((\text{Close–Lowest Low}) / (\text{Highest High–Lowest Low})) \times 100 = \text{Raw Value}$$

This raw stochastic can be smoothed using a moving average, weighted average, or geometric average. Other applications rely upon consecutive closing price differences.

For example, you can take the difference between today's close and yesterday's close and divide by yesterday's close. This represents the rate of change between sessions. This number can be averaged for a period and multiplied by 100 to create a standardized scale.

Regardless of formula variations, the stochastic will reach a maximum or minimum value by its construction when powerful trends are in place. Further, if a slow and fast stochastic are used to identify "divergence," common volatility in fast-moving trends will cause false signals. The rate of change in consecutive limit sessions will be extreme and remain constant. This "fools" the math and the trader unless another standard is used as a filter to modify the interpretation.

Referencing Coffee Prices in 1994

TechnoFundamentals can provide an appropriate override to this problem. Consider coffee during 1994 (see Figure 7-6). The Brazilian coffee freeze in early July was responsible for pushing prices to their highest levels in almost two decades. Both the RSI and stochastic had issued overbought and reversal signals prior to the freeze because coffee had been rallying since early May.

The freeze caught many traders short or out. While TechnoFundamentals would not have warned of the pending weather problems, analysis of coffee supply and demand trends indicated the rally from May could reach over $1.00. Brazil's policy over the preceding four years unloaded inventories at depressed prices. That process was at an end and supply was finally in balance with consumption. When the $1.00 point was exceeded, the next TechnoFundamental reference point was unusually high at approximately $1.40.

As an advocate of TechnoFundamental referencing, I found the fact that coffee encountered resistance at this level very satisfying. Such exact predictions do not occur often.

Using fundamental weather analysis, it was clear a freeze was possible. Assessing damage represented guesswork, yet the last major freeze that occurred in 1975 gave an indication of how strong coffee could react when facing such uncertainty. Coffee is not a market that stands still while it sorts

Figure 7-6

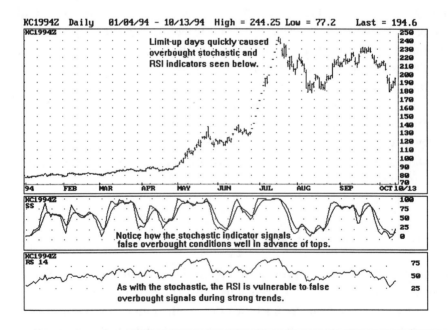

out the damage. A fundamental review of 1975 shows capacity expanded in response to soaring prices. Within five years following the freeze, Brazil recovered while other producing nations filled shortages with additional exports. Even with the rush to build capacity, coffee never returned to its pre-1975 price levels. As a reference, the deficit created by the 1975 disaster was in excess of the 1994 forecast.

Taking the broader 1994 production base into account, the fundamental implication was for a top below the eventual peak that occurred in 1977. Coffee illustrates the importance of a fundamental reference for production, consumption, and time. The 1975 event was the catalyst for a major bull trend. Prices did not reach a top until more than a season later. This warns that the trend could build strength as its full impact reaches the market. In 1975, there were inventories that could be immediately drawn down over the following season. When stored supplies were finally exhausted through 1976, coffee roasters had to depend upon current production on a hand-to-mouth basis.

In contrast, the 1994 freeze caused a more dramatic upward thrust. Within the season, coffee prices increased 300%. Technically, when prices broke through $1.40, the next available reference point was the 1985 interim high of approximately $1.68. This area offered no resistance during the 1994 move. Traders who jumped out at $1.68 made a large profit, but suffered an opportunity loss as prices climbed above $1.80.

During this time, the RSI and stochastic registered overbought conditions. There was no way to determine the appropriate course of action based upon standard rules for these indicators. Restricting market action to technical adjuncts like price oscillators causes a reference vacuum.

Interestingly, the good old moving average was able to effectively track coffee's movement through mid-August 1994 (see Figure 7-7). Whenever a powerful trend is present, the gross price movement from bottom to top or top to bottom is large enough to allow a lagging moving average to capture a healthy portion of the trend. Moreover, if a top forms gradually, the moving average can catch up to the current price for an efficient exit when the trend finally turns.

Fundamentally, the campaign to reduce excess inventories took away a buffer. This suggested that the top formed by August '94 could have been an interim point related to the drought of 1985/86. The market would have to

Figure 7-7
Coffee, December 1994

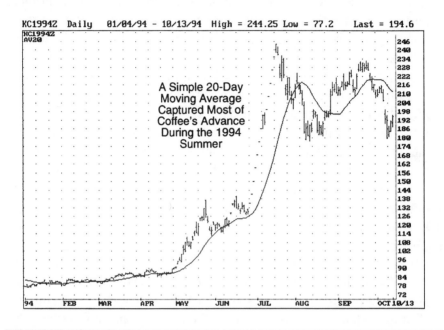

KC1994Z Daily 01/04/94 - 10/13/94 High = 244.25 Low = 77.2   Last = 194.6

A Simple 20-Day
Moving Average
Captured Most of
Coffee's Advance
During the 1994
Summer

digest the actual damage to 1994/95 production to determine whether a true high had been achieved. Roasters accumulated positions in anticipation of the worst. If Brazil's trees could produce more than expected during their summer, roasters would hold overpriced inventories and prices would decline.

Recall that coffee production expanded dramatically from 1976 through 1981. The production chart (see Figures 7-8 and 7-9) shows a trend that formed a consolidation from 1981 through 1988. Interruptions were mainly the result of weather while recoveries lead to expanding capacity. A linear projection placed production above 105,000 bags if the trend remains. This warned that the reversal of the 1994 price trend could be stronger than the advance. Certainly, any downside objective would reference 1993/94 lows. Unless producing nations viewed the 1994 freeze and subsequent price rally as an opportunity to gain control of pricing through quota mechanisms, the pattern called for supply gains.

There was some pain associated with depressed 1993/94 prices. Marginal output was unprofitable. High fertilizer and chemical costs coupled with

Figure 7-8

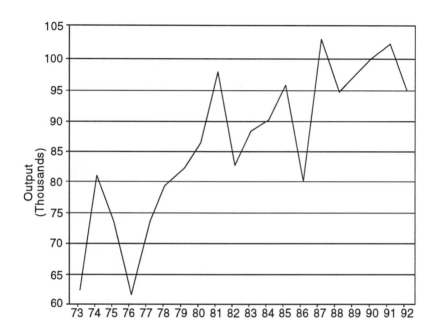

increasing labor demands forced some producers to neglect trees. This was beginning to affect prices in May '94. Just when there was a possibility for the uptrend in production to stall, weather gave an incentive to expand.

We are able to draw conclusions about coffee based upon referencing fundamental patterns relative to price. We can assume production will stall at prices under $1.00 and expand above $1.40. This is the normal range.

Overproduction at prices above $1.40 should bring prices down. An extraordinary event like a freeze or drought will challenge $1.40. If the stochastic or RSI appear overbought at $1.40, reference the normal range versus the extraordinary range. An overbought signal should be more reliable in a normal range, but should not be trusted as prices break out during special circumstances. As simple or obvious as this logic may seem, untold numbers of traders and professional managers still were not using TechnoFundamental referencing in 1994.

Figure 7-9
World Green Coffee (Total) Production in Thousands of 60 Kilo Bags (132.276 Lbs. per Bag)

Crop Year	Angola	Brazil	Cameroon	Colombia	Costa Rica	Ethiopia	Guatemala	India	Indonesia	Ivory Coast	Mexico	Salvador	Uganda	Zaire (Congo, K)	World Total
1973-4	3,200	14,500	1,260	7,800	1,570	1,700	2,200	1,535	2,750	3,255	3,300	2,378	3,100	1,317	62,459
1974-5	3,000	27,500	1,816	9,000	1,390	2,050	2,540	1,630	2,675	4,500	3,900	3,300	3,000	1,150	81,082
1975-6	1,180	23,000	1,482	8,500	1,276	2,677	2,043	1,498	3,049	5,266	3,856	2,530	2,214	1,072	73,008
1976-7	1,131	9,300	1,307	9,300	1,331	2,782	2,213	1,753	3,219	4,867	3,330	2,973	2,664	1,437	61,439
1977-8	1,047	17,500	1,371	11,050	1,449	3,143	2,550	2,147	3,911	3,393	3,401	2,700	1,868	1,129	71,374
1978-9	613	20,000	1,634	12,600	1,749	3,142	2,827	1,842	4,788	4,742	4,022	3,423	1,944	1,293	79,074
1979-80	260	22,000	1,658	12,712	1,522	3,188	2,647	2,495	4,803	3,973	3,600	3,322	2,042	1,316	81,908
1980-1	586	21,500	1,959	13,500	2,140	3,264	2,702	1,977	5,265	6,090	3,862	2,940	2,133	1,526	86,249
1981-2	392	33,000	1,953	14,342	1,782	3,212	2,653	2,540	5,785	4,084	3,900	2,886	2,885	1,425	98,195
1982-3 (1)	430	17,750	1,817	13,300	2,450	3,350	2,593	2,200	4,786	4,260	4,100	2,671	3,200	1,390	82,345
1983-4 (1)	350	30,000	1,900	13,000	2,070	3,350	2,340	2,000	4,895	3,667	4,200	2,453	3,100	1,400	91,657

Crop Year	Papua-N. Guinea	Brazil	Cameroon	Colombia	Costa Rica	Ethiopia	Guatemala	India	Indonesia	Ivory Coast	Mexico	Salvador	Uganda	Zaire (Congo, K)	World Total
1980-1	870	21,500	1,959	13,500	2,140	3,264	2,702	1,977	5,365	6,090	3,862	2,940	2,133	1,526	86,344
1981-2	910	33,000	1,850	14,342	1,782	3,212	2,653	2,540	5,785	4,160	3,900	2,886	2,885	1,425	98,189
1982-3	640	17,750	1,830	13,300	2,300	3,670	2,530	2,170	4,750	4,510	4,530	3,100	3,000	1,354	82,778
1983-4	925	30,000	1,000	13,000	2,070	3,300	2,340	1,667	5,515	1,420	4,530	2,400	2,700	1,350	88,595
1984-5	775	27,000	2,316	11,000	2,516	2,587	2,703	3,250	5,600	4,609	4,250	2,680	2,800	1,540	90,266
1985-6	860	33,000	2,067	12,000	1,514	2,833	2,650	2,033	5,800	4,420	4,826	2,300	2,700	1,610	95,934
1986-7	756	13,900	2,191	11,000	2,566	2,700	2,843	3,350	5,900	4,405	5,297	2,275	2,700	1,875	79,549
1987-8	1,100	38,000	1,251	13,000	2,375	3,200	3,020	2,050	5,965	3,103	4,717	2,538	2,600	2,000	103,231
1988-9	1,175	25,000	1,760	10,700	2,758	3,300	3,022	3,590	6,750	3,989	5,500	1,492	3,300	1,750	94,292
1989-90	1,092	26,000	1,440	13,300	2,453	3,400	3,472	2,150	7,100	4,734	5,100	2,787	2,500	2,000	97,286
1990-1	964	31,000	1,450	14,500	2,565	3,500	3,282	2,970	7,480	3,000	4,550	2,603	2,700	1,695	100,465
1991-2 (1)	784	28,500	1,485	17,980	2,630	3,000	3,444	3,200	7,100	3,967	4,620	2,357	3,000	1,500	102,893
1992-3 (2)	900	24,000	1,350	16,500	2,500	3,000	3,000	2,500	7,500	4,000	4,200	2,400	3,000	1,300	94,850

(1) Preliminary. (2) Estimate.

Source: Foreign Agricultural Service, U.S.D.A. Table provided through Knight-Ridder CRB InfoTech™ CD-ROM.

Wave Theory and Minor Trends

If a particular TechnoFundamental trend is in place, we have a basis for predicting how high or how low prices will go. The reference point is an effective filter that helps avoid the pitfalls of picking tops and bottoms. *The objective is to approximate maximum and minimum price levels.*

When we examine agricultural prices relative to the inflation rate, we see that raw commodities experienced deflation from the 1980s through the first half of the 1990s. Production efficiencies and increased capacity expanded supplies in pace with demand. In many cases, supply outpaced demand. The climbing Consumer Price Index (CPI) was largely the result of wages and inputs rather than raw prices.

This is why TechnoFundamental referencing is effective. There is a practical range that defines "too high" and "too low." Knowing where the highest prices have been under identifiable circumstances permits us to filter out volatility that frequently accompanies tops and bottoms.

At the same time, unusual circumstances that lead to new ranges do appear in supply and demand chart patterns. If we see supply is flat, for example, we know demand influences will dominate. Such was the case for platinum and palladium from 1990 forward. Likewise, if we were to see a reducing slope in silver's production trend, we could anticipate higher prices and a change in interim complexion.

This is an important concept because studies show that *markets exhibit dominant trends over multiple minor trends*. In fact, the theory of major and minor trends has been popularized in "wave theory."

A significant drawback to wave analysis is the inability to accurately identify the major wave and its turning point. Common applications use a "wave count" to estimate when a top or bottom is likely to occur. Unfortunately, the count is often subjectively based, using chart analysis. If the practitioner inaccurately identifies a wave or misses a count, consequences can be unpleasant.

It makes sense to determine the potential for a "final wave" by identifying turning points in supply and demand. Remember that supply and demand usually gain momentum based upon fundamental driving forces. Thus, an underlying minor trend in production can point to the major trend around which there will be cycles or waves.

If a market experiences dislocation, the wave count will turn in an opposite direction. A dislocation takes place when production means are exhausted or economies deteriorate. In the case of the former, the protection of "old stand" forests could constitute dislocation in lumber supplies. Economies deteriorate when the use of or production of a commodity is no longer economically feasible. Using environmental law as an example, pollution control or land reclamation requirements might make strip mining too expensive relative to the end product's current selling price. While unknown, there is a practical limit to how high prices can go before a commodity is abandoned. This price is always relative to alternatives.

Could the reality of cold fusion push palladium prices to $5,000 per ounce? An affirmative answer relies upon the efficiencies of any real cold fusion process and the availability of less costly substitutes. The debate over reality or fantasy is not the pricing consideration.

The question is the influence upon demand. After an initial speculative frenzy, the market will answer the question, "How much palladium do we have and how much do we need?" Prices will strike a balance between supply and demand. We know current supplies and the cost of production. Any incremental increase in production will have an associated cost.

As a hypothetical, consider a process for inexpensive recovery of oil from tar sands and old wells. By some estimates, primary and secondary oil recovery account for less than 20% of total content. The remaining 80% adheres to subsurface structure and is beyond economically viable reach. Yet, if a new process were developed that could inexpensively extract the bulk of well content, a new pricing standard would emerge.

The new process would combine with the existing energy infrastructure to support the use of oil and delay the acceptance or implementation of new energy technologies. Obviously, timing would be a critical element. The new oil recovery process would need to be introduced well in advance of any significant encroachment by alternatives to oil. As long as cars, utilities, and homes were still using fossil fuels, the economics of oil would present a strong argument against a rapid switch.

It is possible such a development could eclipse cold fusion or similar progressive technologies. If price is a sole determinant, oil could maintain its position. If a cost were added for pollution or environmental impact, there would still be a tradeoff unless such costs exceeded energy alternatives.

What would be a possible reference point to determine how low oil might settle? We may not be able to establish a correlation to any technical price pattern because we would be experiencing a totally new set of fundamentals that force the abandonment of previous references.

This brings us to another method of extrapolating a downside objective. Rather than reference a previous price pattern, we can use basic fundamental techniques to analyze the cost of oil recovery using the new technique and the reasonable profit that might be required to satisfy industry requirements.

Further, we would place an emphasis upon oil consumption trends. Technically, we could evaluate demand patterns to see if there would be any offset against an anticipated increase in crude availability. You may question whether this approach provides anything new and different from traditional fundamental analysis. The answer is that our technique is the same, but the context is different.

As with all market analysis, TechnoFundamentals is an evolutionary process. It involves applying known art to new science. This is true for stochastic indicators, relative strength, and even neural networks. Virtually all math associated with these "new" methods has roots established centuries ago. Only recently have these tools been applied in novel ways to forecast market direction and distance.

CHAPTER 8

PATTERN RECOGNITION, NEURAL NETWORKS, AND RELATED SCIENCE

The latest frontier in humanity's attempt to conquer the future using the past is through the sophisticated application of "pattern recognition" systems.

This approach should not be confused with identifying technical price patterns such as flags, head and shoulders, double tops and bottoms, and other "pictures." While new applications can be applied to check the accuracy of traditional chart patterns, the modern approach tries to "learn" market behavior by "recognizing" causal correlation patterns.

This new science is actually an attempt to mimic human learning processes and memory functions. Studies of the brain reveal various stages in thought and learning development. We are just beginning to realize that our thinking is a series of progressive pattern recognition processes.

How is it possible for us to comprehend abstract images or read the diverse handwriting of other individuals? Even the most advanced computers have difficulties with these seemingly simple tasks. Why do grand master chess players consistently outperform machines—at least until 1995?

When is an apple an apple or a face a face? Do all individuals see the same images? Is the color red really red to everyone? Such questions involve a combination of science with philosophy.

Experience shows there are people who exhibit uncanny ability to predict market trends or pick sound investments. There is a sixth sense that allows these individuals to amass great fortunes with seemingly little effort. We may describe these fortunate souls as "experts."

Within the scope of modern technology, we can attempt to dissect the steps associated with expert thinking and reconstruct them into mathematical models and compu. r systems. The term "expert system" refers to this translation of expert skills into an automated methodology.

Over the past several years, the term has been blurred to include computer programs that are not necessarily based upon a particular expertise.

These are not expert systems in the true sense. While much has been written about expert systems, few results have actually been produced that are as good as the real thing: a human practitioner.

The fault may lie in the complexity of our thought processes or the difficulty in translating them into pure computer logic. Studies show the human rational process is not always consistent. We have the ability to intuitively bend our rules to fit new or unique situations.

Computer scientists insist that this adaptive behavior can be emulated by machines. As computers become increasingly powerful, various levels of hierarchical learning appear possible.

Our brains process images and thoughts through pattern recognition and references. We actually mentally supply information for skeletal images to complete pictures. As children we lack a comprehensive reference library from which we can collect all of the required information.

This is believed to be one reason children draw abstract pictures like stick figures. The basic shape of an object becomes a building block for pattern recognition and interpretation.

At what point does a circle become an apple? (See Figure 8-1.) Must it have a stem? Do we need to add a color? Must the circular shape be altered? Perhaps a green leaf might help?

Take the same circle and add two dots for eyes, one dot for a nose, and a curved line for a mouth and we comprehend a face. A simple turn of the curved line produces a happy, sad, or angry face. Add eyebrows, and you can alternate between changing the mouth or the eyes to produce the same interpretation of the image. (See Figure 8-2.)

This implies that we can attach the same meaning to different patterns. How do we know, at the earliest age, that an upturned mouth is happy and a downturned mouth is sad? How do we understand that upturned eyebrows can express uncertainty or surprise? With all of the modern computer's speed, even the definition of a happy or sad face is a hard task.

Figure 8-1

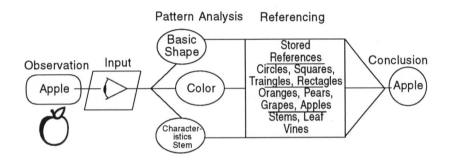

Figure 8-2

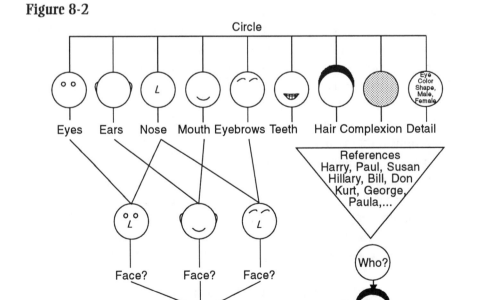

Thinking in Parallel

The computer uses a series of sequential steps to test an image against a static database. When a match is found, a conclusion or solution is at hand. If the database lacks the necessary information for a match, the computer is at a loss.

In contrast, people process the image *in parallel.* If specific information is missing, we use associations to formulate a "best fit."

The parallel process that associates information in order to draw a conclusion is the foundation of neural network technology. The brain uses neurons to store and transmit information. It is an impressive sequence involving many parts of the brain. The incredible network of neurons and synapses process and transmit information involving sight, sound, smell, touch, taste, and creativity from task centers to our ultimate "hard disk" in the cortex. Unlike a computer, when we retrieve information from our hard disk, we collect a vast number of references simultaneously, giving us the ability to instantly recognize objects, situations, and stimuli.

Suppose we could employ the same process using computers. Using formulas that represent known events, we can try to predict new events by association.

Each event or "condition" is held in a neuron. As neurons are combined, they can recognize patterns associated with various outcomes. The natural world displays linear and nonlinear patterns. Statistical methods are well suited for identifying linear patterns, while nonlinear events pose many perplexing problems. Frequently, a nonlinear pattern appears random. Neural networks are particularly adept at analyzing nonlinear situations.

Much of the literature covering artificial neural networks deals with applications rather than constructs. While equations used to create a neural network may be complex, the concepts are relatively easy to grasp.

Our comprehension is believed to emanate from a set of reference "layers." Scientists do not know how much information is actually required to allow reference layers to complete a picture or thought. Some believe our ability to link references is so efficient that we are able to comprehend with very few inputs. This is why we can associate a stick figure with the image of a person.

As more layers are applied, we can distinguish between one face and another. We identify faces we know from those that are unfamiliar. Further, we are able to add priorities and importance to our database. A face we must remember is stored. A face that passes without significance is discarded. This filtering activity prevents our storage system from becoming overburdened with unnecessary information.

For those familiar with computers, our minds have primary and secondary "caching." We immediately store current information in a holding area thought to be the hippocampus. Over time, our system determines what information should be moved to permanent storage in the neocortex and which should be deleted. All of this is necessary to understand how an artificial neural network recognizes patterns.

Will Artificial Intelligence Tame the Markets?

In our earlier chapter on time series, we briefly described tools for analyzing price movements over time. Operations like moving averages, regression, and correlation provide insight into trend, seasonal, cyclical, and random movements. These are broad categories that are assumed to have some repetitive consistency or linear profile.

If a time series is not consistent, a different approach is necessary. In addition, forecasts based upon time series analysis often address long-term outlooks. As traders attempt to shorten their trading horizons, they must deal with increasingly nonlinear behavior.

In an investment environment that responds in seconds, time is of the essence. If it is possible to recognize patterns that lead to immediate consecutive price movements, we gain a substantial advantage over other participants. We may also want to identify when market complexions change.

For example, linear statistics reveal that most commodity markets trend less than 20% of the time. The remaining 80% has been categorized as random "trading range" movements. Of course, these numbers are based upon assumptions about a trend's definition. Nonetheless, the latter description of day-to-day market behavior is generally accepted.

Increasingly, trading departments and investors insist that the market give up returns continuously. This accounts for the intense quest for models and systems which recognize and predict nontrending movements.

By recognizing when a market is trending or in a trading range, an artificial intelligence program can adjust algorithms and methods to fit the market. This is not a new concept. Many moving average systems have been used which altered the length of the average to more appropriately mimic market action. However, the process for fitting models without artificial intelligence has been crude and subject to error.

If markets do indeed experience repetitive nonlinear patterns, a neural network can be trained to recognize when a market is moving progressively higher or lower, when prices are consolidating, and when direction is turning. This assumes the network can link a pattern to future behavior.

Of course, any neural network or artificial intelligence program will be constrained by its experience. The most popular construction of models gain experience or "training" by examining past data, a method known as "back propagation."

This is not to say that back propagation is the only widely used method. Training can be based upon observations or empirical studies that provide inputs and outputs for the network to examine and optimize. If a market undergoes structural change, back propagation or assumptions based upon observations can provide spurious training going forward. This is why many networks continue to train and evaluate in "real time" to allow for structural changes.

There is no model that can predict exogenous events like the death of a world leader, an earthquake or volcanic eruption, war, a significant discovery or announcement, or other random and instantaneous events, none of which are within the capabilities of any system. Unless someone invents a real crystal ball, we will always be at the mercy of unforeseen events.

TechnoFundamentals + Neural Networks

However, a system can be trained to *react* to these events with speed, accuracy, and objectivity. This means a system can quickly measure the potential influence and impact of an event and react accordingly. If a disaster influences buyers and sellers, measuring the influence over each side of the market can provide insight into the most likely continuation.

The introduction of TechnoFundamental analysis opens a new window for neural network technology. It is possible to train a system to recognize technical supply and demand patterns and make a forecast. (See Figure 8-3.)

This cutting-edge application shows significant promise. Initial studies show neural networks have an uncanny ability to pick which markets are

Figure 8-3

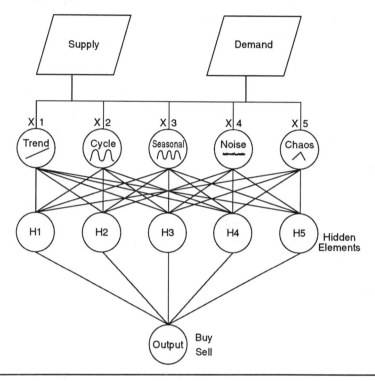

more likely to experience bull and bear trends. Models can also define parameters for highs and lows.

Finally, timing overlays can identify intervals during which certain objectives are likely to be achieved. For example, one adaptation of a neural network was taken from a model used to evaluate environmental changes for predicting ice ages, global warming, and disaster cycles.

The network was trained on astronomical events that included shifts in the earth's magnetic fields, sun spots, planet alignment, orbital irregularities, and other identifiable conditions. Further inputs included estimates of atmospheric and ocean conditions, life cycles, and land characteristics.

The result was an accurate model of various ice ages, greenhouse eras, and other global conditions. Substituting commodity production and consumption trends, a similar neural network structure would seem to be able to identify periods when particular markets would make major moves or experience unusual volatility.

With only three inputs, the neural network can identify market patterns that include seasonal, cyclical, and trending movements (see Figure 8-4). This is not to say that traditional statistical analysis cannot produce the same information. However, the network appears more agile for daily trading applications.

What is a reasonable expectation for random noise or trend strength? The network exhibits an intuitive feel for "what's real and what's not." Without adding volatility as an input, the simple network can still sort out appropriate high/low expectations. This objective sensitivity to probable behavior is extremely valuable when approaching markets like coffee in 1975–77, 1980, and 1994.

The predictions for a slow deterioration in silver prices and eventual climb in copper also provide valuable market insight. While the network can't predict weather, it can extrapolate reactions to weather. This permits expanding the model to include "what if" scenarios for agricultural commodities.

Figure 8-4

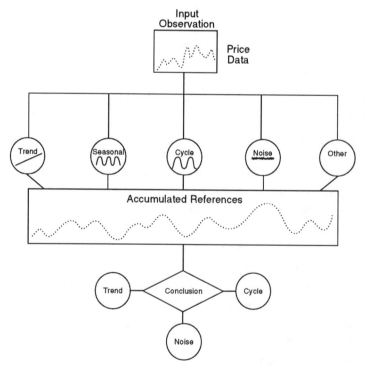

There have been attempts to construct "causal correlation tables" for news events such as the release of government statistics.

These tables can take many forms. In general, they show market conditions, the expected news item, the actual news item, and the result. Secondary columns acts as a spreadsheet that reacts to changes in values.

In the simplest construct, the table applies only three conditions: greater than, less than, and equal to. More complexity is involved when incorporating quantitative measurement to "greater than" and "less than" conditions.

When is "greater than" important? After the release of significant news or statistics, the causal correlation table attempts to objectively evaluate human response within the affected market. Using experience, most likely outcomes are immediately computed within certain confidence levels. Based upon historical testing, the model can determine which circumstances or patterns occur within calculated probabilities. The degree to which these probabilities remain consistent (don't change over time) is an indication of how "confident" you can be about the forecast. Those who have studied statistics know this as the "confidence interval."

Creeping Complexity

As more layers of information are added, there is a presumption that the model will gain accuracy. Unfortunately this is often not the case. Complexity frequently lowers accuracy because the neural network can receive conflicting patterns without an ability to prioritize. One pattern may say "up" while another points down. It is easy to see how this might happen in basic commodity markets like grains, meats, metals, softs, and energy.

Financial markets are even more susceptible to conflicting pattern recognition. In the beginning of 1994, several groups were working on "Grand Unification Models," a phrase borrowed from physics. The attempt was to unify inputs into a giant neural network that would sort out and prioritize patterns to provide the "near perfect" forecast. (See Figure 8-5.)

To the best of my knowledge, this Grand Unification Model remains an elusive goal. Yet, with ever increasing computer power and accessibility, there is a chance someone will eventually crack the market's hidden formula. To be sure, there are:

- highly accurate weather forecasting models with time horizons of one to five days;

Figure 8-5

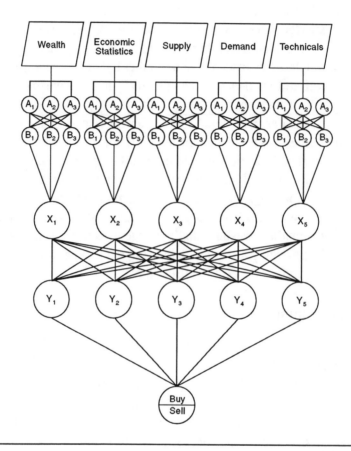

- increasingly accurate velocity formulas for predicting consecutive price movements;

- "chaos models" that can adjust for chaotic and random introductions of price influencing events;

- new parallel processing technologies that can process billions of instructions in a second.

All of these developments bring us closer to answering, "Where, when, and how far will prices move?"

Reality is different from anticipation. In 1992, I attended an artificial intelligence symposium in New York City. I was introduced to a neural network model that used global supply and demand statistics for wheat, corn, and soybeans that had been trained on five years of data and tested on the next subsequent five-year period.

The network had impressive paper trading and actual results. The model was also applied to cotton, orange juice, and oats with less exciting performance. This was attributed to a lack of movement or input correlations. On the basis of the 10-year record, the developers were raising funds for trading. I admit, the proposal was tempting.

Fortunately, other financial commitments foreclosed my participation. However, I was given the privilege of monitoring the actual performance in real time.

As luck would have it, 1993 rainfall was an anomaly for the model. Previous training produced an experience of falling prices with higher precipitation. While the network eventually concluded it was on the wrong track, the floods of 1993 washed out the entire endeavor (see Figure 8-6). "If it sounds too good to be true, it probably is!"

How Much Does the System "Know"?

The inherent problem with back propagation learning is that the learning period may not provide a domain of all possible experiences. Without a complete education in crop production, any neural network lacks a frame of reference to recognize unusual situations. As human beings, we can reason that waist-high water across a cornfield might not be good for the crop. What seemed particularly foolish about the neural network implementation was the fact that the founders did not intervene before it was too late.

This brings up the point of recognizing structural change. Networks trained on data *before* a significant structural change will probably fail when such change is encountered. The literature discusses "learning nets" that reevaluate data within a current time frame. These systems are supposed to increase their efficiency as the data domain grows. However, even learning networks are not endowed with truly intuitive skills.

Further, the human mind possesses unique methods of prioritizing and categorizing references (memories) to actually create totally new thoughts and references. This "creative process" is extremely important for interpreting new situations.

Figure 8-6
Neural Net Model for Corn, Summer 1993

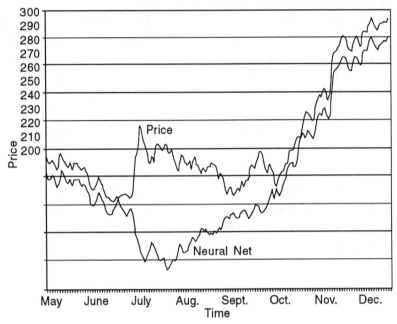

The neural network trained on rainfall was unable to predict price action during the 1993 summer floods.

Scientists have determined that our thought processes are also emotionally formed. Survival situations stimulate our "fight or flight" response. Raised emotions heighten our ability to remember. Thus, life-threatening situations make a lasting impression. These memories can be quickly recalled and referenced allowing us to react properly if the same problematic circumstances arise.

Unfortunately, as of this writing, computers and programs are not advanced enough to accomplish the same tasks with equal accuracy and efficiency. In contrast with predictive neural networks, a simple moving average filter can be more effective in capturing large profits under unusual circumstances. The average simply tracks price movement until the trend flattens or reverses.

Certainly, a moving average is not predictive as much as reactive. Yet reaction is frequently all that is required to capture healthy returns. Fortunately, neural networks can be trained to be both predictive and reactive. The decision process can be limited by static filters like moving averages or technical indicators such as the Relative Strength Index, Advance/Decline Index (ADX), stochastic measurements, and others. Some neural network experts believe static filters form "hybrid nets."

It is interesting to note that many hybrids exhibit excellent documented results in comparison with theoretical performances of pure neural network systems. This could be due to the linear nature of some market activities.

Consecutive limit up or limit down days would be viewed as a linear event. Slope would appear as a constant straight line. An accelerating trend would be a curvilinear event subject to standard statistical measurement, evaluation, and extrapolation.

The Quest for the Perfectly Efficient Market

A number of neural networks studies mention a tendency for market efficiency to doom systems to failure. This is because systems themselves influence markets. There is an underlying assumption that inefficiencies are required to provide profit opportunities. This defines "efficiency" and "inefficiency" as abstract concepts.

We should not ignore built-in mechanisms for limiting efficient market performance. The imposition of daily limits on price changes for non–spot futures contracts restricts efficiency. Stocks are regulated to curb effects of "programmed trading" and avoid meltdowns when equity values are overstated.

Facts and behavior suggest market pricing mechanisms are not efficient. A neural network which adapts to changing efficiencies should remain viable indefinitely or as long as free markets exist. Efficiency has always been a function of human behavior.

I suppose there may come a time when computers make pricing decisions based upon some fixed formula for efficient pricing. If that time comes, there will no longer be a need for bid/ask markets. Machines will determine who should pay what price for particular commodities, investments, or services.

Neural networks have recognized patterns in supply and demand that influence prices. TechnoFundamental models identify growth, contraction, and static conditions within the context of pricing. The steps are relatively simple. First, the system is allowed to review historical prices. This is defined as the "outcome." Once the network knows the outcome you are seeking, you provide the input from which the outcome is to be derived or extrapolated. The computer sets out to identify any linear or nonlinear relationship between outcome and input patterns.

In addition to obvious patterns, a network can be trained to recognize relative probabilities. Most of us are familiar with the construct, "if—then." If a certain condition exists, what is the probability you will see a certain result? If multiple correlations are encountered, what is the level of assurance associated with combined probabilities?

This approach has been used to measure the accuracy of moving average crossover systems. Several moving averages are tested to see how effective a crossover is for predicting a price continuation. Assume you select a three-day, five-day, 10-day, and 15-day moving average. The market is tracked each time one of the averages is crossed by the closing price.

You might discover that there is a 40% chance prices will continue in the direction of the crossover when the three-day average is violated. Each of the other averages also has an associated probability measured by examining test data. You want to determine if combining events increase the observed probability prices will continue.

While some statisticians may argue that you could measure the combined probability by observing the occurrence of multiple events, neural networks can establish asset allocation parameters based upon the occurrence of individual as well as multiple events.

Should you buy one contract when the three-day moving average is crossed by price to the upside? Several contracts? Should you add contracts if the five-day joins the three-day? At what point is the probability of a continuation diminished?

If supply is increasing at an average annual rate of 5% per year, what is the probability prices will remain static or move lower? If demand increases at the same rate, what is the impact of general inflation upon price? If U.S. dollar parity deteriorates against European currencies, do we observe a measurable effect upon price?

These relationships can be the training ground for neural networks. In addition, the slope of a supply chart or its tendency to level off provide patterns that we can use within the context of making short, medium, and long-term forecasts.

Some surprising results have been derived from these studies. Today, the popularity of short-term trading has rendered long-term strategies obscure and almost obsolete. Traders want action at any price.

Yet, had an investor remained consistently short gold and silver from 1980 through 1992, a gross profit was assured. Many short-term traders became casualties as they attempted to identify an ever-shifting bottom for these metals.

Certainly, seasonal commodities are not as prone to consistent long-term declines or advances. Common sense dictates that certain commodity complexes must be followed on a weekly or daily basis. However, it is helpful to keep an open mind about position trading.

Few situations illustrate this as well as the interest rate decline from 1990 forward. While not intentionally investing in this trend, millions of homeowners favorably participated in the interest rate decline through their variable rate mortgages. By not jumping into and out of their mortgages, the gross return achieved in savings was greater than many trading strategies that tried picking tops and bottoms.

"Refinement" is a word used to describe an objective of modern market models. We may know from experience that very high corn prices will encourage greater planting in the following season. We may know low prices will discourage planting or inspire government intervention to prop up values. The key is to *quantify* this observation.

Is there a pattern associated with the amount farmers will plant relative to prices and profit margins? Over the years, how much have government set-aside programs affected actual yields? Is price the only consideration or do farmers respond to general economic conditions as well? For example, how much of a role do interest rates or energy prices play in a farmer's decision to plant or let fields lie fallow? Weather is decisive in determining years of scarcity or plenty.

In turn, weather cycles precipitate government programs. Neural networks can help refine input dependencies that display some consistency. Was the Payment In Kind program of 1983 predictable? Was the drought? Even if both were random, could we have reacted to the outcome in time to profit?

Studies indicate that we can create systems that react in time to participate in market responses. Repetitive patterns develop from similar circumstances. This strongly supports the TechnoFundamental philosophy.

Recall our discussion of market bias. A season following a bumper crop tends to have a downward bias while a previous shortage establishes a bullish bias. Moves toward the market bias are stronger because the trend is anticipated.

If oil-producing nations abandon cooperative quotas, there is little doubt bias will be bearish. Neural networks can refine or quantify the bias by recognizing trading patterns. If you have traded agricultural markets that are sensitive to weather, you know that the slightest dry spell following a poor crop year blasts prices higher. Rain relieves pressure, but not to the same extent. The pattern culminates in an intensification of bullish bias if there is less rain, or a bias reversal if ideal weather conditions persist. "Patterns, patterns, everywhere" but which ones do you pick?

While some researchers are dedicated to refinement, there is an equally impressive pursuit of intermarket analysis. In this book's Introduction, I pointed out that there was a relationship between Treasury Bonds and soybeans by virtue of government support programs and Federal Reserve policy. The dependence or "interdependence" of markets is the focus of intermarket analysis. I have never been able to draw a distinction between dependence and interdependence; however, you should be aware that the insertion of "inter" has become fashionable regardless of its impact upon meaning. Intermarket analysis examines relationship patterns rather than fundamentals or technicals that independently influence each market. This is a very exciting field because it recognizes the trend toward market dependence in the context of "globalization." Markets are global and market dependence is global. Thus, world crops affect domestic prices, world subsidy programs translate into global pricing mechanisms, political decisions change economics, tax structures influence production and capital expenditures, and the list continues.

In 1985, Robert P. Regan introduced a commercial hedging service through a new company called Federal Interest Rate Protection Corporation. Based in North Andover, MA, his company used intermarket analysis to forecast short-term interest rates with an emphasis upon the prime lending rate. His model was called "PRO-TECT" and relied upon correlations between various cash interest rate instruments to make forecasts. Forecasts were converted into trading strategies that used futures and options markets. The primary objective was to protect real estate developers and large borrowers against rising interest rates by hedging. The PRO-TECT model discovered relationships between 19 different markets. By linking analysis with specific trading strategies, Federal Interest Rate Protection Corporation promoted a "symbiotic" analysis.

For those unfamiliar with the term, symbiosis is a mutually beneficial and highly dependent relationship between different organisms. For example, termites rely upon certain bacteria to help digest wood. The bacteria rely upon the termites as a host environment. Pilot fish clean sharks and whales by eating barnacles and other potentially harmful growths. When borrowed by market analysts, symbiosis suggests that one type of analysis depends upon another for survival or viability. The symbiotic system introduced by Mr. Regan was actually a precursor of the explosion in "derivatives." In Regan's case, the "interdependence" between his correlation of 19 markets and his futures trading strategy translated into a form of derivative that was bound by the cash transaction. The combination of a futures or options position and a cash or loan position created a totally new transaction with different characteristics than either component. (See triangle illustration, Figure 8-7.)

Assuming a reasonable correlation between the Eurodollar and U.S. prime rates, a variable interest rate bank loan could be changed into a fixed rate loan by selling Eurodollar futures in an amount equal to the loan. If the prime rate and Eurodollar rate increased, the additional interest payment required on the loan would be covered by the Eurodollar profit. Hence, the loan has been transformed and a derivative transaction exists. Had companies used intermarket analysis in connection with interest rate derivatives during 1994's rapid interest rate advances, billions in losses could have been avoided. There is little question that millions will be spent to hone intermarket analysis. In fact, the combination of intermarket analysis with technical and fundamental analysis is the basis for another hybrid approach that was introduced by Lou Mendelsohn, President of Mendelsohn Enterprises, Inc. of Wesley Chapel, FL, in 1991 called "Synergistic Analysis." (See Figure 8-8.)

In his literature, Mendelsohn describes combining market-specific technical and fundamental analysis with intermarket analysis to form a synergistic forecast. The synergistic approach uses neural networks to "quantify relationships and find hidden patterns between related financial markets." The result of Mendelsohn's studies is a unique and increasingly popular software product called "VantagePoint." (Trademark of Mendelsohn Enterprises, Inc.) (See Figure 8-9.)

Since the training and implementation of neural networks is a complex exercise, many traders prefer a packaged approach. Products like Vantage-

Figure 8-7

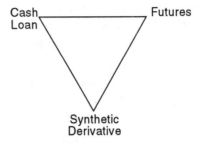

A variable rate loan can become a synthetic fixed rate loan by selling highly correlated financial futures as a hedge against rising rates.

Figure 8-8

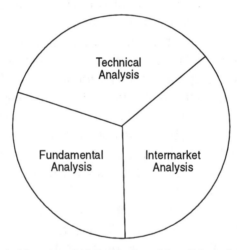

"Synergistic Market Analysis" combines technical, fundamental, and intermarket analysis.

Point are already designed and trained for specific markets like Treasury Bonds, S & P 500, OEX, Eurodollar, Swiss Francs, Japanese Yen, Deutschmarks, Canadian Dollar, and Nikkei. Synergistic Analysis is markedly different from TechnoFundamentals in its method of combining technical and fundamental measurements. Yet, it illustrates a move toward combined strategies that will evolve at an accelerating pace.

Figure 8-9

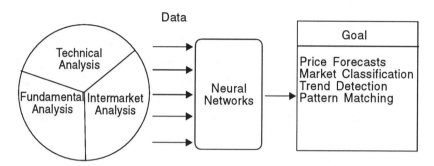

Vantage Point™ software combines Synergistic Analysis with neural networks to complete the model.

Prior to developing VantagePoint, Mendelsohn introduced "ProfitTaker" and "Trader" software packages. The evolution is obvious when you consider that ProfitTaker remains a very popular technical analysis system and Trader is a "spreadsheet type" of program for analyzing fundamental data.

Mendelsohn's Synergistic Analysis leads to even more intriguing neural network applications that are exemplified by the work of Dr. Amir Atiya and Ashraf Azmi. Using intermarket analysis, these gentlemen have applied neural networks to develop position/asset allocation models. Relationships between markets raises the question, "Which markets are best to follow at any point in time." Since traditional portfolio design criteria do not necessarily apply to futures and options, the science of position allocation has emerged as a mirror discipline. Determining the right market at the right time is a function of the forecast, risk assessment, exposure-to-capital ratios, and complimentary positions. Since futures and options may be purchased and sold with equal ease, portfolio design is a complex exercise because it involves evaluation of a position relative to a forecast. This requires an assumption of an accurate forecast. Obviously, all forecasts are subject to error. Further, subjective and even objective forecasting is vulnerable to variations in error. In other words, performance is not always consistent over time.

The following performance summary illustrates the application of Dr. Atiya's neural network to the well-known COMMODEX® trading system. COMMODEX tracks 47 U.S. futures markets with as many as 100 contract months. Trading all positions can require upwards from $250,000 in margin.

How can an individual with less than this amount objectively and success-fully use the COMMODEX system? Dr. Atiya's network is trained on the COMMODEX system results and price action for the 47 markets. External filters allow the model to select trades based upon "associated probabilities." The neural network is told that it has starting equity of $60,000 with a round-turn commission rate of $60. The model dynamically adds and sub-tracts commodities from the portfolio based upon the amount of available equity and the filtering system. Without the network, a trader using COM-MODEX might make subjective choices about which contracts to trade.

PROCESSING DATE: DECEMBER 30, 1994

Total amount of money invested: $60,000.00

Total profit (after commission): $252,569.50

Percentage total profit: 420.9%

Maximum drawdown: $92,058.90

Total profit divided by maximum drawdown: 3.465

PROFIT BY COMMODITY AND MONTH FOR NEURAL NETWORK APPLIED TO THE COMMODEX SYSTEM

month: instrument	JAN.	FEB.	MARCH	APRIL	MAY	JUNE
AUST. $	0.0	0.0	1590.0	−2080.0	2280.0	−2790.0
BONDS	−1047.5	11265.0	3718.8	−1245.0	−13016.3	−1305.0
CRB INDEX	0.0	−1520.0	−1735.0	2175.0	5530.0	−3890.0
CORN	92.5	−622.5	377.5	415.0	−285.0	0.0
CAN. $	0.0	0.0	2060.0	−1780.0	30.0	−1580.0
COFFEE	0.0	−712.5	−1342.5	−705.0	34672.5	35347.5
CRUDE OIL	−790.0	−780.0	810.0	0.0	0.0	0.0
COTTON	0.0	0.0	−3370.0	555.0	−3275.0	−505.0
COCOA	0.0	−710.0	370.0	680.0	2090.0	−1040.0
COPPER	0.0	0.0	15.0	930.0	2237.5	−345.0
US $ INDEX	1920.0	−4200.0	−1170.0	6610.0	−6200.0	−6570.0
D-MARK	0.0	0.0	−970.0	1042.5	−1045.0	−2895.0
EURO $	0.0	0.0	2145.0	2025.0	−935.0	1265.0
FEEDERS	−1365.0	−615.0	−535.0	765.0	1565.0	765.0
FRENCH FRANC	0.0	0.0	0.0	1445.0	−1200.0	−1045.0
ORANGE JUICE	0.0	0.0	−165.0	0.0	0.0	1440.0
PORK BELLIES	0.0	0.0	0.0	976.0	−280.0	−48.0
5-YEAR NOTES	483.8	9249.4	19496.9	812.5	−8816.3	4778.1

month:	JAN.	FEB.	MARCH	APRIL	MAY	JUNE
GOLD	0.0	−240.0	−450.0	990.0	280.0	−550.0
HEATING OIL	−880.8	−797.4	−948.6	1044.6	−270.0	−429.6
GASOLINE	−1757.4	−1327.8	−2114.4	0.0	946.8	−391.8
YEN	0.0	0.0	2580.0	1505.0	−2072.5	18020.0
K.C. WHEAT	−140.0	−1230.0	775.0	−752.5	−1350.0	102.5
LIVE CATTLE	−2724.0	−36.0	340.0	564.0	1980.0	−1488.0
LIVE HOGS	840.0	−640.0	−188.0	−232.0	0.0	32.0
LUMBER	0.0	0.0	16360.0	12672.0	−5368.0	−1856.0
MUNI BONDS	−4922.5	7447.5	6377.5	−1937.5	−9081.3	4880.0
MAJOR MARKET	0.0	0.0	0.0	0.0	0.0	0.0
NATURAL GAS	12270.0	−4320.0	−150.0	−720.0	2890.0	−530.0
BRITISH POUNDS	0.0	0.0	−7.5	1202.5	−991.3	2040.0
OATS	55.0	−12.5	−45.0	0.0	0.0	0.0
PALLADIUM	0.0	−110.0	−420.0	585.0	−670.0	0.0
PLATINUM	−835.0	−530.0	−565.0	0.0	−1030.0	−2025.0
SOYBEANS	0.0	0.0	−1492.5	−1292.5	−1895.0	−3812.5
SWISS FRANCS	−2502.5	0.0	−1020.0	−535.0	0.0	−1045.0
SOY MEAL	0.0	−540.0	−2040.0	−640.0	−360.0	−2420.0
SUGAR	−849.6	2022.4	1358.4	0.0	−284.0	−1352.8
SOY OIL	0.0	−222.0	−834.0	0.0	0.0	258.0
S & P 500	0.0	0.0	0.0	0.0	0.0	0.0
SILVER	0.0	−145.0	1290.0	−1065.0	300.0	−2245.0
T-BILLS	0.0	0.0	0.0	440.0	−525.0	0.0
T-NOTES	−2946.3	19298.8	11343.8	−2641.3	−2078.8	2848.8
2-YEAR NOTES	−135.6	3275.6	2002.5	734.4	−3443.1	−2417.5
VALUE LINE	5065.0	−7020.0	9355.0	3265.0	−3300.0	1940.0
WHEAT (CHI)	−507.5	140.0	102.5	−70.0	−735.0	417.5
NYFE INDEX	0.0	0.0	0.0	0.0	0.0	0.0

month:	JULY	AUG.	SEPT.	OCT.	NOV.	DEC.
instrument						
AUST. $	−3500.0	−430.0	−2070.0	200.0	5480.0	1960.0
BONDS	−1810.0	0.0	2140.0	−4425.0	−235.0	4440.0
CRB INDEX	340.0	580.0	−2140.0	2120.0	5520.0	605.0
CORN	0.0	0.0	0.0	0.0	0.0	0.0
CAN. $	−500.0	−920.0	−90.0	−790.0	0.0	0.0
COFFEE	8193.8	5141.3	3097.5	17445.0	14238.8	−1882.5
CRUDE OIL	0.0	−320.0	−1310.0	0.0	0.0	0.0
COTTON	−2195.0	820.0	5200.0	−240.0	3430.0	17665.0
COCOA	810.0	−680.0	−250.0	−1840.0	420.0	−610.0
COPPER	−745.0	405.0	−310.0	3680.0	190.0	3417.5

month:	JULY	AUG.	SEPT.	OCT.	NOV.	DEC.
US $ INDEX	−40.0	−260.0	20.0	980.0	10240.0	−880.0
D-MARK	0.0	0.0	0.0	3017.5	0.0	290.0
EURO $	−305.0	−1760.0	165.0	−1010.0	270.0	420.0
FEEDERS	1840.0	1230.0	965.0	330.0	−370.0	2060.0
FRENCH FRANC	−25.0	−45.0	−420.0	2330.0	3300.0	−640.0
ORANGE JUICE	−615.0	−37.5	900.0	0.0	0.0	0.0
PORK BELLIES	6440.0	−7248.0	2668.0	−3592.0	1860.0	364.0
5-YEAR NOTES	−3354.4	−1037.5	853.8	506.9	−865.0	−401.3
GOLD	−460.0	−680.0	650.0	−700.0	0.0	480.0
HEATING OIL	1526.4	−3553.8	−1959.0	−236.4	−1490.4	118.2
GASOLINE	−144.0	3789.0	1501.2	2142.0	−1010.4	594.0
YEN	−3407.5	−3807.5	−1395.0	2105.0	1367.5	2150.0
K.C. WHEAT	1242.5	0.0	0.0	−320.0	0.0	−570.0
LIVE CATTLE	1512.0	−732.0	−620.0	−2300.0	1192.0	4200.0
LIVE HOGS	108.0	−796.0	628.0	−476.0	0.0	0.0
LUMBER	2748.0	−15496.0	37028.0	−6576.0	−5464.0	0.0
MUNI BONDS	−591.3	−870.0	−398.8	2413.8	4505.0	67.5
MAJOR MARKET	0.0	0.0	0.0	0.0	0.0	0.0
NATURAL GAS	0.0	1820.0	210.0	−210.0	2630.0	−2710.0
BRITISH POUNDS	−3507.5	−2523.8	1005.0	2902.5	2167.5	−1401.3
OATS	0.0	0.0	0.0	0.0	0.0	0.0
PALLADIUM	0.0	0.0	−740.0	650.0	−365.0	−135.0
PLATINUM	625.0	0.0	−1405.0	−550.0	0.0	20.0
SOYBEANS	872.5	192.5	3680.0	1400.0	645.0	−912.5
SWISS FRANCS	1080.0	−2530.0	−725.0	−457.5	0.0	265.0
SOY MEAL	−130.0	−400.0	1520.0	−1410.0	40.0	−40.0
SUGAR	0.0	−836.8	0.0	160.0	−261.6	861.6
SOY OIL	0.0	0.0	450.0	−426.0	564.0	−456.0
S & P 500	0.0	0.0	0.0	0.0	0.0	0.0
SILVER	−1125.0	1615.0	2975.0	850.0	0.0	0.0
T-BILLS	0.0	−160.0	315.0	−200.0	−110.0	0.0
T-NOTES	−1406.3	−196.3	570.0	−2328.8	−1523.8	2098.8
2-YEAR NOTES	−1388.1	−273.8	−1109.4	132.5	531.3	−713.8
VALUE LINE	80.0	7675.0	−1775.0	−1985.0	0.0	0.0
WHEAT (CHI)	−197.5	0.0	0.0	0.0	0.0	0.0
NYFE INDEX	0.0	0.0	0.0	0.0	0.0	0.0

TOTAL PROFIT FOR 12 MONTHS BY COMMODITY
AUST. $	640.0
BONDS	−1520.0
CRB INDEX	7585.0

CORN	–22.5
CAN. $	–3570.0
COFFEE	113493.8
CRUDE OIL	–2390.0
COTTON	18085.0
COCOA	–760.0
COPPER	9475.0
US $ INDEX	450.0
D-MARK	–560.0
EURO $	2280.0
FEEDERS	6635.0
FRENCH FRANC	3700.0
ORANGE JUICE	1522.5
PORK BELLIES	1140.0
5-YEAR NOTES	21706.9
GOLD	–680.0
HEATING OIL	–7876.8
GASOLINE	2227.2
YEN	17045.0
K.C. WHEAT	–2242.5
LIVE CATTLE	1888.0
LIVE HOGS	–724.0
LUMBER	34048.0
MUNI BONDS	7890.0
MAJOR MARKET	0.0
NATURAL GAS	11180.0
BRITISH POUNDS	886.3
OATS	–2.5
PALLADIUM	–1205.0
PLATINUM	–6295.0
SOYBEANS	–2615.0
SWISS FRANCS	–7470.0
SOY MEAL	–6420.0
SUGAR	817.6
SOY OIL	–666.0
S&P 500	0.0
SILVER	2450.0
T-BILLS	–240.0
T-NOTES	23038.8
2-YEAR NOTES	–2805.0
VALUE LINE	13300.0
WHEAT (CHI)	–850.0
NYFE INDEX	0.0

Total:

month:	JAN.	FEB.	MARCH	APRIL	MAY	JUNE
profit:	−677.4	26367.9	62905.3	25737.7	−13704.6	31558.2

month:	JULY	AUG.	SEPT.	OCT.	NOV.	DEC.
profit:	1971.6	−22326.1	49824.3	13292.5	46895.9	30724.3

DAILY PROFITS: YYMMDD	COMMISSION SUBTRACTED	WITHOUT COMMISSION	CUMULATIVE PROFITS
940103	60.0	180.0	60.0
940104	−964.5	−364.5	−904.5
940105	−1989.7	−1569.7	−2894.2
940106	−9085.5	−8425.5	−11979.8
940107	−914.6	−794.6	−12894.3
940110	4259.4	4679.4	−8634.9
940111	1151.8	1271.8	−7483.2
940112	−6327.7	−5787.7	−13810.9
940113	−1819.5	−1339.5	−15630.4
940114	747.7	747.7	−14882.7
940117	−161.1	−41.1	−15043.8
940118	−426.7	−6.7	−15470.5
940119	4974.0	5334.0	−10496.5
940120	−3218.4	−2618.4	−13714.8
940121	208.6	448.6	−13506.2
940124	−3370.3	−3310.3	−16876.5
940125	4923.3	4923.3	−11953.2
940126	8330.5	8750.5	−3622.7
940127	701.1	821.1	−2921.6
940128	3510.2	3630.2	588.6
940131	−1266.1	−1206.1	−677.4
940201	2416.9	2836.9	1739.5
940202	−7044.4	−6444.4	−5304.9
940203	−7770.4	−7350.4	−13075.3
940204	−2726.0	−1346.0	−15801.3
940207	4292.9	4352.9	−11508.4
940208	−7712.5	−7232.5	−19221.0
940209	−150.7	−30.7	−19371.6
940210	−5852.1	−5552.1	−25223.7
940211	6683.7	6743.7	−18540.1
940214	−2444.9	−2204.9	−20984.9

PROFITS:	COMMISSION SUBTRACTED	WITHOUT COMMISSION	CUMULATIVE PROFITS
940215	1053.9	1173.9	−19931.0
940216	11883.0	11943.0	−8048.0
940217	8604.4	8844.4	556.4
940218	−6186.7	−6126.7	−5630.3
940222	11688.8	11808.8	6058.5
940223	8420.9	8780.9	14479.5
940224	530.4	710.4	15009.9
940225	−7087.2	−6967.2	7922.7
940228	17767.8	17887.8	25690.5
940301	1015.3	1375.3	26705.9
940302	7565.4	7745.4	34271.3
940303	−5472.4	−4992.4	28798.8
940304	−5511.3	−5391.3	23287.6
940307	7191.3	7371.3	30478.9
940308	−1743.9	−1623.9	28734.9
940309	13829.7	14009.7	42564.6
940310	−2518.8	−2278.8	40045.8
940311	6127.8	6607.8	46173.6
940314	−6432.5	−6252.5	39741.1
940315	−8562.5	−7962.5	31178.7
940316	3013.5	3433.5	34192.2
940317	17734.8	17734.8	51926.9
940318	5062.1	5122.1	56989.0
940321	−3268.9	−3028.9	53720.1
940322	−1774.1	−1534.1	51946.1
940323	13126.7	13426.7	65072.7
940324	2286.5	2646.5	67359.3
940325	−7538.6	−7298.6	59820.7
940328	12468.1	13068.1	72288.8
940329	14134.5	14494.5	86423.3
940330	8638.8	8878.8	95062.0
940331	−6466.3	−6466.3	88595.8
940401	21995.4	22175.4	110591.2
940404	−23622.6	−22962.6	86968.5
940405	−2098.1	−1618.1	84870.4
940406	−7149.4	−6789.4	77721.0
940407	11000.6	11120.6	88721.7
940408	2604.5	2724.5	91326.1
940411	−8882.5	−8882.5	82443.6
940412	7360.4	7480.4	89804.0

PROFITS:	COMMISSION SUBTRACTED	WITHOUT COMMISSION	CUMULATIVE PROFITS
940413	5320.4	5380.4	95124.4
940414	−885.9	−885.9	94238.5
940415	18577.1	18637.1	112815.6
940418	2618.2	2738.2	115433.8
940419	−1517.7	−1457.7	113916.1
940420	−15151.5	−15091.5	98764.6
940421	7188.7	7668.7	105953.3
940422	2352.5	2772.5	108305.8
940425	1629.1	1629.1	109935.0
940426	2844.0	2904.0	112779.0
940428	−1069.6	−889.6	111709.4
940429	2624.1	2924.1	114333.5
940502	2708.9	3068.9	117042.4
940503	−8587.3	−8227.3	108455.1
940504	−2574.5	−2214.5	105880.6
940505	20878.3	20878.3	126758.9
940506	6068.3	6188.3	132827.2
940509	−28048.9	−27088.9	104778.3
940510	7361.2	7661.2	112139.4
940511	2188.8	2368.8	114328.2
940512	3920.1	4040.1	118248.4
940513	12414.1	12414.1	130662.5
940516	−14765.4	−14705.4	115897.1
940517	5865.9	6105.9	121763.0
940518	14945.6	15605.6	136708.5
940519	−5016.1	−4176.1	131692.4
940520	11587.4	11587.4	143279.8
940523	−18352.5	−18112.5	124927.3
940524	−11917.1	−11917.1	113010.2
940525	−19764.3	−19764.3	93245.9
940526	5710.4	5830.4	98956.3
940527	4862.0	5522.0	103818.3
940531	−3189.4	−2829.4	100628.9
940601	−4808.5	−4328.5	95820.4
940602	5968.8	6208.8	101789.2
940603	−10312.3	−9892.3	91476.9
940606	−2615.8	−1955.8	88861.2
940607	−2053.8	−1753.8	86807.4
940608	−7719.8	−7479.8	79087.7
940609	−4330.2	−4150.2	74757.5

PROFITS:	COMMISSION SUBTRACTED	WITHOUT COMMISSION	CUMULATIVE PROFITS
940610	–2526.2	–1866.2	72231.3
940613	3225.1	3585.1	75456.3
940614	–2646.6	–2406.6	72809.7
940615	–9172.2	–8512.2	63637.5
940616	4152.5	5052.5	67790.1
940617	–7866.5	–7626.5	59923.5
940620	14609.5	15029.5	74533.0
940621	–23312.1	–23072.1	51220.9
940622	3068.0	3488.0	54288.9
940623	21025.4	21385.4	75314.3
940624	18885.8	18885.8	94200.0
940627	17064.5	17364.5	111264.6
940628	13325.5	13505.5	124590.1
940629	8824.8	8884.8	133414.8
940630	–1227.8	–1227.8	132187.1
940701	–6419.0	–6359.0	125768.1
940705	11844.6	11904.6	137612.7
940706	–6928.0	–6748.0	130684.7
940707	7403.5	7403.5	138088.2
940708	45245.5	45545.5	183333.7
940711	8800.1	9100.1	192133.8
940712	–3173.8	–3053.8	188960.1
940713	–22119.6	–21819.6	166840.4
940714	13837.5	14197.5	180677.9
940715	6484.9	6664.9	187162.8
940718	–16281.5	–16161.5	170881.3
940719	–23464.1	–23284.1	147417.2
940720	9664.1	9784.1	157081.3
940721	–7931.8	–7511.8	149149.6
940722	–19359.3	–19059.3	129790.3
940725	–1002.9	–882.9	128787.4
940726	–1344.1	–924.1	127443.3
940727	9210.5	9630.5	136653.8
940728	2287.7	2527.7	138941.5
940729	–4782.8	–4722.8	134158.7
940801	–3193.4	–2773.4	130965.4
940802	4561.8	5161.8	135527.1
940803	–18735.8	–18495.8	116791.3
940804	7076.7	7196.7	123868.0
940805	16532.8	17132.8	140400.7

PROFITS:	COMMISSION SUBTRACTED	WITHOUT COMMISSION	CUMULATIVE PROFITS
940808	−11801.9	−11321.9	128598.8
940809	8126.0	8726.0	136724.8
940810	−13082.4	−13082.4	123642.5
940811	7664.5	7964.5	131306.9
940812	−20747.8	−20207.8	110559.1
940815	−4010.4	−3830.4	106548.8
940816	837.9	1797.9	107386.6
940817	161.0	221.0	107547.6
940818	4794.7	4914.7	112342.3
940819	13956.3	14316.3	126298.6
940822	−4773.3	−4713.3	121525.3
940823	−9632.3	−9392.3	111893.0
940824	−814.9	−814.9	111078.1
940825	−5792.0	−5732.0	105286.2
940826	3309.8	3489.8	108596.0
940829	4460.5	5120.5	113056.5
940830	−2259.1	−2259.1	110797.4
940831	1035.2	1275.2	111832.6
940901	−3955.2	−3775.2	107877.4
940902	−1047.9	−567.9	106829.5
940906	3260.1	3260.1	110089.6
940907	11467.1	11647.1	121556.8
940908	4545.2	4725.2	126102.0
940909	3028.2	3508.2	129130.2
940912	7574.8	8234.8	136705.0
940913	−6368.0	−5948.0	130337.0
940914	−9657.3	−9417.3	120679.7
940915	24321.9	24441.9	145001.6
940916	−229.7	130.3	144771.9
940919	8463.3	8463.3	153235.2
940920	8189.8	8789.8	161425.0
940921	−9922.9	−9922.9	151502.1
940922	3732.2	4392.2	155234.3
940923	1248.1	1248.1	156482.5
940926	−1001.3	−761.3	155481.2
940927	−8111.4	−8111.4	147369.8
940928	11283.8	11403.8	158653.6
940929	1266.1	1626.1	159919.7
940930	1737.2	1797.2	161656.9
941003	1821.6	1941.6	163478.5

PROFITS:	COMMISSION SUBTRACTED	WITHOUT COMMISSION	CUMULATIVE PROFITS
941004	3456.1	3456.1	166934.6
941005	6025.9	6085.9	172960.5
941006	9826.8	9886.8	182787.3
941007	7513.0	7513.0	190300.2
941010	−9218.2	−8918.2	181082.0
941011	−7043.6	−6863.6	174038.4
941012	599.1	1019.1	174637.6
941013	5353.5	5653.5	179991.1
941014	−11122.5	−10522.5	168868.6
941017	3862.4	4222.4	172731.0
941018	−2492.0	−2372.0	170238.9
941019	3098.2	3578.2	173337.1
941020	−2621.8	−2261.8	170715.3
941021	4058.9	4958.9	174774.2
941024	−4944.4	−4404.4	169829.8
941025	2744.9	2924.9	172574.7
941026	2486.9	2786.9	175061.6
941027	−9161.3	−8861.3	165900.4
941028	6244.1	6304.1	172144.5
941031	2804.9	3704.9	174949.4
941101	10222.9	10462.9	185172.3
941102	−3540.3	−3120.3	181632.0
941103	6701.3	7001.3	188333.2
941104	627.1	627.1	188960.3
941107	−12251.6	−12251.6	176708.7
941108	−1242.0	−1242.0	175466.7
941109	7322.3	7502.3	182789.0
941110	3885.0	4305.0	186673.9
941111	2008.9	2008.9	188682.9
941114	5340.4	5640.4	194023.2
941115	3098.4	3158.4	197121.7
941116	5226.6	5586.6	202348.3
941117	7067.3	7247.3	209415.5
941118	11461.2	11461.2	220876.8
941121	−2379.7	−2259.7	218497.0
941122	−1523.4	−1523.4	216973.6
941123	−638.4	−278.4	216335.3
941125	−6672.0	−6132.0	209663.3
941128	3346.1	3526.1	213009.5
941129	9766.8	9826.8	222776.3

DAILY PROFITS:	COMMISSION SUBTRACTED	WITHOUT COMMISSION	CUMULATIVE PROFITS
941130	−931.0	−931.0	221845.3
941201	22392.0	22392.0	244237.3
941202	−6331.3	−6331.3	237906.0
941205	138.8	198.8	238044.8
941206	−6644.5	−6344.5	231400.3
941207	3540.0	3600.0	234940.3
941208	566.8	866.8	235507.0
941209	−7297.6	−6817.6	228209.5
941212	14159.0	14519.0	242368.5
941213	7667.0	7787.0	250035.5
941214	4530.0	4710.0	254565.5
941215	−12223.3	−12043.3	242342.2
941216	1893.9	1893.9	244236.1
941219	−4756.3	−4396.3	239479.7
941220	5288.2	5288.2	244767.9
941221	2575.6	2635.6	247343.5
941222	5307.0	5967.0	252650.5
941223	7456.4	8116.4	260106.9
941227	−5028.5	−4908.5	255078.4
941228	−1382.5	−902.5	253695.9
941229	−1126.4	−946.4	252569.5
941230	0.0	0.0	252569.5

The variations in performance coupled with correlations of different markets and risk criteria create a nonlinear problem with multiple solutions. In any optimization model you look for the "best fit" among your possible solutions. However, the combination of criteria is sufficiently complex to present many apparent solutions with equally acceptable "fits." Since TechnoFundamental analysis is a new discipline, it has not been extensively studied in conjunction with portfolio selection or asset allocation models. There is little question that an examination of supply and demand trends can provide a set of probabilities that a neural network can use as a "filter" in a selection process. Price referencing will give boundaries against which the asset or position evaluation can be more accurately determined.

As an example, consider the recurrence of a weather phenomenon called "El Niño" mentioned earlier in this text. By tracking reactions to this change in weather, a neural network can evaluate the potential for extraordinary price action in grains. The higher the probability of a fundamentally based trend, the more likely it is that the network will select grains as part of a portfolio. It is also likely that asset allocation will emphasize grains over commodity complexes that have less of a chance for dramatic price movement. It should be noted that many students of El Niño believe there is a correlation with sun spot cycles. There is evidence that the tide ebbs and flows in 7- to 11-year intervals. This supports the incorporation of cycle assumptions into certain neural network systems.

The science of market forecasting is still in its infancy. Just as humanity is attempting to decipher its genetic code, so too are we seeking to unlock a formula for market-driving behavior.

We are years away from the "perfect system." By definition, such a system will be our downfall because it will create "perfect markets." This suggests absolute pricing efficiency which removes profit opportunity. It is an interesting intellectual or philosophical exercise to ponder the perfect world.

However, in the interest of making a profit, we should not dwell on this exercise too long.

CHAPTER 9

PRACTICAL APPLICATIONS

Now that you understand some basic TechnoFundamental concepts, how do you make a profit?

There are several practical tools you can use to begin practicing different levels of TechnoFundamental analysis.

- Simple spreadsheet applications help translate statistics into meaningful data.

- Plotting software adds pictures to the numbers.

- Database management systems provide powerful modeling environments.

- Databases give access to massive amounts of accurate statistics, prices, and measurements.

- Government and private reports yield current and ongoing information.

- Weather services tell you what to expect in the short run.

- Charting software lets you recreate past situations.

- Neural network packages let you construct unique pattern recognition systems.

The number of tools and the depth of these products is exceptional. Even more impressive is the rate of expansion in power and versatility. By the time this book is published and generally read, many applications covered in this chapter may have been developed into commercially available computer products.

For obvious reasons, this book cannot reveal proprietary trading systems. For better or worse, copyright and patent protection remains too vague to protect valuable market formulas.

However, the *building blocks* of several proprietary systems are within the scope of this book. You will see how traders are applying analysis to markets and you can judge the results.

What Spreadsheets Can Do

It is always best to begin with simple techniques. Most traders simply need a starting point from which they can build their own sophisticated routines for tracking markets. Earlier, we covered the importance of following government and private statistics to determine market bias, supply and demand trends, and relative price. Tracking this information can be confusing at best and daunting at worst for both experienced and inexperienced traders.

Fortunately, the development of spreadsheet programs has lessened the pain associated with this task. When faced with pounds, tons, acres, bushels, and content, you can quickly conduct forward and backward analysis by constructing appropriate formulas in relatively simple spreadsheets.

For example, analyzing grains requires you to consider planting intentions, potential yield per acre, domestic consumption, exports, and carryovers. When the U.S. Department of Agriculture releases planting intentions in the spring, you may be faced with translating acres into yields.

Since yield depends upon weather, it is best to use a "best case/likely case/worst case" approach. You can determine from previous years what the average yield has been in good and bad years. Using this information, you can establish three columns in your spreadsheet for each outcome. The formula is simple multiplication:

$$ACRES \times YIELD = TOTAL\ BUSHELS\ (estimated)$$

The result can be translated into tons so you can easily cross reference anticipated yield to other statistics like exports, imports, and carryovers. Using conversion factors for corn, wheat, soybeans, and oats, we have the following:

TOTAL BUSHELS × .027216 = TONS (wheat and soybeans)
TOTAL BUSHELS × .025400 = TONS (corn, sorghum, and rye)
TOTAL BUSHELS × .014515 = TONS (oats)

To gain a global perspective, you would include hectares. Foreign yields are often presented as "quintals per hectare." The conversion formulae are:

BUSHELS PER ACRE × .6725 = QUINTALS PER HECTARE
(wheat and soybeans)

BUSHELS PER ACRE × .6277 = QUINTALS PER HECTARE
(corn, sorghum, and rye)

BUSHELS PER ACRE × .3587 = QUINTALS PER HECTARE (oats)

You should also reverse these formulae to translate foreign statistics into U.S. references. This allows you to see how foreign production compares with U.S. production. It is convenient to include conversions for tons, kilograms, and pounds to make sure that you have quick access to "normalizing" any statistics that could impact the market.

Figure 9-1 lists many of the conversion factors and equations that are extremely helpful for constructing many spreadsheet studies. You will encounter numerous ways of stating fundamental supply and demand statistics. It is always helpful to have a quick reference at your fingertips.

The following provides an example of spreadsheet headings and formulae that can be used for basic statistical translation. With this in place, you can build a reference spreadsheet that allows you to compare current developments with previous years.

*****

GRAINS
WHEAT
Acres Bushels # Hectares Bushels
Planted per acre Bushels Tonnes Pounds Kilograms planted per acre
 0 0 0 0 0 -
CORN
Acres Bushels # Hectares Bushels
Planted per acre Bushels Tonnes Pounds Kilograms planted per acre
 0 0 0 0 0 -
OATS

Acres Bushels # Hectares Bushels
Planted per acre Bushels Tonnes Pounds Kilograms planted per acre
0 0 0 0 0 -
SOYBEANS
Acres Bushels # Hectares Bushels
Planted per acre Bushels Tonnes Pounds Kilograms planted per acre
0 0 0 0 0 -
A1: [W10] 'GRAINS
A3: [W10] 'WHEAT
A4: [W10] 'Acres
B4: [W10] 'Bushels
C4: [W9] ^#
G4: [W9] 'Hectares
I4: [W8] 'Bushels
A5: [W10] 'Planted
B5: [W10] 'per acre
C5: [W9] 'Bushels
D5: [W7] 'Tonnes
E5: [W7] 'Pounds
F5: [W10] 'Kilograms
G5: [W9] 'planted
I5: [W8] 'per acre
C6: [W9] (A6*B6)
D6: [W7] @SUM(B6*0.0254)
E6: [W7] @SUM(B6*60)
F6: [W10] @SUM(D6*1000)
G6: [W9] (A6*0.040694)
I6: [W8] @IF(A5O,(C5/A5)," -")
A9: [W10] 'CORN
A10: [W10] 'Acres
B10: [W10] 'Bushels
C10: [W9] ^#
G10: [W9] 'Hectares
I10: [W8] 'Bushels
A11: [W10] 'Planted
B11: [W10] 'per acre
C11: [W9] 'Bushels

D11: [W7] 'Tonnes
E11: [W7] 'Pounds
F11: [W10] 'Kilograms
G11: [W9] 'planted
I11: [W8] 'per acre
C12: [W9] (A12*B12)
D12: [W7] @SUM(B12*0.0254)
E12: [W7] (B12*56)
F12: [W10] @SUM(D12*1000)
G12: [W9] (A12*0.040694)
I12: [W8] @IF(A120,(C12/A12)," -")
A15: [W10] 'OATS
A16: [W10] 'Acres
B16: [W10] 'Bushels
C16: [W9] ^#
G16: [W9] 'Hectares
I16: [W8] 'Bushels
A17: [W10] 'Planted
B17: [W10] 'per acre
C17: [W9] 'Bushels
D17: [W7] 'Tonnes
E17: [W7] 'Pounds
F17: [W10] 'Kilograms
G17: [W9] 'planted
I17: [W8] 'per acre
C18: [W9] (A18*B18)
D18: [W7] @SUM(B18*0.014515)
E18: [W7] (B12*32)
F18: [W10] @SUM(D18*1000)
G18: [W9] (A18*0.040694)
I18: [W8] @IF(A180,(C18/A18)," -")
A21: [W10] 'SOYBEANS
A22: [W10] 'Acres
B22: [W10] 'Bushels
C22: [W9] ^#
G22: [W9] 'Hectares
I22: [W8] 'Bushels

A23: [W10] 'Planted
B23: [W10] 'per acre
C23: [W9] 'Bushels
D23: [W7] 'Tonnes
E23: [W7] 'Pounds
F23: [W10] 'Kilograms
G23: [W9] 'planted
I23: [W8] 'per acre
C24: [W9] (A24*B24)
D24: [W7] @SUM(B24*0.027216)
E24: [W7] @SUM(B24*60)
F24: [W10] @SUM(D24*1000)
G24: [W9] (A24*0.040694)
I24: [W8] @IF(A240,(C24/A24)," -")

TechnoFundamentals measure changes in basic supply and demand along with momentum and acceleration. Momentum is the slope of the supply or demand trendline. Acceleration is the rate of change in the slope. These are important TechnoFundamental measurements because they give you the market bias. An accelerating supply line implies lower highs and lows if demand is flat. If demand keeps pace with supply, you should see frequent and long price consolidation patterns. Assuming demand is accelerating faster than supply, prices should experience higher highs and lows. Changes in relative momentum that are reflected by acceleration give you clues to major fundamental turning points.

Recall our previous discussion about building capacity. When capacity is playing catch-up to demand, a decrease in demand will have an extended impact because it is difficult to shut down production. Global supply patterns clearly show that countries are able to respond to each other's production problems.

Thus, if Brazil experiences a freeze in coffee regions, other South American and African producers will happily supply the shortfall. As more nations discover crude oil reserves, the importance of OPEC is diminished. (In the Gulf War of 1990/91, you may have noticed how the initial surge in energy prices was offset after Operation Desert Storm as Iraq's and Kuwait's production was replaced with excess capacity of other countries.)

Figure 9-1
Conversion Factors

Commonly Used Agricultural Weights and Measurements
Bushel weights:
wheat and soybeans = 60 lbs.
corn, sorghum and rye = 56 lbs.
barley grain = 48 lbs.
barley malt = 34 lbs.
oats = 32 lbs.

Bushels to tonnes:
wheat and soybeans = bushels x 0.027216
barley grain = bushels x 0.021772
corn, sorghum, and rye = bushels x 0.025400
oats = bushels x 0.014515

1 tonne (metric ton) equals:
2204.622 lbs.
1,000 kilograms
22.046 hundredweight
10 quintals
36.7437 bushels of wheat or soybeans
39.3679 bushels of corn, sorghum, or rye
45.9296 bushels of barley grain
68.8944 bushels of oats
4.5929 cotton bales
(the statistical bale used by the USDA and ICAC contains a net weight of 480 pounds of lint)

Area measurements:
1 acre = 43,560 square feet = 0.040694 hectare
1 hectare = 2.4710 acres = 10,000 square meters
640 acres = 1 square mile = 259 hectares

Yields:
Wheat: bushels per acre x 0.6725 = quintals per hectare
Rye, corn: bushels per acre x 0.6277 = quintals per hectare
barley grain: bushels per acre x 0.5380 = quintals per hectare
oats: bushels per acre x 0.3587 = quintals per hectare

Commonly Used Weights
The troy, avoirdupois, and apothecaries' grains are identical in U.S. and British weight systems, equal to 0.0648 gram in the metric system. One avoirdupois ounce equals 437.5 grains. The troy and apothecaries' ounces equal 480 grains, and their pounds contain 12 ounces.

Troy weights and conversions:
24 grains = 1 pennyweight
20 pennyweights = 1 ounce
12 ounces = 1 lb.
1 troy ounce = 31.103 grams
1 troy ounce = 0.0311033 kilogram
1 troy pound = 0.37224 kilogram
1 kilogram = 32.1507 troy ounces
1 tonne = 32,151 troy ounces

Avoirdupois weights and conversions:
27 11/32 grains = 1 dram
16 drams = 1 ounce
16 ounces = 1 lb.
1 lb. = 7,000 grains
14 lbs. = 1 stone (British)
100 lbs. = 1 hundredweight (U.S.)
112 lbs. = 8 stone = 1 hundredweight (British)
2,000 lbs. = 1 short ton (U.S. ton)
2,240 lbs. = 1 long ton (British ton)
160 stone = 1 long ton
20 hundredweight = 1 ton
1 lb. = 0.4536 kilogram
1 hundredweight (cwt.) = 45.359 kilograms
1 short ton 907.18 kilograms
1 long ton 1,016.05 kilograms

Figure 9-1 (Continued)

Metric weights and conversions:
1,000 grams = 1 kilogram
100 kilograms = 1 quintal
1 tonne = 1,000 kilograms = 10 quintals
1 kilogram = 2.240622 lbs.
1 quintal = 220.462 lbs.
1 tonne = 2204.6 lbs.
1 tonne = 1.102 short tons
1 tonne = 0.9842 long ton

U.S. dry volumes and conversions:
1 pint = 33.60 cubic inches = 0.5506 liter
2 pints = 1 quart = 1.1012 liters
8 quarts = 1 peck = 8.8098 liters
4 pecks = 1 bushel = 35.2391 liters
1 cubic foot = 28.3169 liters

U.S. liquid volumes and conversions:
1 ounce = 1.8047 cubic inches = 29.6 milliliters
1 cup = 8 ounces = 0.24 liter = 237 milliliters
1 pint = 16 ounces = 0.48 liter = 473 milliliters
1 quart = 2 pints = 0.946 liter = 946 milliliters
1 gallon = 4 quarts = 231 cubic inches = 3.785 liters
1 liter = 1.0567 quarts = 1,000 milliliters
(1 milliliter = 0.033815 fluid ounce)
1 liter = 33.814 fluid ounces
1 imperial gallon = 277.42 cubic inches = 1.2 U.S. gallons = 4.546 liters
1 U.S. barrel = 42 U.S. gallons
1 short ton = 6.65 barrels
1 tonne = 7.33 barrels

Energy Conversion Factors

U.S. Crude oil (average gravity):
1 U.S. barrel = 42 U.S. gallons
1 short ton = 6.65 barrels
1 tonne = 7.33 barrels

Barrels per tonne for various origins:

Origin	Barrels per tonne
Abu Dhabi	7.624
Algeria	7.661
Angola	7.206
Australia	7.775
Bahrain	7.335
Brunei	7.334
Canada	7.428
Dubai	7.295
Ecuador	7.580
Gabon	7.245
Indonesia	7.348
Iran	7.370
Iraq	7.453
Kuwait	7.261
Libya	7.615
Mexico	7.104
Neutral Zone	6.825
Nigeria	7.410
Norway	7.444
Oman	7.390
Qatar	7.573
Romania	7.453
Saudi Arabia	7.338
Trinidad	6.989
Tunisia	7.709
United Arab Emirates	7.522
United Kingdom	7.279
United States	7.418
USSR	7.350
Venezuela	7.005
Zaire	7.206

Figure 9-1 (Continued)

Approximate Heat Content of Petroleum Products
(Million Btu per barrel, 1 British thermal unit is the amount of heat required to raise the temperature of 1 pound of water 1 degree F.)

Petroleum Product	Heat Content
Asphalt	6.636
Aviation Gasoline	5.048
Butane	4.326
Distillate Fuel Oil	5.825
Ethane	3.082
Isobutane	3.974
Jet Fuel, Kerosene	5.670
Jet fuel, Naptha	5.355
Kerosene	5.670
Lubricants	6.065
Motor Gasoline	5.253
Natural Gasoline	4.620
Pentanes Plus	4.620

Refined Products
The number of barrels contained in a tonne of each, of the following products is:

Aviation gasoline	8.90
motor gasoline	8.50
kerosene	7.75

jet fuel	8.00
distillate, including diesel	7.46
residual fuel oil	6.45
lubricating oil	7.00
grease	6.30
white spirits	8.50
paraffin oil	7.14
paraffin wax	7.87
petrolatum	7.87
asphalt and road oil	6.06
petroleum coke	5.50
bitumen	6.06
LPG	11.60

Petrochemical Feedstocks:

Naptha less than 401 degree F	5.248
Other Oils equal to or greater than 401 degree F	5.825
Still Gas	6.000
Petroleum Coke	6.024
Plant Condensate	5.418
Propane	3.836
Residual Fuel Oil	6.287
Special Napthas	5.248
Unfinished Oils	5.825
Unfractionated Stream	5.418
Waxes	5.537

Source: U.S. Department of Energy

Natural Gas Conversions

Although there are approximately 1,031 Btu in a cubic foot of gas, for most applications the following conversions are sufficient:

Cubic Feet			MMBtu
1,000	(one thousand cubic feet)	1 Mcf	1
1,000,000	(one million cubic feet)	1 MMcf	1,000
10,000,000	(ten million cubic feet)	10 MMcf	10,000
1,000,000,000	(one billion cubic feet)	1 Bcf	1,000,000
1,000,000,000,000	(one trillion cubic feet)	1 Tcf	1,000,000,000

Source: Commodity Research Bureau InfoTech™, Knight-Ridder

Most spreadsheet programs like Microsoft's EXCEL, Borland's Quattro, and Lotus 1-2-3 include graphing capability. After accumulating a reasonable number of data points, you can plot supply and demand statistics to determine trends, tops, bottoms, consolidations, equilibrium, and common technical formations we have reviewed like head and shoulders, flags, and others.

You select time as your x-axis and the supply or demand statistics as your y-axis. For comparison, you can plot both on the same graph. Your study can be expanded for TechnoFundamental referencing by adding price as a variable on a third axis.

Several programs allow you to construct a second scale on the right hand margin of your graph. This lets you see how price interacts with supply and demand.

It is important to properly correlate time frames for all variables in this graphical analysis. Make sure you use monthly price data if you intend to use monthly supply and demand data. When using annual data, use average price over the year as your yearly data point. Understand that you can focus upon supply and demand subsets like beginning and ending stocks, imports/exports, domestic consumption, government reserves, and other statistics to gain an understanding of trends among market components. Frequently, a component's trend will change market bias when it becomes a significant factor.

For example, a slow decrease in coffee reserves prior to the 1994 Brazilian freeze accentuated supply concerns. Having reduced inventories over the previous two years, it appeared Brazil would not be able to make up for crop deficiencies with old crop inventories.

Consider the following excerpt from the July 1993 *Oil Crops: Situation and Outlook Yearbook*:

Acreage Estimates for 1993 Come Full Circle—USDA's June Acreage Report placed U.S. soybean plantings for 1993/94 at 61.1 million acres, up from the March Prospective Plantings Report estimate of 59.3 million. However, the Acreage Report released June 30 was based on surveys conducted between May 31 and June 15 and did not reflect the impact of rain and flooding in several major producing states in the upper Midwest. Consequently, USDA's July World Agriculture Supply and Demand Estimates for U.S. soybeans reflected 59.5 million planted acres—nearly what was projected in March. Final soybean plantings may differ significantly from the June Acreage Report estimates. Updated acreage estimates will be published in the Crop Production Report on August 11, 1993.

Prospects of a 34.1 bushel-per-acre yield and harvested acreage of 58 million acres is expected to result in a 1.975 billion bushel soybean crop in the 1993/94 season. Together with estimated beginning stocks of 290 million bushels, the 1993 crop is expected to result in a total supply of 2.27 billion bushels, the lowest since 1990.

You can see that much of the information you would input into your spreadsheet for soybeans is provided in the report along with some conversions. However, this is not always the case. Interim reports frequently give only basic figures or net changes.

You must determine the meaning of these numbers. Further, private estimates do not always support USDA assumptions. Given the tremendous stakes involved, there is an increasing use of private surveys. For some traders, this involves using airplanes to take aerial photographs of vast regions to determine actual plantings. In some cases, these studies include spectrography and infrared pictures to determine crop condition, ground moisture, and insect population. Prior to planting, pictures are taken to reveal how much acreage is being prepared for planting. These endeavors are worth the effort when you consider that USDA estimates can vary by more than 10%.

In some cases, you may wish to include in your spreadsheets forecasts sponsored by brokerage companies, farm coops, universities, and trading firms. Let the computer compare predictions to see if there is a consensus or significant divergence.

In 1983, there were several different viewpoints and discrepancies associated with the soybean crop. Many traders believed these differences were responsible for wild price swings. The use of a spreadsheet to track soybean data would have identified suspect statistics. This would have avoided overreacting to intermittent price gyrations.

Data gathering can be a tedious process. While you can go back and collect statistics from old USDA reports, modern technology provides some shortcuts. Knight-Ridder Financial Publishing, based in Chicago, produces a biannual update of price, volume, open interest, and fundamental data on a CD-ROM called the "CRB InfoTech." This is an extremely valuable tool for anyone who is serious about TechnoFundamental studies or other market analysis.

On a single CD-ROM, you have access to fundamental data spanning more than twenty years as well as price data for cash, futures, and options stretching back thirty years or more. In most cases, tables are in reasonably fixed column format. This simplifies the process of converting statistical tables into spreadsheets for analysis. In a single process, you can load 20 years of supply and demand data into your study. Thereafter, you simply add information as it becomes available.

It should be noted that statistical tables used in this text were all compiled using the CRB InfoTech ROM. Software supplied by Knight-Ridder allows you to easily locate and extract tables of fundamental data independently or through relational tags known as "hypertags." The database permits multi-level key word searches which are extremely helpful for in-depth studies and determining intermarket relationships. In addition to extracting tables, this author was able to build the supply and demand charts illustrated in this book by extracting data from tables and importing it into QUATTRO PRO 6.0. Standard graph functions were used. (Appendix A provides a list of price, volume, and open interest data available in the CRB InfoTech.)

CRB InfoTech is compatible with the MegaTech charting package from Ret-Tech® Software Incorporated (151 Deer Lane, Barrington, IL 60010, 708-382-3903). The majority of the charts prepared for this text were derived from the CRB InfoTech and the MegaTech software. Technical studies include :

Accumulation/Distribution Index
Advance/Decline Line
Arms Index
Moving Averages
Bollinger Bands
Channel Index
Chaikin Oscillator
Directional Movement Index
New High/Low
Japanese Candle Stick
KR Volatility
MACD Line Charts
MACD Histograms
Moving Average Envelopes
Money Flow Index

Momentum
Nicoski Study
Negative Volume Index
Moving Average Oscillator
Open Interest Overlay/Underlay
Overlay Issues
Volume Oscillator
On-Balance Volume
Parabolic Time/Price
Point & Figure Chart
Positive Volume Index
Percent R
Percent Volume Change
Rate of Change
Relative Strength Index
Fast and Slow Stochastic
Rolling Sum
Spreads
Variable Moving Average
Volume Overlay/Underlay
Volume/Price Trend

For those who use MicroSoft® Windows®, there is an alternative package available from Omega Research (9200 Sunset Drive, Miami, FL 33173, 305-270-0174) called SuperCharts for Windows. This is an extremely impressive package for a very reasonable price that offers substantial flexibility. The same ability to conduct technical studies exists with the added advantage that you can cut and paste or move between applications within the Windows environment. SuperCharts is compatible with CRB InfoTech and can create very detailed charts and studies. In addition, Omega's System Writer program allows you to construct and test your own models.

Perhaps the "Granddaddy" of technical analysis software is the Compu-Trac® package available from Tim Slater (1017 Pleasant Street, New Orleans, LA 70115, 800-535-7990). This is the "original" PC-based charting and technical analysis software. Over the years, many modules have been added to enhance CompuTrac's ability to access data and conduct studies.

As mentioned in Chapter 8, you may be interested in applying neural network models to your trading. The VantagePoint software is available from Mendelsohn Enterprises (25941 Apple Blossom Lane, Wesley Chapel, FL 33544, 800-732-5407). This software has already been trained for specific markets. All that is required to run the models is current market data.

In Chapter 3, I reviewed the components of a time series. The seasonal and cyclical aspects of any commodity give you tools for filtering technical systems. This approach combines technical trading systems with seasonal correlation studies to determine whether the system performance is affected by seasonal changes in the underlying commodity. This is not the same as a seasonal study of the underlying commodity. Instead, it analyzes seasonal aspects of a technical system. Suppose a commodity exhibits a greater tendency to trend in the spring and fall. A "trend-following" technical system would be likely to perform well for this commodity during these two seasons while exhibiting poor performance in the summer and winter. This would be evident through a seasonal study of the system's performance. Logically, you would use the system more in the spring and fall while curbing trading in the summer and winter.

This becomes another tool for asset allocation as it relates to the studies of Dr. Amir Atiya and Ashraf Azmi. By measuring the consistency of a technical system's seasonal behavior, the probability of success or failure of any buy or sell signal can carry a "seasonal weight." These weights can be assigned using conventional statistical techniques or by applying a neural network. For the purpose of illustration, examine the performance of the COMMODEX® System for Treasury Bonds from 1982 through 1994. Figure 9-2 shows cumulative profits generated by COMMODEX with no assumption of starting capital. The graph illustrates an approximate four-year cycle which implies that long-term interest rates experience more consistent trends every other four years. Within the years, there are distinct seasonal patterns that imply that the spring and fall are more likely to experience consistent movements relative to winter and summer. Is it possible the four-year cycle is linked to U.S. presidential terms? Perhaps, but the reason behind the cycle is not required to successfully trade.

Understand that the study illustrated in Figure 9-2 is unique to the COMMODEX system. Another technical approach based upon nontrending market conditions might do better in the summer and winter and worse in the spring and fall. We are measuring the personality of the system rather than

Figure 9-2
Treasury Bonds (1982–1994)

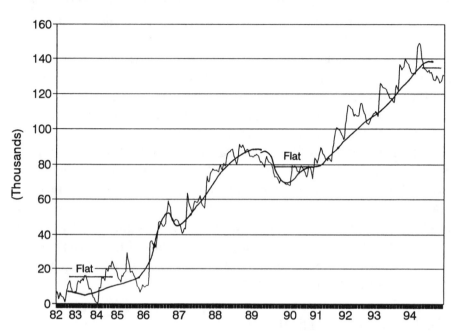

the market. (The COMMODEX System, 7000 Boulevard East, Guttenberg, NJ 07093, 201-868-2600.)

This "seasonal study" of a technical approach can be considered another form of TechnoFundamental analysis. The graphical representation of cyclical and seasonal patterns is a reversal of the applications explained in previous chapters because we are using a fundamental phenomenon to evaluate a technical method. Herein lies another exciting aspect of the new TechnoFundamental science. Consider the combinations of technical/fundamental and fundamental/technical studies that can be perfected. As recently as 1980, such studies were well beyond the reach of most individuals. The data were too difficult to compile and computing power was too expensive. In addition, many of the most exciting markets and instruments did not exist until the late 1970s and were not particularly liquid until the early 1980s.

While the title of this chapter is "Practical Applications," you should be concerned with "what is practical." Is it practical to follow a system that requires $100,000 in capital when you only have $25,000? Is it practical to track a method that requires minute-by-minute monitoring? Is it practical to conduct your own market studies? Is it practical to do your own trading? Practicality is increasingly a function of technology. Our information age is evolving investment strategies that are practical for almost anyone with discretionary funds.

Studies and products mentioned in this chapter have been tested in markets with highly positive results. Specific formulas may have been omitted, but the parameters have been explained with enough detail so that you can construct similar studies or use products. The diversity of applications is enormous. All it takes are resources and a desire to learn.

As demand for easily formatted data increases, it is likely Knight-Ridder and other information companies will make importing and exporting tables easier. With a little practice, you can become proficient at picking apart all types of documents to feed your analysis. There are even programs that conduct "key word searches" on text documents to automatically extract statistics like plantings, yields, exports, imports, and additional data that are easily identified. In the world of investing, information is power and powerful tools are strategic partners in the pursuit of profit.

The Toolbox of Statistical Analysis

These basic spreadsheets are building blocks for more complex TechnoFundamental analysis. Once you have a historical study, you can use it as input for other statistical analysis programs that may include regression, correlation, and probability studies.

Several neural network packages such as Ward System's NeuroShell for DOS or Windows and California Scientific Software's BRAINMAKER let you use spreadsheets as program inputs. This simplifies the process of searching for TechnoFundamental patterns that can be applied to successful trading.

It is important to provide any neural network study with sufficient data for proper training. As mentioned in the previous chapter, you may wish to include some human intuition as a filter for any system that is based upon fundamental correlations. This avoids errors associated with extraordinary conditions like the 1993 summer floods.

In addition, technical analysis should also be enlightened with human intervention. There is a point beyond which certain price action becomes practically impossible. Some technically based neural networks predicted a continuing downtrend in short-term U.S. interest rates toward the end of 1993. When the T-Bill rate sank below 2.8%, logic dictated the downside was limited. Given the economic environment, it was unlikely investors would pay the U.S. Treasury for the privilege of holding short-term debt.

Even if interest rates had declined further, room for profit was limited. However, a model based upon momentum patterns might not see an inevitable turn-around. Thus, tempering a system with common sense is prudent.

Admittedly, there are times when prices defy historical perspectives. Such was the case when silver fell below $5 an ounce and continued a free fall into the mid-$3 range. At $3, a case could be made that the worst a buyer could do would be to lose $3. Of course, the likelihood that silver would be dumped in the streets for free was (and remains) nil. Anyone with sufficient tenacity and deep pockets could have bought silver as it sank below $5. As long-term charts show, silver eventually recovered.

You may consider including in your system studies correlating USDA forecasts with actual outcomes to derive a level of confidence for government predictions. The latter could be compared with price action.

There is a saying, "Buy the rumor, sell the news." More often than not, rumors drive prices more than reality. An anticipatory reaction to a rainstorm or approaching hurricane can be more dramatic than the actual effect. There is more power in *anticipating* what the Federal Reserve will do, as opposed to trying to *react* correctly.

Thus, knowing how well forecasts correlate with reality gives you an edge. Does price react more to the forecast or the outcome? Your spreadsheets hold valuable answers. Demand can be studied in relation to price to determine market "elasticity"—the extent to which consumers become sensitive to higher or lower prices. This provides valuable insight into eventual reactions to increasing prices.

Is elasticity linear or exponential? Is there a consistent drop in demand when prices rise? Is the increase in demand as strong when prices decline? All of these questions set up a trading perspective and framework.

Previously, we defined tops and bottoms in relation to a trader's willingness to buy a higher high or sell a lower low. While we can see technical price, volume, and open interest patterns that conform to tops and bottoms, they are concurrent and may not provide enough time to efficiently trade.

If you isolate demand or supply reactions relative to price levels, you can predict probable tops and bottoms in advance. This sets the stage for more accurate technical evaluations. When price consolidations appear on a long-term chart, you can seek out fundamental supply and demand relationships that may have influenced or caused the formations. If supply and demand conditions remain consistent relative to consolidations, you have a leading indicator for market equilibrium.

In addition, there is a lead time associated with supply and demand reactions to price. Obviously, increasing prices do not instantly translate into falling demand just as rising prices will not immediately induce capacity expansion. If the lead time between action and reaction is consistent, you can build a trading model around the reaction times.

In some cases, lead time can be six months or more. The assumption is that you intend to trade over the long run and are willing to wait for trends to materialize.

In 1987, 1989, and 1990, copper prices reached $1.40 per pound before encountering resistance. The exception was during the last quarter of 1988 and first quarter of 1989 when prices reached $1.65. However, there appeared to be an approximate six-month cycle between reaching market resistance and hitting a consolidation bottom. Each time, the cycle low was below $1.00.

This suggests that copper is too expensive at approximately $1.40 or overproduction is encouraged at such attractive levels. There is a three month lead between the time prices reach resistance and the increase in output by copper producers. Whether observed cyclical patterns are measured logically or using a computer model, desired results are the same. You want to have reliable information for making a profit.

The August 12, 1994 *Wall Street Journal* reported:

Midwest Bumper Crop Exceeds Forecast; Impact on Economy Is Likely to Be Mixed. The USDA said it expects corn farmers to harvest 9.21 billion bushels, up 45% from last year, when excessive rain and record floods limited the harvest to 6.34 billion bushels.

. . . Based on Aug. 1 conditions, U.S. soybean growers are expected to harvest 2.28 billion bushels. The forecast is up 6% from July and 26% bigger than last year's actual harvest.

From this information, you can transform statistics backward into yield-per-acre. Was 1994 becoming an extraordinary year? From the implied yield, which of the scenarios portrayed in your spreadsheet is on track?

If you study yields over the past several years, you will notice an uptrend. New seed and farming techniques account for a steady increase. New chemical treatments and biotechnology could boost yields in corn, soybeans, and wheat by 25% within the next 10 years.

This is an important perspective. Even if planted acreage remains static or declines slightly, overall production will rise. Is the projected increase in line with anticipated demand? Have you examined consumption trends? Is consumption rising, flat, or declining? What is the slope of the consumption line relative to demand? By now, you should recognize these questions as basics of TechnoFundamental analysis. You are examining fundamentals as you would technically evaluate price action. You are attempting to identify trends, tops, bottoms, and reversal points.

Why must you conduct these exercises? After all, with all of the news and advisory services available, someone should already have this type of analysis. As a practical matter, there is no substitute for hands-on experience. You become familiar with the market on a personal level.

You may be using objective programs. However, your trading discipline is likely to be a function of your confidence. Further, many of the self-professed experts who publish advisory services form their opinions using far less analysis than described in this chapter.

Finally, various information sources frequently have hidden agendas. As proof, examine literature published by the Silver Institute, U.S. Mint, and other groups selling precious metals. You will find their information is consistently bullish.

Of course gold has been a monetary standard for centuries, but this does not mean the prices cannot decline. Silver has also been used as coinage. This does not mean silver will always have a high value, however.

For some reason, you will always see projections for deficits in production and surging demand. Your own analysis will test such authoritative sources against reality. Anyone can speculate about what might happen. Using TechnoFundamentals assures a more factual and less emotional structure for making trading decisions. This is not to say that you should not consider advisory services or technical trading systems to supplement your work. Simply keep in mind that you have the ability to determine the validity of someone's analysis by referring to your own TechnoFundamentals.

CHAPTER **10**

SYNTHETIC INVESTING

Investment theory and practice are rapidly changing. If you look back upon the recent "Industrial Age," you will see that investing involved "capital formation." As used here, capital is defined as the means for production and is associated with plant and equipment. You invested in a gold mine or a railroad. Your investment produced tangible products or services that had associated costs, market values, and profit margins. An investor could judge the efficacy of an investment by assessing the product or service relative to alternatives or competitive entities. Life was simple.

In contrast, investing is a process of creation as much as it is a funding of processes. Opportunities are literally created out of paper with less and less of a link to tangible products or services. In effect, investing is "synthesized." This process is alluded to in previous chapters covering combinations of futures and cash instruments to create "synthetic" transactions. However, it is important to end this text with a view of the future and a proper perspective about how the subject matter will apply in coming years. After all, if the investment process continues migrating away from physical reality and more toward synthetic transactions, the study of fundamentals may become extinct. Instead, you might concentrate on the combinations and permutations of option premiums relative to volatility in conjunction with futures and without regard to the underlying commodity or financial instrument.

Consider the following example. You wish to convert a 30-year U.S. Treasury bond into a 90-day instrument. It is December 31. You decide to buy

Treasury bonds and sell corresponding March T-Bond futures against your position. This hedge prevents you from losing if interest rates rise. Assuming you have selected the right cash bonds, you can deliver your instruments upon the expiration of the March futures. The result is a synthetic conversion of the bonds into 90-day instruments. (See Figure 10-1.)

The effectiveness of this transaction depends upon how the futures pricing correlates to the actual bonds. You must make sure you understand the pricing mechanism behind the futures. Figure 10-2, at the end of this chapter, is a series of tables published by the Chicago Board of Trade that provides conversion factors for their financial contracts along with a relevant calendar. This type of information is regularly produced by the exchanges, brokerage houses, and research companies. Using spreadsheets, you can create a program for pricing cash instruments relative to futures for creating synthetic instruments. This is a very simple form of "derivative." The transaction is "derived from" the combination of cash and futures. However, since you are creating the transaction and it is not transferable within an organized market or through a recognized broker/dealer, it is not considered a true "derivative." Yet, the concepts are similar.

Figure 10-1

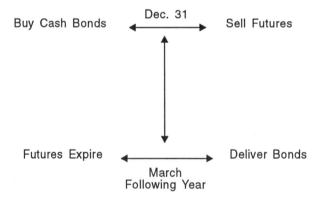

Derivatives are packaged transactions that are sold as complete instruments. There is an aftermarket and derivatives have calculated values based upon the series of transactions that comprise the final obligation. The concern over derivatives is their lack of substance. You end up investing in conceptual relationships backed by contractual obligations. These transactions are truly synthesized. You can see that regardless of debacles in the early and mid-1990s, financial institutions are evolving derivatives at an increasing rate. As organized exchanges provide more futures and options on different commodities and financial instruments, the potential for designing increasingly complex synthetic investments will mushroom.

As mentioned earlier, the introduction of financial instruments has already structurally changed markets. Gold may not be as effective a hedge against inflation as a cross-currency hedge or a T-Bond futures position. The new instruments provide strategies for side-stepping many of the risks associated with rising and falling interest rates, inflation, deflation, and a host of possible evils. As long as there is faith in paper or electronic currency, why invest in gold? In fact, the profit potential of paper may be far greater than any physical product or service. While goods and services will always drive the economy, they may fade as the focal point of investing. Thus, you may be forced to evaluate contractual relationships inherent in a synthetic or derivative transaction rather than the fundamentals associated with supply and demand for an underlying commodity.

For me, this is a distressing development. It is not simply because the fundamental analyst may be destined for extinction, it is because investors may be headed toward disaster. Synthetic transactions are based upon information. Information is only as good as its accuracy. Information is subject to great manipulation. As an example, consider that a majority of business relationships are contractually linked to government indices like the Consumer Price Index (CPI). Labor contracts frequently link wage escalations to the CPI. Business real estate leases are tied to the CPI. Cost of living increases and benefits programs often have a CPI link. Therefore, there is little wonder why so many people held their breath when Federal Reserve Chairman Alan Greenspan suggested to the 1994 Congress that the calculation of the CPI should be changed to reflect a lower inflation rate. Mr. Greenspan stated that the Federal Government and states could save millions or even billions with a simple change in the CPI calculation. By the same token, the performance under every contract linked to the CPI would be changed. These are relationships based upon information.

Social structures are challenged when trust is violated. The move toward investing in transactions that are based upon information exposes the world to unprecedented dangers. Who will control the information? How safe is the information? Who will have access to the information? What will happen if we lose faith in the information? You may believe these questions are beyond the study of TechnoFundamental analysis. Yet, they raise important points about the approach you may be forced to take to protect your wealth in the years ahead. Simply knowing that a change in the CPI will impact rents, wages, and even the cost of some commodities is essential for planning. You may not use such information to invest, but you may want to include a clause in any contract you have that makes sure pricing standards cannot be altered by a change in a statistic.

I believe the evolution of synthetic investing is likely to lead to a revolution back to tangible investing. It may take a meltdown of the information-based investment structure, or it will be a natural progression back to basics. Security agencies around the world are bracing for the ultimate threat to the integrity of "the system." Computer thieves known as "hackers" have had remarkable success breaking into secured financial systems of banks, brokerage houses, and government agencies. They are able to do everything from creating fictitious people to fake credit cards. A breach of the Federal Reserve system or even the falsification of government information could easily bring world economies to their knees.

I am not saying this as an alarmist. It is simply an observation that relates to investment practices. Should you invest synthetically, or should you concentrate upon tangible relationships? Answering is not easy in light of the exciting returns that can become available from synthetic transactions. After all, gold's net performance from 1980 through 1994 was far from stellar. Writing gold call options provided more substantial profit opportunities. The key is to control your own fate. If you are constructing the synthetic investment based upon your own analysis, you are able to assess your exposure, risk, and progress. If you are given a packaged derivative, you must seek to understand the relationships upon which the instrument is based.

Huge losses in derivatives that were experienced by "sophisticated investors" during 1994 were the result of a lack of understanding and flawed market analysis. The Federal Reserve raised interest rates more rapidly during

1994 than during any other previous period. Like the summer floods across the Midwest in 1993, the speed of interest rate hikes was beyond the realm of assumed probability. Investors became complacent in their belief that rates were down and would stay down. Just a small application of TechnoFundamental analysis would have revealed that government debt had been restructured and, at the very least, short-term rates would not decline further after the second quarter, 1994. The demand for funds was rising and the supply was being controlled through monetary policy.

Remarkably, in this information age, what you hear is not necessarily what you get. Statistics are constantly revised up or down by more than a third . . . sometimes by more than 100%! Statistical philosophy clashes with statistical reality. Nothing made this more apparent than President Clinton's State of the Union Address in January 1995. As he stood before the new Republican controlled Congress, President Clinton boasted about the creation of six million new jobs since he took office. He emphasized the need to create more new jobs and to support programs that would lift people off welfare and place them in productive positions. There was talk about tax relief for the lower and middle income wage earners and tax credits for education. Within the very same week of President Clinton's address, Federal Reserve Chairman Alan Greenspan testified before Congress about his concerns that an unemployment rate of 5.4% was too low and could lead to inflation. Greenspan talked about raising interest rates to slow the economy and, effectively, push people out of work. Ah, the difference between politics and reality!

Creating jobs may sound like an appropriate government endeavor, but not at the expense of inflation. Therefore, what we hear is not often what we should expect. Even the stock market changed attitude so that good economic news was bad and bad news was good. The speed of change literally makes "what's hot today is not tomorrow." Just before President Clinton's 1995 State of the Union, the Mexican Peso had lost more than 40% of its value against the U.S. Dollar. Those who bought the promise of an "emerging market" in Mexico were faced with submerging investment values and almost no way out. Only the assurance that aid would come kept the spirit of investment alive in the face of such calamity.

Within the same time frame, a devastating earthquake shook the Japanese city of Kobe to the ground. Initial damage estimates exceeded $40 billion. Within a week, the Japanese stock market plunged in response to the presumed financial requirements for rebuilding. Other world markets followed.

Could fundamentals have helped avoid financial ruin? The fact is that negative market reactions have followed natural disasters from hurricanes to floods and even fires. Rebuilding requires shifting capital. Funds come from liquidating investments. By observing past patterns, you can forecast the timing and extent of market reactions to disasters.

As we move into the twenty-first century, we know that life will not be the same. Technology is on an exponential fast track and every aspect of living is being altered in some fashion. From virtual reality to reality, investors must sort out an increasingly complex picture that has "gone global" within two decades. There are some who claim markets have lost their reason and a return to basics is essential for financial survival. But, with all the change, certain fundamental facts will endure. Humans must eat. Humans need shelter. Humans will forever produce products and services. With this in mind, we know some things will always have value. Unless and until we evolve to the point where nourishment, shelter, clothing, mobility, and energy are no longer essential, we have things worth our investment.

There are many lessons covered in this text. If you finish these chapters with only the concept that you must know what you are trading, you will have gained value. The simple process of associating a trading vehicle with its fundamental roots can be the key to successful investing. How many pounds are in a bushel of soybeans? At least now you should know.

Figure 10-2
Conversion Factors

T-Bonds (Eligible for Delivery October 1, 1993)

Coupon Maturity		Amount ($ Blns)	Sep 93	Dec 93	Mar 94	Jun 94	Sep 94	Dec 94
1. *6¼	Aug 15, 2023	11.0	0.8023	0.8029	0.8032	0.8037	0.8040	0.8056
2. 7⅛	Feb 15, 2023	7.30	0.9015	0.9019	0.9019	0.9023	0.9024	0.9028
3. 7⅛	Feb 15, 2023	8.26	0.9015	0.9019	0.9019	0.9023	0.9024	0.9028
4. 7¼	May 15, 2016	18.82	0.9223	0.9224	0.9229	0.9231	0.9236	0.9238
5. 7¼	Aug 15, 9022	10.01	0.9159	0.9163	0.9163	0.9167	0.9167	0.9171
6. 7½	Nov 15, 2016	18.86	0.9478	0.9478	0.9482	0.8482	0.9486	0.9487
7. 7⅝	Nov 15, 2022	10.30	0.9579	0.9579	0.9581	0.9580	0.9583	0.9583
8. 7⅞	Feb 15, 2021	11.01	0.9860	0.9863	0.9861	0.9863	0.9862	0.9864
9. 8	Nov 15, 2021	32.33	1.0000	0.9998	1.0000	0.9998	1.0000	0.9998
10. 8⅛	May 15, 2021	11.75	1.0138	1.0136	1.0137	1.0135	1.0137	1.0134
11. 8⅛	Aug 15, 2021	12.01	1.0137	1.0138	1.0136	1.0137	1.0135	1.0137
12. 8⅛	Aug 15, 2019	20.01	1.0134	1.0135	1.0133	1.0134	1.0132	1.0133
13. 8½	Feb 15, 2020	10.06	1.0543	1.0544	1.0540	1.0540	1.0537	1.0537
14. 8¾	May 15, 2017	18.19	1.0789	1.0784	1.0783	1.0778	1.0777	1.0772
15. 8¾	May 15, 2020	10.01	1.0820	1.0816	1.0816	1.0811	1.0811	1.0806
16. 8¾	Aug 15, 2020	21.01	1.0820	1.0820	1.0816	1.0816	1.0811	1.0811
17. 8⅞	Aug 15, 2017	14.02	1.0922	1.0921	1.0915	1.0914	1.0908	1.0907
18. 8⅞	Feb 15, 2109	19.25	1.0941	1.0940	1.0935	1.0934	1.0928	1.0927
19. 9	Nov 15, 2018	9.03	1.1074	1.1068	1.1067	1.1061	1.1060	1.1054
20. 9⅛	May 15, 2018	8.71	1.1200	1.1194	1.1192	1.1186	1.1184	1.1177
21. 9¼	Feb 15, 2016	7.27	1.1287	1.1284	1.1277	1.1273	1.1265	1.1262
22. 9⅞	Nov 15, 2015	6.90	1.1926	1.1916	1.1910	1.1899	1.1892	1.1881
23. 10⅝	Aug 15, 2015	7.15	1.2683	1.2674	1.2659	1.2649	1.2634	1.2624
24. 11¼	Feb 15, 2015	12.67	1.3293	1.3280	1.3262	1.3249	1.3230	1.3216

Total eligible for delivery $334.08 billion   *Most recently auctioned 30-yr. T-bond eligible for delivery

Figure 10-2 (Continued)
Conversion Factors

10-Year T-Notes (Eligible for Delivery October 1, 1993)

Coupon Maturity		Amount ($ Blns)	Sep 93	Dec 93	Mar 94	Jun 94	Sep 94	Dec 94
1. **5½	Apr 15, 2000	18.80	0.8752	—	—	—	—	—
2. *5¾	Aug 15, 2003	11.03	0.8495	0.8522	0.8547	0.8576	0.8607	0.8631
3. *6¼	Feb 15, 2003	10.75	0.8870	0.8892	0.8912	0.8936	0.8956	0.8980
4. 6⅜	Aug 15, 2002	22.34	0.8990	0.9012	0.9031	0.9053	0.9073	0.9097
5. 7½	Nov 15, 2001	24.23	0.9709	0.9713	0.9722	0.9727	0.9736	0.9741
6. 7½	May 15, 2002	11.07	0.9696	0.9700	0.9709	0.9713	0.9722	0.9727
7. 7¾	Feb 15, 2001	11.01	0.9863	0.9868	0.9870	0.9875	—	—
8. 7⅞	Aug 15, 2001	12.01	0.9927	0.9931	0.9930	0.9934	0.9934	0.9938
9. 8	May 15, 2001	12.40	1.0000	0.9998	1.0000	0.9998	1.0000	—
10. 8½	Nov 15, 2000	11.07	1.0264	1.0255	1.0250	—	—	—
11. 8¾	Aug 15, 2000	10.50	1.0383	1.0374	—	—	—	—
12. 8⅞	May 15, 2000	10.03	1.0437	—	—	—	—	—

Total eligible for delivery $165.25 billion   *Most recently auctioned 10-yr. T-note eligible for delivery
**Most recently auctioned 7-yr. T-note eligible for delivery

5-Year T-Notes (Eligible for Delivery October 1, 1993)

Coupon Maturity		Amount ($ Blns)	Sep 93	Dec 93	Mar 94
1. 6	Dec 31, 1997	11.26	0.9290	—	—
2. 5⅝	Jan 31, 1998	11.50	0.9143	—	—
3. 5⅛	Feb 28, 1998	11.00	0.8947	—	—
4. 5¼	Jul 31, 1998	11.02	0.8914	0.8961	0.9008
5. 5⅛	Mar 31, 1998	11.01	0.8931	0.8980	—
6. 5⅛	Apr 30, 1998	11.02	0.8914	0.8963	—
7. 5⅜	May 31, 1998	11.03	0.8993	0.9039	—

Total eligible for delivery $110.87 billion   *Most recently auctioned 5-yr. T-note eligible for delivery

Figure 10-2 (Continued)
Conversion Factors

2-Year T-Notes (Eligible for Delivery October 1, 1993)

Coupon Maturity		Amount ($ Blns)	Sep 93	Dec 93	Mar 94	Jun 94	Sep 94
1. *3⅞	Sep 30, 1995	16.02	—	0.9338	—	—	—
2. 3⅞	Aug 31, 1995	16.09	0.9280	—	—	—	—
3. 4⅛	Jun 30, 1995	16.00	0.9378	—	—	—	—
4. 4¼	Jul 31, 1995	16.00	0.9371	—	—	—	—
5. 8½	Aug 15, 1995	8.88	1.0086	—	—	—	—
6. 4⅝	Aug 15, 1995	18.00	0.9410	—	—	—	—
7. 8½	Nov 15, 1995	9.02	—	1.0086	—	—	—
8. 5⅛	Nov 15, 1995	15.56	—	0.9498	—	—	—
9. 4⅝	Feb 15, 1996	15.65	—	—	0.9410	—	—
10. 4⅜	Aug 15, 1996	16.67	—	—	—	—	0.9367
11. 7⅞	Feb 15, 1996	9.06	—	—	0.9977	—	—

Total eligible for delivery $212.20 billion   * Most recently auctioned 2-yr. T-note eligible for delivery

CBOT Financial Calendar

T-Bond and T-Note Futures

Contract Month	First Position	First Notice	First Delivery	Last Trading	Last Delivery
DEC	Nov 29	Nov 30	Dec 1	Dec 21	Dec 31
MAR 94	Feb 25	Feb 28	Mar 1	Mar 22	Mar 31
JUN	May 27	May 31	Jun 1	Jun 21	Jun 30
SEP	Aug 30	Aug 31	Sep 1	Sep 21	Sep 30

2-Year T-Note Futures

Contract Month	First Position	First Notice	First Delivery	Last Trading	Last Notice	Last Delivery
MAR 94	Feb 25	Feb 28	Mar 1	Mar 29	Mar 30	Apr 4
JUN	May 27	May 31	Jun 1	Jun 28	Jun 29	Jul 1
SEP	Aug 30	Aug 31	Sep 1	Sep 28	Sep 29	Oct 3
DEC	Nov 29	Nov 30	Dec 1	Dec 29	Dec 29	Jan 4, 1995

Figure 10-2 (Continued)
Conversion Factors

T-Bond and T-Note Options				Muni Bond Index Futures and Options		30-Day Interest Rate Futures	
Contract Month	First Trading	Last Trading	Expiration Day	Contract Month	Last Trading	Contract Month	Last Trading
DEC	—	Nov 19	Nov 20	DEC	Dec 20	NOV	Nov 30
JAN 94	Nov 15	Dec 17	Dec 18	MAR 94	Mar 22	DEC	Dec 30
FEB	Dec 13	Jan 21	Jan 22	JUN	Jun 21	JAN 94	Jan 31
MAR	—	Feb 18	Feb 19	SEP	Sep 21	FEB	Feb 28

Deliveries for Sep 1993 Treasuries

T-Bonds

Sep	Total Del	$11\frac{3}{4}$ 11/2014	$9\frac{7}{8}$ 11/2015	$8\frac{7}{8}$ 2/2019	$13\frac{1}{4}$ 5/2014	$12\frac{1}{2}$ 8/2014	$11\frac{3}{4}$ 11/2014	$11\frac{1}{4}$ 2/2015	$7\frac{1}{4}$ 5/2016	$7\frac{5}{8}$ 11/2022
24	5	1	1	3	—	—	—	—	—	—
29	—	—	—	—	—	—	—	—	—	—
30	31038	—	—	—	711	6094	20540	3690	1	2
Total	31043	1	1	3	711	6094	20540	3690	1	2

	10-Yr. Notes			5-Yr. T-Notes			2-Yr. T-Notes	
Sep	Total Del	$8\frac{7}{8}$ 5/2000	$8\frac{7}{8}$ 5/2000	Total Del	6 12/1997	6 12/1997	Total Del	$4\frac{1}{8}$ 6/1995
24	—	—	—	—	—	—	—	—
29	25	25	—	60	60	—	—	—
30	7809	—	7809	1153	—	1153	1189	1189
Total	7834	25	7809	1213	60	1153	1189	1189

Appendix A

KNIGHT-RIDDER INFOTECH™ PRICE DATA

The following is a listing of price data available on the CRB-InfoTech™ CD-ROM.§

KR-CRB / Commodity Indices

Futures/Cash Description	Futures Exchange	Futures Start Date	Cash Basis	Cash Start Date
KR-CRB Currency Sub-Index (1977)			KRF	09/25/79*
KR-CRB Energy Sub-Index (1967)			KRF	05/01/85*
KR-CRB Energy Sub-Index (1977)			KRF	09/01/83*
KR-CRB (BLS) Fats & Oils Sub-Index			KRF	01/07/47*
KR-CRB (BLS) Foodstuffs Sub-Index			KRF	01/07/47*
KR-CRB Futures Price Index	NYFE	06/12/86	KRF	09/04/56*
KR-CRB Grains Sub-Index			KRF	09/23/71*
KR-CRB Imported Sub-Index			KRF	09/23/71*
KR-CRB Industrials Sub-Index			KRF	09/23/71*
KR-CRB Interest Rates Sub-Index (1977)			KRF	01/02/84*
KR-CRB Livestock & Meats Sub-Index			KRF	09/23/71*
KR-CRB (BLS) Livestock Sub-Index			KRF	01/07/47*

---

§ Text of table supplied on disk by Knight-Ridder CRB-InfoTech™.
* Futures volume and open interest not included.
+ Closing values only.

Futures/Cash Description	Futures Exchange	Futures Start Date	Cash Basis	Cash Start Date
KR-CRB (BLS) Metals Sub-Index			KRF	01/07/47*
KR-CRB Oilseeds Sub-Index			KRF	09/23/71*
KR-CRB Precious Metals Sub-Index			KRF	01/17/75*
KR-CRB (BLS) Raw Industrials Sub-Index			KRF	01/07/47*
KR-CRB (BLS) Spot Price Index			KRF	01/07/47*
KR-CRB (BLS) Textiles Sub-Index			KRF	01/07/47*
KR-CRB Miscellaneous Sub-Index			KRF	10/03/86*
FOSFA International Edible Oils Index	CBOT	09/23/94	CBOT	10/01/87*
Dow Jones Futures Index			WSJ	01/03/33*
Dow Jones Spot Index			WSJ	01/03/50*
Goldman Sachs Nearby Index	IOM	07/28/92	IOM	01/02/70*
GSCI Agricultural Sub-Index			IOM	12/31/69*
GSCI Energy Sub-Index			IOM	12/31/82*
GSCI Industrial Metals Sub-Index			IOM	12/31/76*
GSCI Livestock Sub-Index			IOM	01/01/70*
GSCI Precious Metals Sub-Index			IOM	01/01/73*
GSCI Total Return Index			IOM	03/31/94*
JOC Industrial Price Index			JOC	01/02/85*
JOC Metals Index			JOC	01/02/85*
JOC Textiles Index			JOC	01/02/85*
JOC Miscellaneous Index			JOC	01/02/85*
JOC Crude Oil & Benzene Index			JOC	01/02/85*
Reuters United Kingdom Index			WSJ	11/17/59*

Currencies

Futures/Cash Description	Futures Exchange	Futures Start Date	Cash Basis	Cash Start Date
Australian Dollar / Japanese Yen			24-HR KRF	05/23/88
Australian Dollar / New Zealand Dollar			24-HR KRF	08/08/89
Australian Dollar / U.S. Dollar	IMM	01/13/87	24-HR KRF	01/04/82*
Australian Dollar / U.S. Dollar	MIDAM	01/06/95		
British Pound / Japanese Yen			24-HR KRF	05/23/88
British Pound, Rolling Spot	IMM	06/15/93		
British Pound / Swiss Franc			24-HR KRF	05/23/88
British Pound / U.S. Dollar	FINEX	12/09/94		
British Pound / U.S. Dollar	IMM	05/16/72	24-HR KRF	04/03/72*

---

* Futures volume and open interest not included.
+ Closing values only.

Futures/Cash Description	Futures Exchange	Futures Start Date	Cash Basis	Cash Start Date
British Pound / U.S. Dollar	MIDAM	01/02/86		
British Pound / U.S. Dollar	SIMEX	07/06/92		
Canadian Dollar / Japanese Yen			24-HR KRF	06/02/88
Canadian Dollar / U.S. Dollar	IMM	05/16/72	24-HR KRF	03/30/72*
Canadian Dollar / U.S. Dollar	MIDAM	01/02/86		
Deutsche Mark / British Pound	FINEX	06/17/94	24-HR KRF	05/23/88*
Deutsche Mark / French Franc	FINEX	06/17/94	24-HR KRF	06/30/89
Deutsche Mark / Italian Lira	FINEX	08/08/94	24-HR KRF	06/08/89
Deutsche Mark / Japanese Yen	IMM	02/26/92	24-HR KRF	05/23/88
Deutsche Mark / Japanese Yen	FINEX	07/13/94		
Deutsche Mark, Rolling Spot	IMM	09/14/93		
Deutsche Mark / Swedish Krona			24-HR KRF	03/08/93
Deutsche Mark / Swiss Franc			24-HR KRF	06/15/88
Deutsche Mark Forward	IMM	09/12/94		
Deutsche Mark / Spanish Peseta	MEFF RF	09/91–06/93+	24-HR KRF	12/04/92
Deutsche Mark / U.S. Dollar	IMM	05/16/72	24-HR KRF	03/30/72*
Deutsche Mark / U.S. Dollar	FINEX	06/17/94		
Deutsche Mark / U.S. Dollar	MIDAM	01/02/86		
Deutsche Mark / U.S. Dollar	SIMEX	07/06/92		
ECU (European Currency Unit)	FINEX	01/86–03/94*	24-HR KRF	01/05/79*
French Franc / U.S. Dollar	IMM	12/30/74*	24-HR KRF	08/22/74*
Japanese Yen, Forward	IMM	01/17/95		
Japanese Yen, Rolling Spot	IMM	01/17/95		
Japanese Yen / U.S. Dollar	FINEX	12/09/94		
Japanese Yen / U.S. Dollar	IMM	05/16/72	24-HR KRF	03/30/72*
Japanese Yen / U.S. Dollar	MIDAM	01/02/86		
Japanese Yen / U.S. Dollar	SIMEX	07/06/92		
New Zealand Dollar / U.S. Dollar			24-HR KRF	08/03/87
Swiss Franc / Japanese Yen			24-HR KRF	05/23/88
Swiss Franc / U.S. Dollar	FINEX	12/09/94		
Swiss Franc / U.S. Dollar	IMM	05/16/72	24-HR KRF	03/30/72*
Swiss Franc / U.S. Dollar	MIDAM	01/02/86		
U.S. Dollar / Austrian Schilling			24-HR KRF	03/04/92*
U.S. Dollar / Belgian Franc			24-HR KRF	05/23/88*
U.S. Dollar / Canadian Dollar			24-HR KRF	03/30/72*
U.S. Dollar / Danish Kroner			24-HR KRF	05/23/88*
U.S. Dollar / Deutsche Mark			24-HR KRF	03/30/72*

---

* Futures volume and open interest not included.
+ Closing values only.

Futures/Cash Description	Futures Exchange	Futures Start Date	Cash Basis	Cash Start Date
U.S. Dollar/Deutsche Mark, Deferred Spot	SIMEX	11/01/93		
U.S. Dollar / Finnish Markka			24-HR KRF	03/04/92*
U.S. Dollar / French Franc			24-HR KRF	08/22/74*
U.S. Dollar / Greek Drachma			24-HR KRF	03/04/92*
U.S. Dollar / Hong Kong Dollar			24-HR KRF	05/23/88
U.S. Dollar / Irish Punt			24-HR KRF	04/07/92
U.S. Dollar / Italian Lira			24-HR KRF	05/23/88
U.S. Dollar / Japanese Yen			24-HR KRF	03/30/72
U.S. Dollar / Japanese Yen	TIFFE	08/24/93+		
U.S. Dollar / Japanese Yen, Deferred Spot	SIMEX	11/01/93		
U.S. Dollar / Malaysian Ringgit			24-HR KRF	03/04/92
U.S. Dollar / Mexican Peso			24-HR KRF	07/11/94
U.S. Dollar / Netherlands Guilder			24-HR KRF	05/23/88*
U.S. Dollar / Norwegian Krone			24-HR KRF	05/24/88
U.S. Dollar / Portuguese Escudo			24-HR KRF	03/03/92
U.S. Dollar / Singapore Dollar			24-HR KRF	05/23/88
U.S. Dollar / South African Rand Financial			Barclays	09/08/94
U.S. Dollar / Spanish Peseta			24-HR KRF	10/14/91
U.S. Dollar / Swedish Krona			24-HR KRF	03/05/92
U.S. Dollar / Swiss Franc			24-HR KRF	03/30/72*
U.S. Dollar Index	FINEX	11/20/85	24-HR KRF	01/04/71*

Energy

Futures/Cash Description	Futures Exchange	Futures Start Date	Cash Basis	Cash Start Date
Butane			Mt. Belvieu, TX	09/03/91*
Crude Oil / Arab Light, European			Free Market	09/28/78*
Crude Oil / Global Spot	IPE	07/24/89	KRF	10/01/85*
Crude Oil / Global Spot	NYMEX	03/30/83	KRF	01/03/77*
Crude Oil / Sour, Midland, TX	NYMEX	02/92–11/92*	West Texas	05/06/91*
Diesel Fuel / .05 S. Low Sulphur			New York	10/29/93*
DuBai Crude Oil / Global Spot			KRF	06/08/92
Gasoline, Unleaded Gulf Coast		11/94–1/95*	New York	11/08/94*
Gasoline, Unleaded Premium Non-Oxy			New York	09/29/89*
Gasoline, Unleaded Premium Oxy			New York	10/05/94*

---

* Futures volume and open interest not included.
+ Closing values only.

Futures/Cash Description	Futures Exchange	Futures Start Date	Cash Basis	Cash Start Date
Gasoline / Unleaded Regular Non-Oxy	NYMEX	12/03/84	New York	09/28/78*
Gasoline / Unleaded Regular Oxy			New York	10/05/94*
Gasoline, Unleaded	IPE	01/27/92		
Gas-Oil-Petroleum	IPE	06/03/86		
Heating Oil #2 / Fuel Oil	NYMEX	11/14/78	New York	09/27/78*
High Sulphur Fuel Oil	SIMEX	08/14/90		
Propane	NYMEX	08/21/87	Mt. Belvieu, TX	01/10/83*
Natural Gas	NYMEX	04/04/90		10/29/93*

Financial Instruments

Futures/Cash Description	Futures Exchange	Futures Start Date	Cash Basis	Cash Start Date
Bank Accepted Bills	NZFOE	01/26/94		
Bank Accepted Bills	SFE	01/02/80		
Canadian Bankers Acceptance, 1-Month	ME	12/16/92+		
Canadian Bankers Acceptance, 3-Month	ME	04/22/88		
Canadian Government Bond, 5-Year	ME	01/19/95		
Canadian Government Bond, 10-Year	CBOT	04/08/94		
Canadian Government Bond, 10-Year	ME	03/29/90		
Catastrophe Insurance, Eastern	CBOT	12/11/92		
Catastrophe Insurance, Midwest	CBOT	05/11/93		
Catastrophe Insurance, National	CBOT	12/11/92		
Catastrophe Insurance, Western	CBOT	02/25/94		
Catastrophe Insurance, Western Annual	CBOT	04/15/94		
Commercial Paper, 30-Day			WSJ	01/02/76*
Commercial Paper, 60-Day			WSJ	06/01/93*
Commercial Paper, 90-Day			WSJ	06/01/93*
Certificate of Deposit, 3-Month			New York	10/23/84*
Certificate of Deposit, 6-Month			New York	10/23/84*
Certificate of Deposit, 1-Year			New York	10/23/84*
Discount Rate			Federal Reserve	01/02/76*
ECU, Long Bond	MATIF	10/18/90		
ECU, 3-Month	LIFFE	10/27/89		

---

* Futures volume and open interest not included.
+ Closing values only.

Futures/Cash Description	Futures Exchange	Futures Start Date	Cash Basis	Cash Start Date
Eurodollar, 3-Month	IMM	12/09/81	Garvin-Guybutler	12/15/92*
Eurodollar, 3-Month	LIFFE	09/30/82		
Eurodollar, 3-Month	MIDAM	08/21/92		
Eurodollar, 3-Month	SIMEX	11/03/89		
Eurodollar, 1-Year Mid-Curve options	IMM			
Eurodollar, 2-Year Mid-Curve options	IMM			
Euro Lira, 3-Month	LIFFE	05/12/92		
Euromark Rate, 3-Month	LIFFE	04/20/89		
Euromark, 3-Month	IMM	04/26/93		
Euromark, 3-Month	SIMEX	09/20/90		
Euroswiss, 3-Month	LIFFE	02/07/91		
Euro Yen, 3-Month	SIMEX	10/30/89		
Euro Yen, 3-Month	TIFFE	02/12/90+		
Euro Yen, 1-Year	TIFFE	07/14/92+		
Federal Funds / 30-Day	CBOT	10/06/88	Federal Reserve	03/20/89*
Federal Funds, Overnight			Garvin-Guybutler	03/31/89*
FIBOR	DTB	03/18/94		
German Bond, (Bund)	DTB	12/03/90+		
German Bond, (Bund)	LIFFE	09/29/88		
German Bond, Long-Term (BOXL)	DTB	03/11/94		
German Bond, Medium-Term (BOBL)	DTB	03/09/92		
German Bond, Medium-Term (BOBL)	LIFFE	01/23/93		
Gilt, Long	LIFFE	11/18/82		
HIBOR, 3-Month	HKFE	12/16/91+		
Italian Government Bond (BTP), 10-Year	LIFFE	09/19/91		
Italian Long Bond	MIF	09/11/92+		
Italian 3–5 Year BTP	MIF	12/14/92+		
LIBOR, 1-Month	IMM	04/05/90		
LIBOR, Overnight			BBA	08/04/86*
LIBOR, 1-Week			BBA	10/22/90*
LIBOR, 1-Month			BBA	06/13/88*
LIBOR, 2-Month			BBA	10/22/90*
LIBOR, 3-Month			BBA	06/13/88*
LIBOR, 6-Month			BBA	06/13/88*

---

* Futures volume and open interest not included.
+ Closing values only.

Futures/Cash Description	Futures Exchange	Futures Start Date	Cash Basis	Cash Start Date
LIBOR, 9-Month			BBA	10/22/90*
LIBOR, 1-Year			BBA	10/22/90*
MIBOR '90	MEFF RF	10/22/90+		
MIBOR, 360-Day	MEFF RF	10/01/93+		
Muni-Bond Index	CBOT	06/11/85	CBOT	01/02/85*
Notional Bond, 10-Year	MATIF	02/20/86	Banque Paribas	01/24/90*
Notional Bond, 3-Year	MEFF RF	03/16/90+		
Notional Bond, 10-Year	MEFF RF	04/10/92+		
PIBOR, 3-Month	MATIF	09/08/88		
Prime Rate			WSJ	01/02/76*
Short Sterling, 3-Month	LIFFE	11/04/82		
Swiss Bonds	SOFFEX	08/24/93+		
Treasury Bill, U.S., 3-Month	IMM	01/06/76	on-the-run coupon	04/29/86*
Treasury Bill, U.S., 3-Month	MIDAM	12/16/92		
Treasury Bill, U.S., 3-Month			Bid/Ask Yield	08/14/86*
Treasury Bill, U.S., 6-Month			on-the-run coupon	04/29/86*
Treasury Bill, U.S., 6-Month			Bid/Ask Yield	08/14/86*
Treasury Bill, U.S., 1-Year	IMM	03/28/94	on-the-run coupon	04/29/86*
Treasury Bill, U.S., 1-Year			Bid/Ask Yield	08/14/86*
Treasury Note, U.S., 2-Year	CBOT	06/22/90		
Treasury Note, U.S., 2-Year	FINEX	03/19/91		
Treasury Note, U.S., 2-Year			on-the-run coupon	08/19/86
Treasury Note, U.S., 2-Year			Bid/Ask Yield	08/14/86*
Treasury Note, U.S., 3-Year			on-the-run coupon	08/15/86
Treasury Note, U.S., 3-Year			Bid/Ask Yield	08/14/86*
Treasury Note, U.S., 5-Year	CBOT	05/27/88		
Treasury Note, U.S., 5-Year	FINEX	03/19/91		
Treasury Note, U.S., 5-Year			on-the-run coupon	08/19/86
Treasury Note, U.S., 5-Year			Bid/Ask Yield	08/14/86*
Treasury Note, U.S., 7-Year			on-the-run coupon	06/26/87

---

* Futures volume and open interest not included.
+ Closing values only.

Futures/Cash Description	Futures Exchange	Futures Start Date	Cash Basis	Cash Start Date
Treasury Note, U.S., 7-Year			Bid/Ask Yield	08/14/86*
Treasury Note, U.S., 10-Year	CBOT	05/03/82	on-the-run coupon	10/03/88
Treasury Note, U.S., 10-Year			Bid/Ask Yield	09/08/88*
Treasury Bonds, U.S., 30-Year	CBOT	08/22/77	on-the-run coupon	01/02/81*
Treasury Bonds, U.S., 30-Year			Bid/Ask Yield	05/13/88*
Treasury Bonds, U.S., 30-Year	MIDAM	08/01/90		
Treasury Bonds, Australia, 3-Year	SFE	05/17/88		
Treasury Bonds, Australia, 10-Year	SFE	12/05/84		
Treasury Bonds, U.S., 30-Year	TSE	09/02/92+		
Yen Bond, Japan, 20-Year	LIFFE	07/13/87		
Yen Bond, Japan, 10-Year	SIMEX	10/01/93		
Yen Bond, Japan, 10-Year	TSE	10/21/85+		
Yen Bond, Japan, 20-Year	TSE	03/30/90		
Treasury Bonds, New Zealand, 3-Year	NZFOE	01/26/94		
Treasury Bonds, New Zealand, 10-Year	NZFOE	01/26/94		

Fixed Income

Futures/Cash Description	Futures Exchange	Futures Start Date	Cash Basis	Cash Start Date
30-Year FNMA 6.0%			KRF	08/13/93
30-Year FNMA 6.5%			KRF	02/24/93
30-Year FNMA 7%			KRF	11/29/88
30-Year FNMA 7.5%			KRF	07/28/87
30-Year FNMA 8%			KRF	11/28/88
30-Year FNMA 8.5%			KRF	07/28/87
30-Year FNMA 9%			KRF	11/28/88
30-Year FNMA 9.5%			KRF	07/28/87
30-Year FNMA 10%			KRF	07/27/87
30-Year FNMA 10.5%			KRF	07/28/87
30-Year FNMA 11%			KRF	07/28/87
30-Year FNMA 11.5%			KRF	07/28/87
30-Year FNMA 12%			KRF	07/28/87
30-Year FNMA 12.5%			KRF	07/28/87
30-Year FNMA 13%			KRF	10/05/87

---

* Futures volume and open interest not included.
+ Closing values only.

Futures/Cash Description	Futures Exchange	Futures Start Date	Cash Basis	Cash Start Date
30-Year FHLMC 7%			KRF	02/01/88
30-Year FHLMC 7.5%			KRF	07/27/87
30-Year FHLMC 8%			KRF	07/28/87
30-Year FHLMC 8.5%			KRF	07/28/87
30-Year FHLMC 9%			KRF	07/28/87
30-Year FHLMC 9.5%			KRF	07/27/87
30-Year FHLMC 10%			KRF	07/28/87
30-Year FHLMC 10.5%			KRF	07/28/87
30-Year FHLMC 11%			KRF	07/28/87
30-Year FHLMC 11.5%			KRF	07/28/87
30-Year FHLMC 12%			KRF	07/28/87
30-Year FHLMC 12.5%			KRF	12/23/87
30-Year FHLMC 13%			KRF	10/05/87
30-Year GNMA 6%			KRF	02/24/93
30-Year GNMA 6.5%			KRF	08/31/93
30-Year GNMA 7%			KRF	11/29/88
30-Year GNMA 7.5%	CBOT	01/92–04/92*	KRF	11/10/87
30-Year GNMA 8%			KRF	07/27/87
30-Year GNMA 8.5%	CBOT	03/91–12/91*	KRF	07/27/87
30-Year GNMA 9%	CBOT	07/89–11/91*	KRF	11/28/88
30-Year GNMA 9.5%	CBOT	06/89–03/91*	KRF	07/27/87
30-Year GNMA 10%			KRF	07/27/87
30-Year GNMA 10.5%			KRF	07/29/87
30-Year GNMA 11%			KRF	07/27/87
30-Year GNMA 11.5%			KRF	07/27/87
30-Year GNMA 12%			KRF	07/27/87
30-Year GNMA 12.5%			KRF	07/27/87
30-Year GNMA 13%			KRF	07/28/87

Foodstuffs

Futures/Cash Description	Futures Exchange	Futures Start Date	Cash Basis	Cash Start Date
Butter, AA			Chicago	08/02/46*
Cheddar Cheese	CSCE	06/15/93	Nat'l Cheese Ex.	06/11/93*
Cocoa/Ivory Coast	CSCE	07/01/59	New York	10/17/80*

---

* Futures volume and open interest not included.
+ Closing values only.

Futures/Cash Description	Futures Exchange	Futures Start Date	Cash Basis	Cash Start Date
Cocoa	FOX	06/03/86		
Cocoa	KLCE	09/15/93+		
Coffee 'C'/Colombian	CSCE	01/03/66	New York	01/02/48*
Coffee/Brazilian			New York	01/02/47*
Coffee, Robusta Dollar	FOX	03/01/91		
Eggs, Large White, Dozen			Chicago	01/02/48*
Flour, Hard Winter Wheat			Kansas City	01/02/53*
Lard			Chicago	01/02/40*
Milk, Non-Fat Dry	CSCE	06/15/93	Western Region	06/11/93*
Orange Juice, Frozen Concentrate	NYCE	02/01/67	New York	11/82–07/84*
Potatoes	FOX	08/06/91		
Potatoes	MATIF	08/19/92		
Sugar #14/Domestic Raw	CSCE	07/07/87	New York	01/47–12/82*
Sugar #11/World Raw	CSCE	01/04/61	New York	01/03/49*
Sugar #7, Raw	LCE	10/1/93		
Sugar #5, White	FOX	04/11/90		
Sugar, U.S. Dollar White	MATIF	11/02/90		

Grains/Oilseeds

Futures/Cash Description	Futures Exchange	Futures Start Date	Cash Basis	Cash Start Date
Azuki Beans	TGE	05/06/93+		
Barley, Canadian/No.1	WCE	11/01/93	Thunder Bay	05/19/94*
Barley, Feed	WCE	01/77-05/94	Thunder Bay	08/01/91*
Barley, EEC	FOX	08/06/91		
Barley, Western / No.1	WCE	02/27/91	Lethbridge	08/01/91*
Barley / Malting, Top Quality			Minneapolis	01/03/72*
Bran / Wheat, Middling, Kansas			Kansas City	09/03/91*
Canola / No. 1	WCE	04/30/74	Vancouver	08/04/81*
Coconut Oil / Crude			New Orleans	01/03/49*
Corn Gluten Feed			Midwest	09/03/91*
Corn Oil / Crude Wet Milling			Chicago	09/03/91*
Corn Oil / Crude Dry Milling			Chicago	09/03/91*
Corn / No. 2 Yellow			Central Illinois	01/02/40*
Corn / No. 2 Yellow	CBOT	07/01/59	Chicago	01/02/40*

---

* Futures volume and open interest not included.
+ Closing values only.

Futures/Cash Description	Futures Exchange	Futures Start Date	Cash Basis	Cash Start Date
Corn	MIDAM	12/16/92		
Corn / No. 3 Yellow, cif Rotterdam			Rotterdam	01/08/87*
Corn, No. 3	TGE	05/19/94		
Cottonseed Meal			Clarksdale, MS	01/02/53*
Cottonseed Oil			Mississippi Valley	01/02/48*
Flaxseed / No. 1	WCE	08/02/83	Thunder Bay	01/02/48*
Hominy Feed			Central Illinois	09/03/91*
Oats / No. 2 Milling	MGE	02/27/91	Minneapolis	01/02/75*
Oats / White Heavy	CBOT	07/01/59	Chicago	01/02/40*
Oats	WCE	06/12/87	Thunder Bay	08/01/91*
Oats	MIDAM	12/16/92		
Palm Oil	KLCE	09/14/93+		
Palm Kernel Oil, Crude	KLCE	11/12/92+		
Palm Oil / Refined, Bleached			New Orleans	02/20/76*
Palm Oil, Crude / cif N.W. Europe			Rotterdam	05/07/87*
Rape Oil / Dutch, fob ex-mill			Rotterdam	05/07/87*
Rapeseed, Deutsche Mark	MATIF	10/28/94		
Rapeseed, French Franc	MATIF	10/28/94		
Rapeseed, U.S. Dollar	MATIF	10/28/94		
Rough Rice	CBOT	08/20/86		
Rye / No. 2			Minneapolis	06/04/47*
Rye / No. 1	WCE	01/02/86	Thunder Bay	01/02/51*
Soybeans / No. 1 Yellow	CBOT	07/01/59	Central Illinois	01/02/40*
Soybeans	MIDAM	12/16/92		
Soybeans / U.S., cif Rotterdam			Rotterdam	01/08/87*
Soybeans, IOM	TGE	05/06/93+		
Soybean Meal / 48% Protein	CBOT	07/01/59	Decatur, Illinois	12/01/47*
Soybean Meal, Hi-Pro	FOX	03/06/91+		
Soybean Meal	MIDAM	12/16/92		
Soybean Meal / 44–45% protein, fob ex-mill			Rotterdam	01/08/87*
Soybean Oil / Crude	CBOT	07/01/59	Decatur, Illinois	01/03/49*
Soybean Oil	MIDAM	01/13/95		
Soybean Oil / Dutch, fob ex-mill			Rotterdam	04/02/87*
Sun Oil / any origin, ex-tank, Rotterdam			Rotterdam	05/07/87*

---

* Futures volume and open interest not included.
+ Closing values only.

Futures/Cash Description	Futures Exchange	Futures Start Date	Cash Basis	Cash Start Date
Wheat / No. 2 Soft Red	CBOT	07/01/59	St. Louis	01/02/40*
Wheat	MIDAM	12/16/92		
Wheat, EEC	FOX	08/06/91		
Wheat / No. 2 Hard Winter	KCBT	01/05/70	Kansas City	01/02/40*
Wheat / Spring 14% Protein	MGE	01/02/79	Minneapolis	01/02/40*
Wheat, Soft White	MGE	02/27/91		
Wheat / No. 2, 14% protein, cif Rotterdam			Rotterdam	04/02/87*
Wheat, Domestic Feed/No. 3	WCE	11/18/85	Thunder Bay	08/01/91*

Industrials

Futures/Cash Description	Futures Exchange	Futures Start Date	Cash Basis	Cash Start Date
Burlap/10 oz. 40″			New York	01/03/50*
Cocoons, Maebashi Dried	MDCE	05/06/93+		
Cotlook World Index	NYCE	10/92–10/94	Cotlook, Ltd.	01/06/77*
Cotton/1 1/16″	NYCE	07/01/59	Memphis	01/02/79*
Cotton, 1 1/16″			7 Market Average	03/23/67*
Cotton, 1 3/32″			7 Market Average	01/02/85*
Cotton Yarn #40	TOCOM	12/21/92+		
Cotton Yarn #40, Nagoya	NTE	05/06/93+		
Cotton Yarn #40, Osaka	OTE	05/06/93+		
Cotton Yarn #20, Osaka	OTE	05/06/93+		
DAP-Diammonium Phosphate	CBOT	10/18/91	Central Florida	04/19/89*
Gum Rosin/Pine Oil, 80% Alcohol			New York	12/10/85*
Hides/Heavy Native Steers			Chicago	01/03/52*
Lumber/Spruce-Pine-Fir 2 x 4	CME	10/01/69	Random Length	01/21/71*
Mercury			New York	02/03/47*
NH3-Anhydrous Ammonia	CBOT	09/11/92	Gulf	01/27/93*
Plywood Sheathing (1/2″–B)			Random Length	08/29/75*
Print Cloth/DNR 48″ 78 × 76			New York	12/10/85*
Rubber/Ribbed Smoked Sheets			New York	01/02/47*

---

* Futures volume and open interest not included.

+ Closing values only.

Futures/Cash Description	Futures Exchange	Futures Start Date	Cash Basis	Cash Start Date
Rubber #3	TOCOM	12/21/92+		
Rubber RSS #3	KRE	05/06/93+		
Silk, Raw	KRSE	05/06/93+		
Structural Panel Index	CBOT	01/25/94	CBOT	01/25/94*
Sorghum/(Milo) No. 2			Gulf Coast	01/03/89*
Tallow/Bleachable			Chicago	01/03/49*
Tallow/Edible			Chicago	09/03/91*
Wool, 64's, Staple, Terr. Del.			Boston	01/03/49*
Wool Tops			Boston	12/10/85*
Wool Yarn #48	TOCOM	12/21/92+		
Wool Yarn, Osaka	OTE	05/06/93+		

Livestock/Meats

Futures/Cash Description	Futures Exchange	Futures Start Date	Cash Basis	Cash Start Date
Broilers, Composite Average			12-City	01/15/65*
Broilers/Dressed 'A', 1¾ to 3½ lb.	CME	2/91–7/93	New York	08/19/68*
Feeder Cattle/Average	CME	11/30/71	Oklahoma City	09/06/77*
Live Cattle/Choice Average	CME	11/30/64	Texas/ Oklahoma	01/02/48*
Live Cattle	MIDAM	12/16/92		
Live Hogs/Average	CME	02/28/66	Omaha	01/02/40*
Live Hogs	MIDAM	12/16/92		
Live Pigs	FOX	08/06/91+		
Meat-Bone Meal/50% Protein			Illinois	09/03/91*
Pork Bellies/12–14 lbs.	CME	09/18/61	Chicago/ Midwest	01/02/63*
Shrimp, Frozen	MGE	07/12/93		
Shrimp, Black	MGE	11/14/94		

---

* Futures volume and open interest not included.
+ Closing values only.

Metals

Futures/Cash Description	Futures Exchange	Futures Start Date	Cash Basis	Cash Start Date
Aluminum Alloy, Cash			LME	10/06/92
Aluminium Alloy, 3-Month Forward			LME	10/06/92
Aluminum/Pig Ingots	COMEX	12/83–7/93	Midwest	01/02/51*
Aluminum, High Grade, Cash			LME	11/25/88
Aluminum, 3-Month Forward			LME	11/22/88
Aluminum, 3-Month Forward			KRF	01/01/80
Copper/Electrolytic Cathodes	COMEX	7/59–12/89	Conn Valley	01/02/48*
Copper High Grade/Scrap No. 2 Wire	COMEX	07/01/59	New York	01/04/71*
Copper, Dollar Cash			LME	05/09/91
Copper, Dollar 3-Month Forward			LME	07/01/93
Copper, Dollar 3-Month Forward			KRF	01/03/77
Gold	SIMEX	07/06/92		
Gold	CBOT	09/17/87		
Gold	HKFE	08/20/90+		
Gold	MIDAM	12/17/92		
Gold	TOCOM	12/21/92+		
Gold	COMEX	12/31/74	KRF	03/20/68*
Gold Coins, Krugerrands				11/02/78*
Gold, 1-Kilo	CBOT	04/12/83		
Gold, London A.M. Fix			London	05/03/94*
Gold, London P.M. Fix			London	01/02/68*
Lead, Dollar Cash			LME	04/26/91
Lead, Dollar 3-Month Forward			LME	07/01/93
Lead, Dollar 3-Month Forward			KRF	02/01/77
Lead Pigment			New York	01/03/50*
Lead Scrap, Smelter's Heavy, Soft			New York	12/10/85
Nickel, Cash			LME	12/24/87
Nickel, 3-Month Forward			LME	11/02/87
Nickel, 3-Month Forward			KRF	04/23/79
Palladium	NYMEX	01/03/77	New York	01/02/68*
Palladium	TOCOM	12/21/92+		
Platinum	NYMEX	03/04/68	Free Market	10/26/67*
Platinum	MIDAM	12/17/92		
Platinum	TOCOM	12/21/92+		
Silver, 1000 oz.	CBOT	03/27/81		

---

* Futures volume and open interest not included.
+ Closing values only.

Futures/Cash Description	Futures Exchange	Futures Start Date	Cash Basis	Cash Start Date
Silver, 5000 oz.	CBOT	03/31/75		
Silver	MIDAM	12/17/92		
Silver	TOCOM	12/21/92+		
Silver	COMEX	06/12/63	KRF	01/02/47*
Silver Coins, $1,000 Face Value			New York	11/02/78*
Steel Scrap, No. 1 Heavy			Chicago	01/07/47*
Tin	KLCE	09/15/93+		
Tin, Cash			LME	06/29/89
Tin, 3-Month Forward			LME	06/02/89
Tin, 3-Month Forward			KRF	05/31/89
Tin Straights, Composite			New York	02/03/47*
Zinc, HG Special, Cash			LME	11/03/87
Zinc, HG Special 3-Month Forward			LME	11/03/87
Zinc, HG Special 3-Month Forward			KRF	01/03/77
Zinc, SP High Grade				01/03/47*
Zinc, Prime Western, Domestic				01/03/47*

Stock Indices

Futures/Cash Description	Futures Exchange	Futures Start Date	Cash Basis	Cash Start Date
All Ordinaries Share Price Index	SFE	03/03/83	SFE	01/01/80*
Bio Tech Index			CBOE	05/28/92
CAC-40 Index	MATIF	08/18/88	MATIF	10/27/89
Capital Share Price Index	NZFOE	01/26/94		
DAX German Index	DTB	11/28/90+	DTB	02/14/90
Dow Jones Industrial Index (30 stocks)	(Theoretical)		NYSE	01/02/01*
Dow Jones Industrial Index (30 stocks)	(Actual)		NYSE	01/02/01*
Dow Jones Transportation Index (20 stocks)			NYSE	01/02/70
Dow Jones Utilities Index (15 stocks)			NYSE	01/02/70
Dow Jones Composite Index (65 stocks)			NYSE	02/06/85
EuroTop 100 Index	NYMEX	10/26/92	COMEX	10/21/92
FT-SE 100 Index	IOM	10/15/92		
FT-SE 100 Index	LIFFE	05/03/84	LIFFE	11/17/86
FT-SE MID 250 Index	LIFFE	02/25/94		
Freight Index	LCE	08/26/88	LCE	01/04/85*
Gold/Silver Index			PSE	06/10/86

---

* Futures volume and open interest not included.
+ Closing values only.

Futures/Cash Description	Futures Exchange	Futures Start Date	Cash Basis	Cash Start Date
IBEX 35 Index	MEFF RF	09/29/92+	MEFF RF	09/29/92
Hang Seng Index	HKFE	08/06/87+	HKFE	07/22/87
Hang Seng, Commerce & Industry	HKFE	12/15/92+	HKFE	03/30/92
Hang Seng, Financial Sub-Index	HKFE	12/15/92+	HKFE	03/30/92
Hang Seng, Property Sub-Index	HKFE	12/15/92+	HKFE	03/30/92
Hang Seng, Utilities Sub-Index	HKFE	12/15/92+	HKFE	03/30/92
Major Market Index (MMI)	IOM	08/06/85*	IOM	01/02/80*
MCSI Hong Kong Stock Index	SIMEX	07/12/93+	SIMEX	12/31/82*
Nagoya 225 Index			NSE	09/27/93
NIKKEI 225 Index	CME	09/25/90		
NIKKEI 225 Index	OSAKA	06/19/90+	OSAKA	05/01/90
NIKKEI 225 Index	SIMEX	09/03/86	SIMEX	01/02/82*
NIKKEI 300 Index	OSAKA	02/14/94+	OSAKA	05/01/90
NIKKEI 300 Index	SIMEX	02/03/95	SIMEX	02/03/95
NYSE Composite Index	NYFE	05/06/82	NYFE	01/02/68
Russell 1000 Index			CBOE	12/03/87
Russell 2000 Index	IOM	02/04/93	CBOE	12/29/78*
Russell 3000 Index			CBOE	12/03/87
S&P 100 Index	IOM	08/82–09/86	CBOE	01/02/76*
S&P Mid Cap 400 Index	IOM	02/13/92	IOM	01/02/81*
S&P 500 Index	IOM	04/21/82	IOM	01/02/28*
Swiss Market Index	SOFFEX	04/17/91+	SOFFEX	04/17/91
TOPIX Index	TSE	08/14/90+	TSE	11/16/88
Toronto 35 Index	TOR	05/27/87	TOR	01/04/82*
Toronto 100 Index	TOR	05/20/94	TOR	10/07/93
Toronto 200 Index			TOR	10/07/93
Toronto 300 Index			TOR	05/27/87*
Value-Line/Arithmetic Index	KCBT	02/24/82	KCBT	01/03/83*
Value-Line, Mini Index	KCBT	08/24/83		
Value-Line/Geometric Index			KCBT	06/30/61*
Volatility Index			CBOE	01/03/86

APPENDIX B

PRECIOUS METALS

The following text is reprinted from a fundamental analysis produced by the author in 1993.

Overview

Since the explosive precious metals markets of 1979/80, upside performances for gold, silver, and the platinum group have been negative. Even with prospects for long-term inflation, investors have not found precious metals as attractive as stocks, bonds, and other paper assets.

Despite the 1993 second and third quarter surges in precious metals, the traditional linkage to economic and political uncertainties seems broken. Reactions to crises have been modest, at best.

There are several structural and fundamental changes that are responsible for poor performances in precious metals. New markets like futures and options on financial instruments have "structurally" changed relationships between precious metals and monetary values. This structural change provides investors and traders with alternative ways to guard against adverse fluctuations in interest rates, inflation, and currency parities.

New technologies threaten to alter supply and demand equations forever. Thus, formerly valid fundamental analysis must give way to new thinking. Few precedents exist that would allow the formulation of new fundamental approaches. Investors will be forced to reevaluate supply and demand relationships for each individual metal.

It is important to understand that rules which have existed for millennia can fall victim to modernity. Yes, mankind has always been fascinated by gold and silver. Yes, both metals have been used as "de facto" currencies up to date. However, the picture is changing.

This report is not intended as a recommendation to buy or sell precious metals. It is simply designed to broaden perspectives and provide a more complete foundation upon which investors can build sound strategies.

Much of today's news concerning precious metals is from interest groups. Mining concerns as well as industry associations have released news with an upward bias despite the consistent downtrend since 1980. Understandably, these groups want to encourage buying.

While there have been reports painting negative pictures, most have narrowly focused upon basic deflation/inflation arguments. This report draws a distinction between monetary and industrial applications. It examines developments in production and application technologies. There have been subtle developments that may have enormous effects upon gold, silver, platinum, and palladium.

Gold

Gold is a monetary metal. Traditionally, gold was used as currency. Therefore, gold has retained its reputation as a "valuation standard." Most demand comes from investment interest. Less than 25% of newly mined gold is used for industrial purposes. Approximately 33% is consumed in jewelry and the arts and about 8% is used in dentistry and medical applications. The remainder is hoarded or used as exchange.

Of the industrial applications, gold's main use is for electrical contacts and electronic components. Long range forecasts for the growth in the electronics sector have been mixed. A significant number of communications switches are being converted to fiber optical cable. Gold that was formerly used to bridge copper wire will not be required for fiber applications.

Gold is also used as a nonreactive coating in high temperature applications such as jet engine fans and electric generators. Here, too, new technology may allow substitution of ceramics, polymers, or less expensive metals. Gold coated glass is used to reflect sunlight and retain heat. However, other energy saving coatings are in development.

Gold Demand 1992

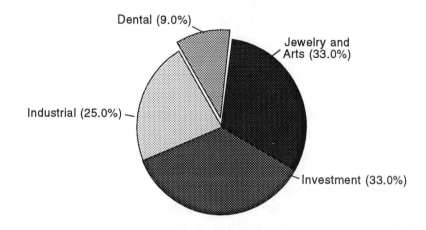

Dental (9.0%)

Jewelry and Arts (33.0%)

Industrial (25.0%)

Investment (33.0%)

Obviously, gold's industrial appeal is linked to its price. When gold reached beyond $800 per ounce in 1980, significant attempts by several industries to seek substitutes resulted in a decrease in the growth of industrial applications for gold.

Industrial demand is an important element to consider. Not only could we see a decrease in industrial use, we could also see an increase in scrap recovery as certain electronic and electrical components are retired.

Jewelry plays a major role in the demand for gold. Of course, jewelry consumption is a function of general economic conditions and consumer spending. While not substantiated, some gold analysts believe there was a cyclical boost in gold demand paralleling marriages of the "baby boomers" during the 80s. Whether demand was related to marriages or economic growth is debatable.

Certain societies use large quantities of gold for traditional or religious purposes. India and China are examples of very large populations capable of drawing down substantial production. As these nations westernize, there is little doubt that their gold appetite can increase.

Advances in fluoride treatments and composite reconstructive materials in dentistry threaten to limit gold demand in this area. Gold is a marvelous material and remains the choice of most dentists. However, advances in the use of palladium, glass, porcelain, and artificial enamels may slowly erode gold's dominant position.

There is significantly less tooth decay among generations that have had fluoridated water and fluoride treatments. Overall, even dentists say this is not a growth area.

The most potent demand for gold comes from investment interests. There are two broad categories. Individual investors buy in small quantities between one and several hundred ounces. Institutional investors accumulate gold in large quantities and tend to use it as a currency alternative or collateral. Governments hoard gold as an asset of last resort.

It is currently estimated that central banks hold 40,000 tons of gold. The average accumulation price is believed to be near $200 per ounce. Estimates are extremely general because central bank hoards can be "old gold" and "new gold." Old gold represents inventories accumulated while the world enjoyed a fixed dollar/gold parity. New gold was purchased after the international gold standard was lifted and prices floated relative to currencies.

Of course, U.S. dollar parity also makes it difficult to estimate an average gold price. Today, currencies can fluctuate 10%, 20%, and more in less than a year. Therefore, pegging a true gold/dollar parity is a questionable exercise.

There has been concern that central banks might abandon gold hoards in favor of investments with associated yields. If this were to happen, gold would be severely depressed. While we have seen some gold divestiture, it is not likely that governments will completely divorce gold. As mentioned, it has always been a last resort.

Turning attention toward supply, there has been remarkable progress in techniques for extracting gold. New leaching and solvent extraction technologies have made surface mining economical. Consider that South Carolina is now the ninth largest gold producing state. The move from nonproducer to producer is based upon new surface mining techniques.

Gold is a rare element. Less than .004 grams per ton of the earth's crust is comprised of gold. However, science is finding more efficient ways of identifying sources and extracting the metal from low grade ores. This is an important consideration. The U.S. went from a net importer of gold to a net exporter in less than a decade. Over the past 10 years, the U.S. has increased gold production by more than 10 times.

Capacity building is not limited to the U.S. One of the largest recent discoveries was in Greenland—a geological area never considered a good candidate for the yellow metal.

Progress in gold extraction technologies dealing with surface mining and secondary recovery has lowered the overall cost of obtaining an ounce of gold. By some estimates, costs have decreased from over $300/oz. to less than $100/oz.

Lower financing, capital equipment, development, refining, and discovery costs have made gold more profitable. This is why some gold stocks have continued to perform well despite falling prices during the '80s and early '90s.

Several analysts as well as various trade groups have called attention to declining "deep shaft" mining operations. Deep shaft mining requires more capital intensive development and has been flat as a result of low gold prices. While deep shaft mines have been responsible for significant production, a decline in this sector does not imply a net decrease in gold output.

This argument has been used to lure investors into gold while prices were declining. It is based upon incorrect assumptions and is contradicted by the facts.

Other technological considerations have far reaching implications for gold. Sea water has large concentrations of gold in solution. However, recovery costs have been far more than the retail gold price.

Recently, scientists have applied water purification techniques to mineral recovery experiments. Using reverse osmosis and centrifugal separators, some experiments imply that mining sea water for gold and other minerals will be cost effective before this decade ends. The boost in production could be enormous.

While there have been reports on declining output in South Africa and the former Soviet Union, statistics paint a different picture. It is likely that the world will continue to increase gold production. New technologies will be applied to new discoveries. The result will be lower relative costs per ounce.

There is little question that gold capacity is rising—not falling. There is little doubt that sustained prices above $300/oz. will keep most gold producers highly profitable. With this in mind, we should turn our attention back to demand.

Gold demand has remained remarkably strong throughout the '80s and '90s. While falling prices gave the impression that gold lost its luster, the fact is that gold has maintained a strong following. From 1988 through 1991, total world mine production increased 18.314%; from 1,862 kilograms to 2,203 kilograms. Even with this increase in new output coupled with divestitures by central banks, the former Soviet Union, and investors, there has been sufficient demand to absorb supplies without a major decline in relative prices.

Any other commodity that experienced a similar increase in supplies would have fallen proportionally more. Indeed, there were several forecasts for gold's decline below $300/oz. after the October 1987 stock market crash.

The "deflation" since 1987 was held responsible for gold's lackluster performance. Tight money and high interest rates during the '80s were also cited as reasons investors turned away from gold. Why hold gold with no yield when you can put money in funds that were providing 10%, 14%, and more? Yet, most analysts neglected to consider enormous production increases. There was simply more gold placed on the market.

During the Nixon Administration, a Gold Commission was established to evaluate the efficacy of gold as a monetary standard. A primary reason gold was abandoned was limited supply. Gold production could not keep up with expanding free world economies. In addition, South Africa and the Soviet Union were the primary producers.

The report concluded that gold supplies were too restricted for it's effective use as a money supply. In addition, South Africa and the Soviet Union would be unjustly enriched if gold remained the global monetary standard.

When gold rocketed beyond $800/oz. in 1980, the high price forced government away from a standard even more. Pegging a currency to gold at such a high price would have completely destroyed paper currency.

Logically, gold prices must be sufficiently low and supplies sufficiently high to accommodate economic growth without currency dislocation. Today's currency mechanisms cannot easily be adjusted to a single standard.

However, if currency volatility increases over the next few years, governments may be forced back to some valuation standard to avert a global confidence crisis. It is important to understand that confidence in paper currency is not simply a question of inflation in today's complex economic environment. As we move closer to "globalization," parity could become as critical as price levels.

Parity is the relative value between currencies. We have seen European, Far Eastern, and North American currencies fluctuate as much as 20% against the U.S. Dollar in less than a 12-month period. At some stage, such volatility could disrupt trade and dilute our trust in the ability to maintain the paper system. Under such circumstances, a revolution back to gold is quite possible; even likely.

The question most investors ask is whether gold will soar as it did in 1979/80. This is the wrong focus. In the event gold is brought back as a standard, those who own the metal will be assured of maintaining purchasing power—regardless of the paper exchange rate.

Of course, the assumption is that individuals will be allowed to own gold. We should not lose sight of the fact that when all else fails, governments can confiscate gold. Today's environment would probably make a government recall extremely difficult. A black market would develop instantly.

Conclusion

Gold's supply and demand picture does not seem to hold the promise of an explosive bull market over the next several months. There are few indications that gold production is declining. On the contrary, many developments suggest gold output will continue to rise—perhaps at an accelerating rate.

Problems with the Commonwealth of Independent States have not stopped the hot pursuit of joint ventures by the U.S., Japan, and other nations. At some stage, foreign capital formation will rebuild former Soviet capacity. It seems inevitable that Russia and her sister states will become a bigger player over the next several years.

South Africa is not consolidating gold operations. All indications point to higher capacities and expanded exploration. There are several major thrusts into new and promising fields that could become productive as early as 1995.

Unless there is a panic associated with an unexpected burst of inflation, long-term prospects will be a function of currency stability. The consolidation of European currencies before the end of this century could turn attention back to gold. If members of the European Community cannot agree on a European Currency Unit (ECU), gold may become the standard of convenience. This is probably why European central banks are reluctant to divest gold holdings.

Gold remains an excellent crisis hedge. From an investment standpoint, gold may not offer as much of a return as conventional paper vehicles. However, as an insurance policy, current gold prices represent a reasonable premium.

Global interest rate trends coupled with current (1993–94) economic growth patterns imply that investors must rationalize between low yields and low inflation. Traditional arguments that low interest rates will encourage a switch into gold are not presently valid. This seems due to the fact that we have both low interest rates and low inflation.

Therefore, gold's main hope rests upon a confidence crisis which has yet to materialize.

Silver

Silver has been both a monetary standard and an important industrial metal. More recently, silver's role as an industrial metal has dominated its pricing mechanism.

Like gold, silver has suffered from a combination of deflation and growing supplies. Over the past several years, silver has been a by-product of other base metals such as copper, zinc, tin, and lead. More effective extraction processes recover silver from base metal slags or tailings without significantly adding to the marginal cost of processing the primary base metal.

Silver Demand 1992

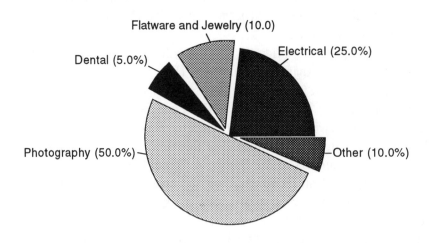

The impact of by-product production became apparent when copper prices moved up beyond $1.40/lb. At such a high price, there was a "copper rush" which boosted ancillary silver output.

Less than 40% of new silver production comes from silver mines. The remaining 60% comes from refinement of gold, platinum group metals, and base metals. Approximately 13,000 metric tons of silver were mined in 1985. Since then, world production has increased about 151% to roughly 15,000 metric tons.

Photographic processes account for more than half of silver's consumption. Another 25% is consumed by electronics and electrical applications. The remaining 25% is used for silverware, jewelry, coatings, mirrors, and brazing alloys.

From 1973 through 1990, annual world silver consumption rose from 507 million troy ounces to 570.2 million troy ounces. However, consumption declined as low as 353 million troy ounces in 1981—just after cash silver prices peaked at $38.27/oz.

In 1973, the average silver price was $2.56/oz. Given the present ratio of consumption to production, a 1993 price below $4.50/oz. is justified. However, on an inflation adjusted basis, silver should be trading near $9.00/oz.

Silver has not been a standard of value since the 1960s. Significant industrial demand could create too much potential volatility. Therefore, silver has been considered too dangerous to use as currency backing. This could easily change.

While interest groups and organizations such as The Silver Institute have projected major growth in silver usage, reality suggests otherwise. Most people are aware of the advances in computer and video imaging. Home movie cameras have been rendered virtually obsolete with the advent of video cameras and players. This technology is rapidly advancing.

New "still shot" video cameras are presently being marketed by Canon, Sony, and several other manufacturers. These new devices record pictures on computer disks which can be played directly on standard televisions. Processors facilitate printing on papers with the same quality as standard photographic development.

While the resolution of current "filmless photography" is not as good as silver-based professional films, the versatility of computer and video imaging is substantially greater. Even with inexpensive editors, users are currently able to alter colors and enhance underexposed and overexposed pictures. Technologies on the horizon hold the promise of far greater resolution, color rendition, and overall quality using non-film-based imaging.

There is little doubt about the future capability of filmless photography. Presently, medical X-Rays, CAT Scans, and magnetic resonance imaging are recorded onto removable disks and viewed on high resolution monitors.

The printing industry has new methods of making lithographic plates without using film. Eventually, the extremely high resolution technology that is presently used by our satellites will be commercialized for consumer and industrial photographic applications.

In addition to obvious advantages filmless photography has over silver-based processes, we must consider environmental questions. Film processing uses large amounts of fresh water and several toxic chemicals. Film results in considerable waste which must be managed.

The environmental movement has already demanded minimal packaging and recycling of film and associated products. As pressure mounts, film manufacturing and processing will become more expensive—regardless of silver prices.

The development of filmless technologies will have the most extreme long term impact upon silver. As mentioned, more than 50% of all silver is consumed by photographic processes. Just as the compact disc has replaced conventional vinyl records, so may filmless technology erode conventional imaging.

This means that "free stocks" of silver could double within this decade. It is only a matter of time before prices for filmless cameras and associated processing units fall to reasonable consumer levels.

We must also consider the explosion in computer technology and "multimedia." Software giants like Microsoft, Borland, IBM, and AT&T are developing new systems combining imaging with sound and computational ability. There are several proposals for national computer communication networks that will allow consumers to view movies, television, or their telephone calls on monitors linked to communications highways. These developments will have a negative impact upon silver-based photography.

This implies that silver is not the metal of choice as a long-term investment. While prices could be sensitive to inflation fears or supply disruptions today, any deterioration in photographic consumption can severely depress prices.

Is there a "silver lining?" The "deindustrialization" of silver provides the perfect scenario for remonetization. In many ways, silver could make a more ideal backing for currency than gold. Since silver is in greater supply, it could be controlled to provide appropriate monetary growth while instilling confidence in paper currency values.

As silver divorces from industrial processes and increases as a by-product of other mining, its position as a monetary metal may improve. Ideally, governments want a metal with a low raw cost and a high perceived value.

Silver continues to be viewed as a precious metal. Yet, the supply and demand balance could easily lower its intrinsic value to less than a dollar before the year 2000. If anything is certain, it is that nothing is certain. Obviously, there could be new technologies employing silver. It is fair to assume that no new technology will have the same potential as photography.

Many analysts are operating under the spurious assumption that filmless technology is far off into the future. It is interesting to note that when compact discs were introduced a short time ago, similar arguments prevailed. Analysts claimed that there were too many conventional phonographs and records in existence for compact discs to make any impact. Tape cassettes using Dolby hiss reduction were considered "good enough" to satisfy most listeners. It was believed that only wealthy audiophiles would adopt digital music technology. Less than a decade later, the standard has changed.

There are rumors that several manufacturers are working on attachments for conventional 35mm cameras which will provide video or computer capabilities. While not confirmed, there is evidence that a small computer imaging device can be manufactured in the form of a film cartridge. A thin reception screen can fit over the normal film track. Such a device would obviate the need for altering camera backs. If true, the move away from film will be accelerated.

Conclusion

Silver is known as the "poor man's gold." In the short term, silver prices could be sensitive to inflation fears. Further, the anticipation of a new bull silver market could become a self-fulfilling prophesy as investors rush to buy. However, the long-run picture is tenuous.

Silver should be regarded as a "trading vehicle" rather than a "buy-and-hold" precious metal. Holding silver as a hedge against inflation could be extremely dangerous if we consider prospects for filmless technology.

There is no present shortage of silver. Alarm over the closing of silver mines should be quelled by the increase in scrap recovery and secondary production. Overall, capacity is growing rather than diminishing. This is why silver prices slumped below $4.00.

If remonetized, silver is likely to have two tiered pricing. Cash silver in ingot form will probably be inexpensive. Face value for silver coinage will carry a high premium. Governments will only remonetize silver if the face value can be realistically set well above the ingot price. Governments do not want to see coinage melted down for intrinsic value. The object is to make a profit on minting.

Regardless of rallies, silver should be viewed with caution. We are at the dawn of filmless imaging. Things may only get worse.

Platinum

Platinum group metals represent the rarest of the industrial precious metals. Their primary importance is for chemical processes. However, platinum also has appeal as jewelry and for investment.

As with all precious metal investments, platinum has no yield. Investors must rely upon price appreciation alone. High interest rates throughout the '80s coupled with deflation during the '90s kept downward pressure on platinum.

Approximately 4 million ounces of platinum will be mined next year. Primary producers are South Africa at about 2.8 million ounces and the former Soviet Union at about 760,000 ounces. Another 200,000 ounces are produced in North America. South America, Australia, and Asia account for remaining quantities.

More than one-third of all platinum is used for automotive catalytic converters. Platinum has been the primary component of converters. However, recent changes in emission standards along with new developments may tip the scale in favor of palladium over the next several years.

Other applications include jewelry at 40%, investment at 7%, chemical at 6%, electrical at 4%, petroleum refining at 3%, and glass at 2%.

As of 1992, there was an approximate 20,000 ounce surplus. Currently, problems with certain Russian facilities and unrest in South Africa are likely to bring supply and demand into balance. New sources in the United States,

Platinum Demand in the Western World 1992

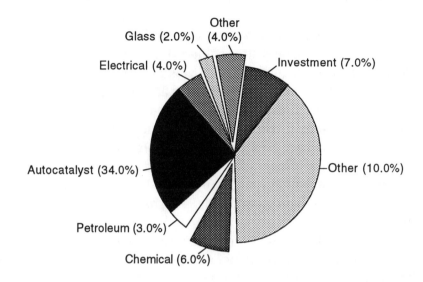

Canada, and South America can make up for any shortfall over the next two years.

Europe's adoption of catalytic converters has increased potential demand for platinum. The outlook for platinum will improve quickly if there is even a modest pick-up in European and North American economies.

As with silver, platinum faces threats from modern technology. While platinum's industrial future seems brighter than silver's, auto manufacturers are developing alternatives to catalytic converters.

The most promising new idea is called "lean burn." Lean burn engines use computer controlled fuel and ignition systems to precisely combine gasoline with air, and time the combustion process. Lean burn engines are estimated to be 10% more efficient than conventional engines and sufficiently clean to forego catalytic converters.

The European Community evaluated lean burn as an alternative to mandating catalytic converters. At the time of the study, computer systems required to regulate engines were more bulky and expensive than catalytic converters.

An exponential leap in computer technology has reversed the picture. Today, it is possible to build onboard automotive computers that are less expensive than catalytic converters. Computers can actually monitor driving habits and record results onto high speed hard disks for subtle engine performance adjustments.

Lean burn engines address two problems simultaneously. First, tail pipe emissions are reduced to meet strict California standards which are likely to be adopted by all states. Second, fleet mileage is increased to meet new Federal MPG (miles per gallon) standards. Finally, lean burn eliminates price risk and supply uncertainty associated with platinum group metals.

Over the past several years, auto manufacturers, petroleum refineries, and chemical plants have been stockpiling platinum to build strategic reserves. Companies use inventories to guard against excessive price volatility or the possibility of supply disruptions. By some estimates, platinum reserves are in excess of 4 million ounces. This is approximately one year's new production.

As a catalyst, platinum is extremely resilient. Much of the metal used in chemical and petroleum processing is recoverable. This is another reason why platinum stockpiles have been building.

Reprocessing car and truck catalytic converters accounted for 245,000 ounces in 1991. The bulk of this recovered platinum came from North America. As more effective methods for collection and processing old converters come on line, this source should grow to more than 400,000 ounces within the next two to four years.

The global recession has been held responsible for delays in junking old vehicles in favor of new purchases. The ratio of recycling relative to new demand is likely to favor supplies because production requirements are already in inventory. Of course, this could change if we see vast improvements in auto sales.

Trends in petroleum refining have not been positive for platinum. New refining technologies have reduced the use of platinum in cracking processes. Oxygenated gasolines that conform to the 1990 Clean Air Act are not processed using platinum group metals.

The glass sector has seen a large decrease in platinum usage as global recessions have reduced demand for fiberglass in boats and other recreational vehicles. Certain nonflammable foam insulators have gained acceptance over traditional fiberglass insulation to further reduce the potential for a comeback in the glass industry.

Advances in the use of other fiber materials for plastic reinforcement such as carbon fiber, Kevlar, and Spectra will also dampen demand for platinum in glass processing.

On the positive side, electrochemical fuel cells that employ platinum are rapidly advancing. These devices combine hydrogen and oxygen to create electricity, water, and heat.

With advances in fuel cell technology, demand for platinum could substantially increase. This area, alone, could replace demand in all other areas combined. However, current technology is not yet commercially feasible. Projections call for commercial applications no earlier than 1994/95 with widespread development coming well beyond 2000.

Yet, long-term prospects for platinum are very good. Assuming another technology does not supplant platinum-based fuel cells, the future in this area appears bright.

On the supply side, several potential joint ventures between Japanese interests and various Commonwealth of Independent States members as well as U.S. joint ventures hold the promise of greatly increasing platinum supplies over the next decade.

Initial prospects for production from the Noril'sk Nickel Combine appeared dim. Already, estimates call for a 15% to 30% decline in platinum group metals over the next two years. Russia lacks the internal financing to rebuild capacity or expand capabilities.

However, mineral reserves at Noril'sk are enormous. The temptation to capitalize upon availability by the U.S., Japan, and European interests has continued to push negotiations forward. There is little doubt that productive ventures will be formed before the turn of this century.

Political stability is a critical factor in platinum pricing. There is no question that we can expect surprises as the Commonwealth of Independent States attempts to form a unified coalition.

In the short run, platinum prices can and will surge if there are any possible supply disruptions from Russia or South Africa. Tension among the Baltic States as well as members of the new Commonwealth (CIS) seems likely to cause several scares. Strategically, reactions will offer the best returns using futures or options rather than investing in the physical metal.

In the meantime, South Africa should be increasing overall production. Large capital programs in several areas began production last year. As projects at Rustenberg, Lebowa, Potgietersrust, Impala, Northam, and other mines are brought up to speed, we can expect to see healthy long-term growth in South African platinum group output.

Recent improvements in palladium prices coupled with new uses for palladium should boost associated platinum output. Mines in North America that are principally dedicated to palladium production were scaled down in 1991 when palladium prices sank below $80/oz. However, with palladium trading at four-year highs, there is a new thrust to activate and expand palladium production.

Conclusion

While platinum fundamentals are a mixed bag of positives and negatives, the longer term picture seems more encouraging than for silver and possibly gold. Technology that threatens to displace platinum in catalytic converters is not yet in place. New uses for platinum are rapidly being developed.

We should keep in mind that technology offers relief from price inelasticity. Formerly, platinum users have been faced with simply accepting higher prices. Over the next several years, platinum prices can be held in check by alternative technologies. If prices climb too high, lean burn engines will be placed on a fast track.

What constitutes too high? Platinum could easily sustain a price rise beyond $600/oz. before there would be a scramble to curb requirements. This implies that platinum has significant upside potential as of this writing.

Palladium

Palladium has been the "little sister" in the platinum group. For the past several years, palladium has traded in a wide range from a high of $189/oz. in the spring of 1989 to a recent low of $78/oz. in June of 1992.

Palladium has gained popularity over the last year as a result of technological developments and anti-pollution legislation. Announcements of palladium-based catalytic converters for automobiles and trucks by Ford Motor Company, Nissan, and Allied Signal set the stage for a long-term rally.

Equally positive are new emission standards for California that require reductions in hydrocarbon emissions by 1994. Platinum-based catalytic converters are not as effective as platinum/palladium/rhodium combinations for reducing overall emissions. Platinum is very effective against oxides like carbon monoxide and moderately effective against hydrocarbons. But, palladium can be as effective at reducing hydrocarbons to carbon dioxide and water. New designs for palladium-based converters permit palladium to become active from a cold start very quickly. This had been a drawback.

While palladium is more susceptible to contamination from sulfur, lead, and other impurities, palladium impregnated substrates have addressed this problem.

The emphasis upon total emission reductions adds real fundamental strength to palladium. This is particularly true when we consider that palladium is mined in approximately the same quantity as platinum. Approximately 3.9 million ounces of palladium were produced in 1991.

The trend for production has been up. New mines in the U.S. and Canada hold the promise of increasing overall global output by another 10% within the next two years.

Almost all palladium is consumed by industrial applications. Very little is used for jewelry and there has not been much of an investment interest—until now. Between 1991 and 1992, a surplus developed which was quickly removed from the market by Japanese hoarding.

Palladium is used alone and in conjunction with silver for manufacturing electronic components like capacitors. The trend toward making smaller components has reduced the amount of palladium used in each component. However, the surge in overall component manufacturing has actually increased usage.

Electronic applications consume nearly half the annual palladium production. Dentistry accounts for another 29%. Autocatalysts has been a relatively small area—only consuming 8%. Alloying for jewelry takes about 6%. Chemical processing uses about 8%.

All indications point to dramatic changes in the traditional demand equation. As long as palladium remains cheap in comparison to gold, dental demand should continue to grow. However, recent strength in palladium may promote using alternatives in certain electronic applications. In particular, palladium "pastes" or paints have been used to draw circuit boards. Palladium and palladium-silver pastes are more desirable than copper. Yet, as palladium prices move beyond $130/oz., other metals become attractive substitutes.

Certainly, demand for catalysts is on the rise. Autocatalysts could account for more than 25% of usage within the next three to five years. Catalyst usage could significantly accelerate if Europe, Japan, and other nations adopt stricter emissions standards before the turn of the century.

The surge in prices since June 1992 has sparked investment interest. Despite a projection of a 200,000 ounce surplus for 1992/93, palladium prices rocketed... almost doubling within a 12-month period.

By far, palladium has been the best performer among the precious metals. The future for this relatively unknown metal could become even more exciting.

The projected 200,000 ounce surplus accounted for 5.1% of 1992 production. Virtually all of the surplus was taken up by hoarding. This implies that investor interest could become a factor over the next several years.

As with platinum, there will be an increase in the amount of palladium recovered from spent catalytic converters. Since palladium was not a major component of previous converters, this will not become a significant factor for some time.

The most intriguing development on the horizon is the continuing experimentation with "cold fusion." The last significant palladium rally occurred in 1989 immediately following an announcement by two professors that they had discovered a way to generate a fusion reaction at room temperature using palladium cathodes in a solution of heavy water.

On the basis of the cold fusion announcement, palladium prices soared to just above $189/oz. Shortly thereafter, cold fusion was discredited because other scientists were unable to immediately duplicate results presented by Professors Pons and Fleischmann.

However, many scientists continued working on cold fusion experiments. Over the past four years, there have been several confirmations of the cold fusion phenomenon. In June 1992, Professor Akido Takahashi of Osaka University presented a paper to M.I.T. in which he claimed to produce 70% energy surplus using a palladium cold fusion device.

Coincidentally, palladium prices began a steady rise since the presentation of that paper—regardless of economic and political gyrations in other precious metals. Several Japanese companies have begun stockpiling palladium. *The New York Times* carried an article in its science section entitled, "Cold Fusion Derided in U.S. is Hot in Japan." Apparently, U.S. scientists are more concerned with what cold fusion is rather than how it can be commercialized. Japan has exactly the opposite point of view.

Approximately 20,000 ounces of palladium were used experimentally last year. Prior skepticism aside, many scientific papers that have been presented form a strong case for cold fusion. Enough positive evidence exists to have prompted the Electric Power Research Institute to commit $12 million to cold fusion research last year. In Japan, an estimated $100 million will be spent on developing palladium-based cold fusion reactors this coming year.

Price implications associated with cold fusion are enormous. This process, if commercially feasible, holds the promise of unlimited clean energy. Such an astounding prospect could easily make palladium the most valuable metal on earth.

Price elasticity would certainly come into play if palladium became too expensive for feasible energy production. With current supplies limited to under four million ounces per year, it is doubtful that palladium can fulfill even modest global energy requirements.

Still, a price rise to approximately $400 per ounce could stimulate a doubling of production. Therefore, palladium supplies could conceivably keep pace with modest implementations of cold fusion plants or reactors.

Politically and economically, cold fusion represents more of a threat than a benefit. There is an incorrect assumption that the world is interested in finding an alternative to fossil fuels. Altruistically, cold fusion appears desirable. However, millions of people are employed by energy industries. Billions of dollars are invested in energy companies. Middle East economies and other areas are supported by energy trade. It is not likely that cold fusion will be politically promoted—regardless of the environmental benefits.

Still, high-tech energy dependent countries like Japan have a sizable long term interest in alternative energy. Perhaps that is why Japan is currently the most aggressively pursuing cold fusion.

Unfortunately, palladium has not been readily available to individual investors. As an industrial metal, the most common selling unit has been 100 ounces. Palladium futures have been traded on the New York Mercantile Exchange since 1968. Futures trading has a high degree of exposure and risk associated with leverage. The futures contract represents 100 ounces of .9995 pure palladium.

As the popularity of palladium increases, investors are likely to precipitate the minting of small palladium bars, medallions, and coins. Recently, there have been announcements of palladium medallions in 1-ounce and 1-ounce sizes that have been manufactured using the cold fusion marketing theme. These appear to be the only .9995 fine palladium medallions available in less than one-ounce weights.

Conclusion

Palladium appears to have the most fundamental upside potential of any actively traded precious metals. This assumes global monetary stability. In the event we experience a surge in inflation or a monetary confidence crisis, gold and silver may be more responsive.

However, absent a flight to quality, prospects appear good for a protracted rise in palladium prices—even in the face of declining silver, gold, and platinum.

A current stumbling block to palladium investment is its lack of physical availability in small quantities. Those interested in buying the actual metal will be forced to pay hefty premiums over spot market prices as long as there are only a few suppliers of medallions and small bars.

Two mining companies warrant mentioning. The Stillwater mine in Nye, Montana is a joint venture between Chevron Resources and Manville Corporation. This mine primarily produces palladium. Current plans call for forming a separate corporation which will be offered to investors. This is an excellent way to participate in palladium's potential through stock ownership.

In Ontario, Canada, the government recently approved mining at Lac des Iles. The mine is owned by North American Palladium Company (formerly Madeleine Mines) which is traded on the Toronto Exchange. The stock should become available on NASD shortly.

Of course, there is always the ability to speculate in futures traded on the New York Mercantile Exchange. As previously mentioned, futures imply higher risks.

Summary

This is an exciting time to be tracking precious metals. The structural changes in both the supply and demand side of gold, silver, platinum, and palladium already provide exceptional profit potentials.

However, it is important to keep long-term prospects in mind when developing an investment strategy for specific metals. Which metals offer the best short-term profits? Which are better to hold for the long run? What are the best vehicles for taking advantage of price movements?

Certainly, we must consider technological advances that could adversely affect silver, platinum, and palladium. Filmless photography and lean burn engines may eventually reduce industrial demand for silver, platinum, and palladium. Gold, on the other hand, could maintain value as a monetary instrument regardless of industrial precious metals trends.

There is little doubt that production of all precious metals is on the rise. Whether increasing production can keep pace with demand is the underlying question that will drive these markets in the months ahead.

The response to inflation during the 1993 second quarter proved that there is still significant investor interest in gold and silver. Although the components responsible for driving inflation in the first and second quarter abated, new developments like rising grain and meat prices could fuel inflation concerns.

An examination of price trends reveals that current inflationary patterns are due to rising costs associated with nonmonetary factors. This is extremely important. There are two basic categories of inflation; cost-push and demand-pull. When rising prices are due to natural scarcity induced by droughts, floods, wars, or disasters, monetary policy cannot effectively control inflation.

Immediately following the OPEC's oil embargo of the U.S. in the early '70s, we experienced severe inflation with negative economic growth. This was a contradiction of traditional thinking which was brought about by structural changes in global energy markets. The result was termed "stagflation."

If the U.S. Federal Reserve attempts to combat cost-push inflation with monetary policy, we could easily experience another stagflation. Investors should recall that the eventual recovery from stagflation resulted in sensational metals markets of 1979/80 when silver reached beyond $45/oz., gold topped $800/oz., platinum moved over $1,000/oz., and palladium passed $400/oz.

It should be noted that one year before the explosive trends of 1979/80, most experts predicted falling gold and silver prices. Inflation was considered under control. Indeed, the peak in the inflationary cycle came before precious metals reached their 1980 tops.

However, the loss of confidence in the U.S. Dollar and the possibility of a gold or silver standard caused an unexpected rush into precious metals. A combination of the Hunt brothers participation in silver and a failed currency intervention by Jimmy Carter caused a short-term lapse of our faith in paper.

For the past 25 years, governments have had the freedom to move away from asset-backed currency. Gold was replaced with Special Drawing Rights (SDRs) to keep cash flows in balance between wealthy nations and developing members of the system.

It was the very divorce from gold that provided the unique profit opportunities associated with gold and silver over the past 15 years. When gold can be used as both a hedge against currency values and a speculative vehicle, there is sufficient price volatility and fluctuation to produce profit potentials.

However, when gold is adopted as a monetary standard, currencies linked to gold stabilize while gold's value is determined by government exchange rates. This implies that gold could lose its luster if it returns as a standard—a fact most investors seem to miss. This is also a reason why gold and silver investing must be carefully evaluated.

Over the next seven years, we face monumental economic challenges that are bound to bring gold and silver into play. The two most significant developments are European unification which includes the formation of a single western European currency and the integration of the former Soviet Union into the western economic system.

Given currency volatility over the past 10 years, it is hard to imagine Europe with a unified currency. The only standard mankind has seemed to accept for the past several thousand years has been gold. Is a return to the yellow metal inevitable? If so, what form will such a return take? Will the public be permitted to own gold? Is there a danger that gold will be confiscated?

If and when silver usage declines with the popularization of computer imaging and video technology, will governments jump on the opportunity to remonetize silver to head off a paper confidence crisis?

Gold and silver will be the monetary metals positioned as standards if all else fails. But, investment returns will depend upon political aspects which remain very tentative.

Platinum and palladium offer different opportunities. Their prices can still be carried by gold and silver. Yet, they are more sensitive to industrial demand. Price elasticity plays a more important role because platinum and palladium users will seek alternatives if prices climb too high.

If we eliminate the possibility of lean burn technology over the next three years, platinum and palladium appear to have favorable fundamentals. Demand is presently growing faster than supply.

A truly extraordinary opportunity will exist if scientists can commercially develop cold fusion using palladium. Such a breakthrough will completely change the complexion of palladium, platinum, and energy markets.

The infrastructure of global energy markets represents an enormous roadblock to the development of cold fusion. However, there is an ever growing

"Green Movement" demanding that economic incentives be put aside for the good of the planet. The Green Movement could gain sufficient strength to force the development of palladium-based cold fusion as well as platinum-based fuel cells. In short, a grass roots uprising in the name of clean air, fewer oil spills, and less energy dependency could bring palladium and platinum to the forefront.

By some estimates, the price of a single ounce of palladium could exceed $1,000 if commercial cold fusion becomes a reality. So far, evidence supporting some type of energy producing process is mounting. Whether the process is truly fusion or some unknown phenomenon may be debated. But, if palladium can produce clean, inexpensive, safe energy, there is no limit to its profit potential.

Over the next several months there will be many arguments in favor of gold, silver, platinum, and palladium. Most will center on the standard inflation and currency valuation logic.

Investors who bought the same arguments in the early 1980s lost huge sums. Some forfeited sensational returns available in stocks and bonds. Obviously, precious metals can be hazardous to your wealth.

When deciding upon any precious metals investment, look at the long-term fundamentals. Understand how the metal is produced. Is supply increasing or decreasing? Is new technology likely to improve supply economics by reducing production costs while increasing output? Who are the producing countries? What are the economic and political conditions that could impact production?

Go beyond inflation and deflation. Understand how each metal is consumed. Put the metal into historical perspective. Remember that anything is possible.

Never forget that governments may use gold and silver as standards of last resort. If so, we must be prepared for the same action we saw during the 1930s. The price of gold was officially set and ownership was illegal.

Precious metals can be provide rapid profits and protection against economic disaster. But, structural changes in supply, demand, and alternative investments have changed the picture. Unfortunately, most information sources and reports have neglected to evaluate this changing picture. Investors have not been made fully aware of advances in mining or technologies that use gold, silver, platinum, and palladium.

After evaluating the facts, it seems apparent that significant supply disruptions or a major global confidence crisis will be required to push precious metals substantially higher. Holding large inventories of silver and gold does not seem as strategically sound as trading futures for quick returns or stocks associated with production.

As a footnote, we should consider that technology is affecting many other areas that could eventually impact precious metals. Advances in genetics could double or triple crops over the next decade and lower overall food prices.

If and when the Commonwealth of Independent States becomes politically stable and modernizes, we could see tremendous increases in global oil and gas supplies, base and precious metals, forest products, and more. Understand that the former Soviet Union spans two continents and nine time zones. By some estimates, the CIS controls more than 33% of the most strategic natural resources.

Each development will eventually trickle down to influence precious metals. It is up to the astute investor to keep the broad perspective in mind when formulating an investment program that may include gold, silver, platinum, and palladium.

INDEX